HUGH
JACKMAN
THE BIOGRAPHY

ANTHONY BUNKO

JOHN BLAKE

Published by John Blake Publishing Ltd,
3 Bramber Court, 2 Bramber Road,
London W14 9PB, England

www.johnblakepublishing.co.uk

www.facebook.com/Johnblakepub facebook
twitter.com/johnblakepub twitter

First published in hardback in 2012
This edition published in paperback in 2014

ISBN: 978-1-78219-914-4

British Library Cataloguing-in-Publication Data:

A catalogue record for this book is available from the British Library.

Design by www.envydesign.co.uk

Printed in Great Britain by CPI Group (UK) Ltd

5 7 9 10 8 6 4

Papers used by John Blake Publishing are natural, recyclable products
made from wood grown in sustainable forests. The manufacturing
processes conform to the environmental regulations of the country
of origin.

Every attempt has been made to contact the relevant copyright-holders,
but some were unobtainable. We would be grateful if the appropriate
people could contact us.

'If you love something, or someone, whatever, just go for it!'

Hugh Jackman

CONTENTS

ACKNOWLEDGEMENTS

I would like to thank all of the people who went out of their way to help me write this book, especially Mam, Sen Sen and Jackie, Allie, and John Blake for giving me the opportunity.

Also for my two daughters, Danielle and Georgia, for putting up with me during my madness.

Stay Free

CLAWS AND PAWS

21 April 2009

With his shock of grey hair, his smart suit and his suntanned face, Jay Leno looked relaxed as he stood on the makeshift platform in front of Grauman's Chinese Theater. In front of him, pressed up against the barriers in the stifling heat of the LA sunshine, were 500 fans, many clutching homemade Wolverine claws. To his right, an army of photographers were all vying for the best position; opposite them a host of dignitaries sat in folding chairs trying to keep cool under the shade of a large marquee.

'Straight guys love him... gay guys love him... women love him, in fact I don't know anyone who doesn't want to be him,' Leno's voice boomed out.

The crowd clapped and hollered. Backstage, Hugh Jackman broke away from the two bodyguards, who looked as though they had just come off the set of *Men In Black,* to sign autographs and talk politely with two women handing out water bottles.

Hugh could hear his good friend and TV presenter, Leno, finishing off the rest of his short introduction. The Hollywood actor made his apologies to the women and headed towards the exit. He stood there nervously, pinching himself to make sure it wasn't all a dream. It had been a hell of a year. He had recently been crowned Sexiest Man Alive by *People* magazine, beating off old favourites like George Clooney and Brat Pitt. Then he was asked to host the Oscars, and was so well received that before the last of the awards had been handed out, his name was already being pencilled in for the next year's event. And now, to top it all off, he was waiting to be inducted into the Hollywood Walk of Fame.

'He hosted the Academy Awards,' Leno added, 'he sings, he dances, acts... everything I can't do... Ladies and gentlemen, Hugh Jackman!'

On cue, the 6ft 3in Australian appeared through the beautifully ornate Chinese doors onto the red carpet in a blue polo shirt, dark trousers and the coolest of sunglasses. He looked like a rock star with the body of an Olympic swimmer and arms that an American football quarterback would die for.

He waved and smiled, acknowledging friends and family, and in particular, the fans.

'By the way,' Leno added, 'Hugh's going to put his face in the cement, unlike the normal stars who only put their hands and feet into it.'

They both laughed. Hugh had been on Leno's *The Tonight Show* many times during his rise through the ranks of Hollywood, and on each occasion Leno found him to be the perfect gentlemen and a model star to interview. 'One of the nicest guys I've ever had the pleasure to work with,' Leno has often said.

'Thanks, everyone,' Hugh took over the microphone. 'This is a dream come true for me... Jay Leno, my opening act.' The mutual respect was evident as the good friends ribbed each other.

Behind him, massive posters of Hugh in full Wolverine costume, including the outrageously epic sideburns, were draped over the walls. They announced the fourth X-Men movie, *X-Men Origins: Wolverine*, to be released on 1 May. It was latest in the series of superhero blockbusters that had propelled Jackman into the spotlight and made him hot property in Tinseltown.

He stared across to where his wife Deborra-Lee Furness, his eight-year-old son Oscar and his three-year-old daughter Ava were sitting in the VIP section with a group of Hollywood bigwigs, including the owner of the Twentieth Century Fox film studio that was releasing the movie, Rupert Murdoch. It was a proud moment for them all.

'I have to tell you,' the Sydney-born forty-year-old said, 'this particular block of real estate has brought me two moments in my life I thought would never ever happen...' As all good actors do, he left a small pause before continuing. 'Hosting the Oscars, and now here today. It means the world to me.'

He continued to thank the people who had supported and helped him to achieve the honour before he promptly switched his attention towards the ones he loved most. Full of pride, he looked over at them as he told the world that if it hadn't been for his family, none of it would have been possible, and without them by his side, it certainly wouldn't have been as much fun.

He turned to his son. 'How I am doing, Oscar?' he asked.

Everyone stared at the little boy; camera crews focused in on Oscar's cute little face. Hugh held his breath thinking back to earlier in the day when Oscar had told him that he was only coming to the ceremony if he didn't do a long, boring speech.

So over breakfast, Hugh had discarded the more 'formal' speech he'd written and in typical laid-back Australian style, promised his son he wouldn't talk for too long, although he couldn't guarantee that it wouldn't be boring.

Under the shade of the tent, the little boy gave Hugh the thumbs-up, then immediately turned his head away to start checking out the 'hot chicks', which according to Hugh was his new fascination. Hugh smiled and carried on.

'It's a very humbling moment as an actor to be here. You look down at the names, from Fred Astaire to Cary Grant, Clint Eastwood, Al Pacino, Steve McQueen, John Wayne, and to think that those have been immortalised and pretty soon I'll be putting my hands in wet cement.'

Another loud cheer rose up from the crowd as six men carried the cement and placed it in front of the stage.

Hugh kneeled down, placing his hands and feet into the wet concrete. He held up his dirty paws to the great delight of fans and to the flashes of hundreds of cameras; across his face was spread the biggest of grins.

To date, there had been just over 2,000 stars privileged enough to have their hands and footprints immortalised forever outside Hollywood Boulevard's historic Grauman's Chinese Theater. Now he, Hugh Michael Jackman, would be joining some of his very own heroes; the stars he had watched on television or at the cinema while he was growing up. And to make it extra-special, his position on the pavement was in between two of the biggest legends of all time, Marilyn Monroe and John Wayne. He knew it didn't get much bigger than that: he was joining a select and elite band of fellow Australians who had also had their foot and handprints immortalised in the theatre's iconic forecourt over the past 70 years – the likes of Cate Blanchett, Nicole Kidman and Olivia Newton-John. Not even Mel Gibson or Russell Crowe, two of the Antipodes biggest-known stars of recent years, had had their hands set in stone as yet.

However, the deep significance of the humble moment hadn't been lost on the superstar, who had not only wowed audiences with his all-action movies like *X-Men* and *Van Helsing*, but had defied critics with masterful stage performances on New York's Broadway and in London's West End. It was unbelievable to think that only 12 years earlier, on his first visit to LA, the Walk of Fame was the exact Hollywood landmark that he and his wife had come to see first. They'd spent hours walking the stretch of pavement on both sides of the street, reading all the names, taking in all of the history. He remembered placing his hands into the imprints of one of his all-time heroes, the late, great Peter Sellers. Never in a million years did he think that one day he would be doing it for himself.

Looking back, the unassuming star's rise to the top hadn't all been plain sailing. There was his tough, uncompromising childhood, which had led to lots of anger and frustration in the early part of his life, and the bouts of loneliness and self-doubt he'd suffered as a drama student and struggling actor. Yet through the rejections and some bad decisions along the way, he had stayed focused and determined as he climbed the ladder to stardom, to arrive on the rung where he stood at that moment.

He cleaned the cement off his hands and politely posed for photographs with his family as the mass of hungry paparazzi verbally pulled him one way and then the other. He didn't really like bringing his children to publicity events, but on this particular, special occasion Deb had persuaded the soon-to-be 'Walk of Famer' to let them come along and experience the moment first-hand.

His daughter, arms dangling round his neck, whispered into his ear, 'Daddy, how does it feel?'

Hugh whispered back, 'Well, Ava, it's a big day for your daddy, and for all of us, all the family. It's a great honour.'

But the innocence of youth cut him off. 'No, Daddy,

how does the *cement* feel on your hands? Can I draw in it as well?'

He laughed out loud before waving one last time to his army of fans. It was time to enjoy the rest of the day with the people he loved most in the world. He disappeared back through the doors carrying his daughter and his son.

Across the street, Matt Balke, another forty-year-old actor, who made a living dressing as the Wolverine character in his white vest and razor-sharp claws, looked on in admiration at the hero he copied everyday. He had left the spot where he made part of his living posing for photographs along with a host of other lookalikes, such as The Incredible Hulk, Superman, Captain Jack Sparrow and old favourites like Marilyn Monroe, earlier than normal, just to catch a glimpse of his idol. The Wolverine impersonator, too, had the widest of smiles on his side-burned face as he thought about the new movie shortly due for release that would certainly mean continued success for both himself and Hugh Jackman.

'I will be honest; I was touched to receive the accolade on the Hollywood Walk of Fame. My dad does not usually say much, but when he found out he hugged me. He was really proud, and that meant a lot to me.'

Hugh Jackman

CHAPTER ONE

TEN-POUND POMS

'Australia needs you and you need Australia,' the advertisement in the magazine assured readers. It portrayed a suntanned family lying on Bondi Beach with waves crashing in the background. It promised lots of space, good food, a healthy lifestyle and free tertiary educational opportunities. It was a brand new country where you could be a completely different person in a class-free society.

To Chris Jackman, this exciting lifestyle was a million miles away from the England where he was born and bred. A country that, although still nursing an almighty hangover from winning the 1966 World Cup, was balancing on the edge of upheaval, social decline and the rapid loss of family values.

So in 1967, Chris, an accountant with one of the world's largest professional services firms, Price

Waterhouse, who also had a degree from Cambridge under his belt, emigrated with his pregnant wife Grace and their three children, Ian, Ralph and Sonya, to the land of promise as 'Ten-pound Poms'. The aim of this scheme, run by the Australian government at the time, was to attract skilled, educated people from Britain and Canada to their shores: the package offered citizenship and a whole load of incentives, which included sailing an entire family halfway across the world for the grand old sum of 10 English pounds. Employment prospects, housing and a generally more optimistic lifestyle in a land that only 100 years earlier was used as England's penal colony were promised. It was all part of the 'Populate or Perish' policy, which was designed to substantially increase the population of Australia by attracting workers from countries with booming industries (and which, truth be told, was only offered to educated white workers from middle-class backgrounds).

Once in Australia, the Jackman clan quickly settled into life in the leafy middle-class suburb of Wahroonga on Sydney's North Shore, located 20km from Sydney's main business district. Wahroonga, an Aboriginal word meaning 'our home', was first settled in 1822 by Thomas Hyndes, a convict who became a wealthy landowner. In the early days, residents thrived by cutting down the tall trees that grew there and selling on the wood. Later on, the trees were harvested for their fruit instead, and when the railway was built it became a popular place for businessmen to build out-of-town residences with large gardens in the 1920s and 1930s.

The Jackman family's introduction into this new way of life was pretty straightforward, and in sharp contrast with many other British families who had also arrived. Many immigrants were placed in basic hostels and the expected job opportunities were not always readily available. Often they fled back home, escaping 'Pommy bashing' and resentment from Australians for job-stealing. But one statistic at the time claimed that nearly half the families that went back home returned later after reassessing life in England, thus becoming known as the 'Boomerang Poms.'

'My dad is pretty tight-lipped about a lot of things,' Hugh said, 'but I asked him why Australia and he just said that it seemed like a wise decision for the family. He already had three kids with a fourth on the way; I was number five. He was an accountant for Price Waterhouse, and was doing okay, but I think he thought living in London with five kids was going to be a nightmare, so he moved out to Australia. Back then, the country was still a bit of a frontier, not dissimilar to the country we depict in the film *Australia*, and my parents were drawn to the idea that there was space and opportunity to live there.'

Other than the birth of their fourth child, Zoe, their first year was reasonably uneventful as they adapted to the new environment. Chris, as normal, knuckled down and worked hard, some would say too hard, often not arriving back home from the office until late in the evening. However he enjoyed the work and his employer was more than happy with their conscientious new recruit. He quickly got promoted and was given an office along with his own secretary.

Initially, his wife Grace loved the place with all its new experiences, and she was regarded as a pleasant woman who would go out of her way to help anybody she could (a trait not lost on Hugh to this day). However, before too long, their cosy existence became disrupted. Chris, already a devoted born-again Christian, began to get more serious about his religion. Together with his wife, he had been converted to the faith back in Britain years before while attending a crusade by American evangelist Billy Graham. Years later, he would insist on taking Hugh and the rest of his children along to hear Billy Graham lecture when the religious road show came rolling into Oz with all its glamour and glitz.

'My dad was religious. He was converted by Billy Graham and he used to take me to things like that.' Initially, Hugh found something appealing about those itinerant preachers; maybe their power to spellbind a crowd. 'For two or three years I thought I might want to be a minister – I became spiritual – but ultimately, the Christian religion didn't really click with me; it left too many questions unanswered. I couldn't get past the fact that 95 per cent of people on the planet are going to hell because they are non-Christian, so I went soul-searching later in life, which has given a lot more meaning to my life.'

Meanwhile, his mother Grace gradually fell out of love with the Church and lost her faith along the way. She began to drift into serious bouts of depression, bordering on mental illness. Up to that point, she had always been a creative person, very much a free spirit, but the realisation that she was becoming more and more of a corporate wife living in northern suburbia, plus the added pressure of an over-religious husband and looking after four kids with another one on the way, began to take its toll. She slowly disappeared into her own world, becoming more and more distant to those around her.

Then, on 12 October 1968, Hugh Michael Jackman was born, weighing in at a respectable 9lb 6oz. Most hoped the birth of her new son would be the catalyst that would snap Grace out of her poor state of mind, but in fact it had the opposite effect. She suffered postnatal depression so severely that Hugh had to spend the first 18 months of his life with his Australian godparents, Tim and Deborah Collis-Bird, who lived on the next street along from the Jackman family.

'My mother was not well. She was probably suffering from postpartum depression. It may not have been diagnosed, I'm not sure, but she was going through a tough time. Actually, for the first year of my life, I didn't live at home; I went to live with my godparents.'

It was a strange time for everyone, especially Hugh's brothers and sisters, who were still very young themselves, didn't really understand what was going on with their mother or why their new brother wasn't living with them. Their father, a man of few words at the best of times, found it hard to explain this to them.

Chris only saw his new son on weekends, while Grace hardly saw her baby at all because she spent most of the time in the hospital suffering from a list of symptoms that included depression and fatigue. It was only in his later years that Hugh realised just how much of a nightmare it must have been for his godparents to look after a baby for all that time, to have loved that child, and then be forced to give it up. Hugh, now with two children of his own, really appreciates what his godparents did for him and his family: 'They were amazing people. My dad told me they had a huge impact on my life because they were incredibly loving and caring and calming.'

He regrets that he didn't make more of an effort to get to know his godparents when he had the chance, and to share some of his life with them while growing up. 'When I went back home and for years afterwards, I don't think I ever remembered them or rang them. I just went on my merry little way. And I never called them, never said anything to them, and then my godmother died. I found out she'd followed my career and kept things about me, and had prayed for me every night of her life.'

When he finally did come home to live, things still weren't easy in the Jackman household. There was the darkness surrounding his mother's condition and also the high standards set by his vehemently English father. It was a tough time for all the kids. Growing up, Hugh made lots of friends but many of them often refused to come over to his house, disliking the strictness of his father. Hugh's best mate, Gus Worland, who is today still his closest friend, was one of the few that didn't mind the sternness. He did, however, find it bizarre when Hugh's father would suddenly shout, 'Who's for elevenses?' and then serve up flambéed *crêpes Suzettes* when all the children really wanted was ice-cream and lemonade.

Aside from his less-than-normal childhood, though, Hugh enjoyed an active life, spending much of his time on the beach, playing, relaxing and exploring the shoreline, although some of his games were quite peculiar. 'I find it kind of scary because I know what I was like when I was a kid. I used to feed my action figures to the squids that were off the bay I lived near – I tore off their arms, stuck them with pins and did other awful things to them.' He's still not sure if there was some deep hidden meaning to his strange behaviour, or if it was just regular boy behaviour.

At home he staged magic shows and dancing competitions for his brothers and sisters. Hugh's siblings weren't sure if it was just youngest-child syndrome or if this was his way of shutting out the reality of what was going on around them. His sister Sonya has described her little brother as determined to get noticed, while his brother Ian said, 'I don't think we were vying for attention, but Hugh was the youngest of five children, so it's only natural he might have felt a need to express himself more loudly than some of the rest of us, perhaps.'

When Hugh was eight, life in the Jackson household took an even worse turn. One morning, his mother kissed him goodbye before he left for school. When he returned home later that day, she was gone. He knew right away something was wrong. When the rest of the family arrived home later that evening, Hugh told his father that he thought his mother had gone back to England. His father went mad and sent him to bed, but later came up to apologise after finding a note from his wife informing them all that she had decided to return home to spend time with her mother, who was very ill. Even with all the arguing and shouting between the couple prior to their mother's departure, the children thought she was just playing a stunt to get back at their dad, and naively believed she would turn up all smiles and they would suddenly become a normal family again. However, Chris now knew that any signs of normality for them all were just a distant memory.

As expected, the family was devastated. The period of misery following his mother going away is forever seared in Hugh's memory. For a long time after his mother had gone, Hugh wouldn't even go into the house alone after school. He would play outside by himself until one of his brothers or sisters came home.

Hugh and his next oldest brother fought like cats and dogs all the time. 'It was survival of the fittest and I was the smallest. My older brother Ralph used to bully me and one day I chucked a chair at him. It smashed and I picked up the bottom of the chair and swung it at him. He was taunting me and I thought, I'm going to have to kill him because if I just knock him out he's gonna wake up and then he's going to kill me.'

Outside the madness of home life, Hugh felt more exposed than ever. Divorce wasn't new to the area. Lots of couples split up, but it was the father who usually left and normally he lived right around the corner and saw the kids on weekends. There was a lot of attention and sympathy given to Hugh and his siblings from concerned people that made him feel like a leper. He hated it as much as he hated benevolent teachers and other parents always staring, pointing or being overly nice.

'I had some very dark periods as a child,' he admitted. 'I wanted Mum to come back, partly because I felt everyone stared at us. I felt like we were abnormal and weird, and I desperately wanted to be normal.'

A year after his mother left, out of the blue she returned, but only for a brief visit. She soon went back to England once again, leaving her children more confused than ever. After about two years she re-married and had a daughter. Hugh thought this would be the last he would see of her in Australia, but when he was twelve, she came back again. For a while his parents tried their best to reconcile. The children were of course over the moon and extremely pleased to be a family again. Hugh finally felt like the hole inside him had been repaired; he was complete. He had prayed every night to be a normal family again and now his prayers had been answered. For the first time in ages, he couldn't wait to tell everyone the great news that the Jackmans were just the same as every other family he knew.

Regretfully, the reconciliation proved short-lived when after only a few weeks Grace upped and left again, this time never to return. It was then the realisation that his mother and father would never be together for good hit home.

'As a kid it's hard to figure out how your parents don't love each other any more,' Hugh has said. Yet he later admitted that only when he was in a relationship that failed did he fully appreciate and understand how it must have felt for his parents. 'Looking back now, my parents were probably not suited to be together, they were completely different in too many ways.'

And he was more disillusioned and angry than ever when his mother left for the last time. It wasn't easy, especially as he was entering his teenage years. He claimed the loss manifested itself in anger and rebellion. 'High school was tough. I was bullied and probably did some bullying myself. I didn't take to authority at all – I was bit of a smart-arse for a while.' The teachers at his all-boys private school took pity on him, but it seemed to have a negative effect because he got into more trouble, rebelling against everything and everyone for a short time. While playing sport, he turned his anger to his advantage: 'Playing rugby when I was young, if I got tackled very hard, I would kind of go into a little white rage, a bit of uncontrolled violence, often getting into trouble or sent from the field to cool down.'

Hugh also started to look for excitement in other more dangerous forms. He and his mates would go to a place in Sydney called Warriewood Blowhole, where they would jump off an 80ft cliff into the water, swim through a cave which led to a blowhole, and then let the waves wash them up onto a mound of mossy rocks. Although thrilling for a young boy, it was also ridiculously dangerous. He didn't realise just how perilous it was until years later, when he returned with his own son and saw the memorials left to all those people who had perished doing the same stunt.

His home situation only made him more determined in everything he did. He wasn't sure if that determination came from being the youngest of five and needing to survive in a household full of kids or from wanting others not to feel sorry for him.

Over time, the anger that burnt deep inside the teenager began to dissipate as Jackman started to draw great strength from his father, who struggled to bring up the clan single-handedly through discipline and hand-me-downs. The respect Hugh has for his father is evident every time he mentions his name. 'The main thing I love about my dad is I've never heard him say a bad word about anybody, including my mum. The temptation must have been huge. I love that quality about him.'

It was apparent Chris had put his entire life on hold for the kids; they came first, second and third in all his thoughts and actions. 'What really amazes me now that I am older and can see things really clearly, is that for 10 years that man did not have a private moment,' he recalled. 'I mean, there's a whole decade there of supreme effort, just this non-stop commitment to his kids. He cooked, cleaned, shopped, got us dressed, got us off to school, and on weekends he'd go to five different sporting games, stay twenty minutes at each one, and race off to the next one because he didn't want any one of us to feel left out. Then this hard-working man got four weeks off every year and took us camping. So there he was with five kids in the tent, one little gas stove, all squashed in together. We kids absolutely loved it, but looking back now, I realise it wasn't a holiday for him.'

Even to this day, he doesn't know how his father managed to keep it all together and still have the time to come and cheer him on at sporting events. 'There's still a little boy in me that loves to have Dad there. Maybe that's what this acting thing is, me calling out, "Dad, Dad!"'

On the odd occasions when his father had to travel for work, the kids stayed with family and friends. His dad would drop them off along with a huge crate of food. Some people felt sorry for the children, but Hugh loved it. Not only did he get to stay with his friends, but he could escape the regime of his life at home. 'We'd be rostered on jobs to do each day or week. There would be emptying and stacking the dishwasher, ironing, cleaning and everything else.' His dad had all their meals mapped out for the whole week because he only had one morning to do the shopping.

On top of being a stickler for order and structure, Hugh's father was a real idealist whose priority was getting his kids to learn. If Hugh asked for a pair of Nikes when he was growing up, he got a resounding 'No' and was told to go get a job and buy them himself. But if he, or any of the other children for that matter, asked for a saxophone or other musical instrument, one would appear the next day, along with a schedule of lessons. During this time, Hugh learnt to play piano; he also studied guitar and violin. For anything that was to do with education or learning, his father spared no expense; any other fripperies had to be earned. Thus a strong work ethic was nurtured in the children and Hugh's earliest ambition was to follow in his father's footsteps and become an accountant: 'I wanted his job. He had such a calm power about him when he was at work, and he had a secretary.'

Chris Jackman's parenting yielded a remarkable crop of adults. Ian became a Rhodes Scholar and is a Sydney barrister; Zoe became an accountant, living in England. (Hugh once said about her: 'She said, "I'll never marry one, I'll never be one." She did both!') Sonya works as a stage actor in England and Ralph reported on sport for ABC TV in Perth until he changed careers.

Chris eventually remarried, just as Hugh was finishing high school. Hugh found it strange, after being raised on a strict diet of chores and self-reliance, to suddenly have his new stepmother, Elizabeth, around the house. It was a delight in many ways, because she was very easy to talk to and she spoiled him rotten. He remembered her saying things like, 'If you just put your washing out, I'll take care of it.' He thought, 'Wow, how cool is this?'

Although it was nice to have a 'new' mother about, when Hugh hit his teens he began to long to see his real mother. From the age of fourteen, he travelled to England once a year to visit her on what was called the 'milk run'. This was a cheap airline ticket that stopped at several different locations before landing in London. It took forever, but it was during these visits that Hugh finally made peace with his mother and came to terms with their situation. He now maintains that he has a great relationship with her, and even identifies with her slightly mercurial nature. 'I have always been fairly understanding of that situation. I am not going to say it was the easiest of times for me, or the family. Mum and I have come to a peaceful place with it. We got through the hard times and resolved things finally. I've always been close to her and never felt angry at her, which I can't explain, and which some people find hard to understand.'

Obviously a parent leaving in such a manner must have a lasting effect on a child and Hugh believes the experience affected him subconsciously later on in life, especially in the movie-making business. 'Some people find it hard to finish and let go. Not me. I move right on to the next thing, and that's probably a defence from when my mum came to visit and dropped in and out of my life. I had to learn to enjoy her when she was there and get used to the fact that it wasn't permanent. It's ultimately not such a bad quality to have, because nothing really is permanent, is it?'

'I am immensely proud of Hugh and all he has achieved. I stayed in regular contact with him over the years and we are now really great friends. I have watched all his films and I am delighted the way things have turned out. He had great presence even as a young boy. Everybody has always loved Hugh.'

Grace Jackman

CHAPTER TWO

CHICKEN LEGS

Like most of the kids who lived in the wealthy liberal heartland of Wahroonga, Hugh was privileged enough to attend private school. The Australian education system is one of the best, ranking in the top ten on a worldwide scale, year on year. Pymble Public School, the primary school that Hugh attended, prides itself on being a leader in education. For Jackman it was a wonderful place to begin his schooling and, more importantly, a great environment in which to learn about life. The teachers were extremely focused and the classes small enough to allow individual students to flourish.

Even though Hugh's home life was in turmoil, he worked hard in class and seemed to progress well in most subjects. He is remembered as a model student with very good manners, who was always polite to members of staff.

It was at the age of five that he first appeared on stage, in *Camelot*, and he continued to perform through a string of musicals and plays. At the primary school, pupils were strongly encouraged to both contribute to official productions and to put on their own shows. This suited Hugh's creative talent and gave him an escape from the reality of his personal life. He looked and felt at home on the stage regardless of what he had to do or in front of whom he had to perform. 'If I look back, I don't remember why, but I remember when I was about six and there was a group singing. I was the one who was brought out to sing the lead part and I don't think that I was a great singer or anything.'

Around the age of nine, like most developing young males, he started to take an interest in the opposite sex – and if rumours are to be believed, girls also began to take notice of the skinny, good-looking boy. He juggled his fledgling love life between several of them at the same time, even kissing one little girl behind the back of another. It earned young Jackman the reputation of being something of a love rat, in complete contrast to the devoted partner he is today.

In his young and naive mind, Hugh thought that if he didn't get to kiss a girl before he transferred from Pymble Primary to an all-boys school, he wouldn't have the chance to do so for a long time. So, on good advice from a friend, who had assured him that a girl called Sarah was something of a sure thing in the 'handing out free kisses' department, he decided to see if he could break his duck.

Hugh spent an entire week building up enough courage to approach the cute girl, and one day during lunch break, he finally slid up next to her in the playground and told her, 'I want you to know I love you.' Later he admitted he wasn't sure where he had plucked the well-used line from, especially at such a young and tender age, but to his great surprise Sarah informed him that she loved him too. A nervous but extremely excited Jackman then suggested they go down to the cricket field and into the bushes. A very bold move indeed for the inexperienced Christian boy, especially since he had already committed himself to a girl called Martine.

Sarah agreed, and hand-in-hand they marched into the long grass, where a young Jackman puckered up his lips and had his first snog. Afterwards, while walking home, he told his mate that he really didn't know what all the fuss was about!

Sarah, who is now married and the mother of two children, still remembers the kiss, but insists Hugh was no match for her husband. 'I can tell you, my husband is a much better kisser than the Sexiest Man Alive!' she laughed. She further revealed that she and Hugh dated for a couple of terms after dancing together to the soundtrack of *Grease* in dance meetings held before school. 'There was a group of us that would meet every morning and dance to *Grease*. He was my partner and I think that's where it blossomed. I was his girlfriend for nearly the whole year, but then when I left at the end of Year Four, he dumped me for Nikki. And that was that.'

Another classmate, Martine Bruce, was one girl who

didn't succumb to the handsome smile and charm of the schoolboy Hugh. She remembered the time when she turned down the advances of the boy destined for stardom after he kept chasing her around the playground, trying to kiss her. Meanwhile, Hugh recalled picking Martine up after she fell in a running race at primary school. 'My dad said, "Oh, I always knew you were romantic because you were running in a race and Martine fell over, and you stopped and went back and picked her up."'

Martine remembered the young Jackman having a crush on her and often writing her love letters or appearing in her street to throw rocks at her roof to get her attention: 'I wouldn't come out, I would hide from him.'

Yet Hugh didn't really discover what the female form was like until he and his friend Scott Whitehead found a couple of copies of *Penthouse* magazine under Scott's older brother's bed. Hugh was shocked, and although he was drawn to the images on the pages, he was afraid of what his religious father would say if he found out his son was ogling the naked girls. In fact, Jackman later admitted that one of the reasons why he didn't lose his virginity until he was around eighteen was because of the fear that his father would find out, or that he might be struck down by the hand of God.

At the age of eleven, Jackman finally left all the girls behind and moved to Knox Grammar School. The school was established on Sydney's north shore in 1924 by the Presbyterian Church and was named after John Knox. Knox was a 16th-century Scottish reformer who planned a network of similar schools in every church parish. It was a very religious, upper-crust boys' establishment, which became a production line for students who often progressed into high-flying professional careers.

Hugh recalls Knox Grammar School with fondness. 'I am a person who loves to learn new things and challenge myself. I totally credit this quality to the education I received at Knox. One's effort was always held higher than one's results, and a true passion for learning and discovery was at the heart of everything we did.'

Due to his gangly appearance and his skinny 'chicken legs', he picked up the nickname 'Sticks', which stayed with him right through his schooling. The fact that he spent most of his time at Knox wearing a kilt and enjoying a truly Scottish education didn't help.

Yet, Hugh has no regrets about his Celtic connections – or the Scottish skirts. He actually gained a secret passion for the Scottish national dress. 'Despite the blistering heat, my school had the whole Scottish thing going on; it was Presbyterian. We had the thistle in our emblem, as well as a pipe band, and I used to have to wear a kilt to school.' Although wearing a kilt might seem bizarre in Australia, it was very normal for Hugh. 'When I was in the cadets, I had to wear the whole outfit, complete with a sporran, every Friday. Everybody made fun of us because the local school kids thought we were this strange oddity. But because my brothers also went to my school and I grew up seeing them in the kilt, it was normal to me.'

Hugh quickly developed into an all-round sportsman

who excelled in everything he did. He was a skilled rugby player (when he wasn't using it to offload his anger); he also loved cricket, played basketball, took part in high jump, and swam freestyle and butterfly.

During his senior year, in 1986, he was elected school captain. The tradition of a school captain was founded in British Empire-legacy school systems in countries like Australia, New Zealand, South Africa, India and others.

Hugh's name was put forward by members of staff and he was elected by a voting system that involved the student body. To become the school captain was a real honour and the students who filled the position were usually individuals who had achieved a higher degree of commitment, dedication, experience and knowledge above that of the average student. In the role, Hugh acted as liaison between the students at large and the faculty staff, and between the school and the community. He loved the honour and the attention it brought: 'I wasn't particularly a goody-two-shoes, but I was always somehow the guy that would get up onstage to make the speech. I don't know; I remember thinking, "Oh, I've been chosen to do this." So there you go.'

Hugh starred as the lead role in the school production of *My Fair Lady* in 1985. The musical was directed by the headmaster, Dr Ian Paterson, who was impressed by Hugh's confidence and attitude. Brian Buggy, Knox Grammar's music teacher, remembered him as a lovely pupil at school, intelligent with a real passion for theatre.

It was when he first started to dabble with going on stage at school that one story emerged which has gone down in Jackman family folklore. After his performance at the school variety show when Hugh was twelve, a teacher suggested that he should consider taking dance lessons because he showed lots of promise. He came home and told his dad, who was quite supportive of the idea. But his brother overheard the conversation and yelled out, 'Ah, you bloody poof!' Hugh said he wasn't quite sure what a 'poof' was but he knew it didn't sound like something he should be. He never took the lessons. Later in life he recalled how his brother apologised when they went to see a show together and he realised that he had stopped the younger Jackman from 'cleaning up with all the girls.' Hugh was more disappointed he had bowed to peer pressure and missed out on those vital years of learning to dance properly. To add insult to injury, his brother, at the age of thirty, gave up being a sports journalist to do musical theatre!

It was during his yearly trips to see his mother and while going to see numerous shows in London with her that Hugh's real love of the theatre blossomed. On the long return trip back to Oz he would daydream about one day treading the boards in the West End.

Despite his love of theatre and his well-behaved manner, Hugh still had a streak of macho bravado running through his veins. He continued to play crazy and sometimes dangerous games. Often he would get involved in head-butting competitions with his mates to see who could make the biggest dent in the metal lockers at school. One of the most foolish and treacherous regular pastimes was roof-riding. Hugh and his gang of friends would take turns in lying on top of a car, holding on through the windows, while the vehicle raced through the streets or around waste land. Sometimes it reached speeds of well over 100 miles per hour. 'We stopped after an insane driver lost control of the car and it skidded, sending the unfortunate roof-top passenger flying through the air, breaking his leg in several places.'

However, the young Jackman still worked hard at school and his grades were good – but he had given up on the idea of following in his father's footsteps. Instead he decided to attend the city's University of Technology, taking a BA honours degree in communications with the aim of becoming a journalist. By coincidence, this was the same route taken by another famous Hollywood actor who later in life became his friend (and rival): George Clooney.

During his gap year between leaving Knox Grammar and starting at university, Hugh decided to use his time to do a spot of travelling. Like most Australians do at some time in their lives, he bought a cheap airline ticket to get away from the island continent for a while. 'It's your rite of passage. Every Australian travels. We're the great wanderers,' he once said.

He ended up touring and working in Britain when he was eighteen. It was a rewarding experience for him, although on one occasion while drinking in a bar in the beautiful city of Bath, England, he ended up learning about life the hard way. 'I met up with a few Aussies, and got so drunk I ended up singing some Australian songs very obnoxiously. Somebody tapped me on the shoulder and clocked me across the face, laying me out. I don't know how long I was unconscious. All I remember is getting up and smelling blood.' He laughed and added, 'Today that would be on someone's cell phone, right?'

Hugh quickly recovered from the fracas and like most teenagers at that age put the fight down to experience and moved on. Shortly afterwards, he ended up working at the prestigious Uppingham School in the East Midlands. Founded in 1584, it had celebrated its 400th anniversary the previous year. Hugh became an assistant housemaster, helping the teachers with English and drama lessons. His laid-back approach went down a storm with both students and teachers alike, and he left quite an impression on those who worked with him. In a somewhat old-fashioned environment, he was a breath of Australian fresh air. He had a natural gift for putting people at ease and a great sense of humour. On more than one occasion he found himself being drafted in to instruct a class of fourteen-year-olds. He found the whole experience brilliant if not a little ironic: 'Here I was, an eighteen-year-old Aussie teaching English to a bunch of English kids. I thought, if that was my school fees, I'd be pretty annoyed.'

But he loved the olde English quaintness of Uppingham School; all the pomp and ceremony, the rules and tradition, even little things like the small doorways and tiny stairways. He had a ball there and really wanted to stay, but Australia was calling him home.

Richard Boston, retired housemaster of Uppingham

and secretary of the Old Boys' Association said, 'Hugh arrived from Sydney at the age of eighteen. He was a great guy and still is. I remember him coming in as a fresh-faced, young gap student during the winter term. He was a delightful, open sort of person, exactly the same as he is now. A great communicator, and he would have made a brilliant schoolmaster had he continued in that direction rather than with acting. No one at the school was surprised when Hugh reached the height of his fame and best of all, it looks like it hasn't changed him one iota.'

A much more confident and wiser young man returned to his homeland and ploughed into his communication studies. He enjoyed the course and was a very optimistic student, picturing himself working as a freelance correspondent for ABC or the BBC somewhere in the Middle East, learning the art of journalism, filing reports, changing the world. 'I found it something a little different to what I had done before. Journalism combined something very close to intellectual rigour with a close involvement with people.'

Vice-chancellor Professor Ross Milbourne at the University of Technology said, 'The University was proud to have contributed to shaping an individual of such inestimable qualities.'

To pay his way through university, Hugh took a series of low-paid jobs. He moonlighted from midnight to dawn pumping gas at a Shell garage, chatting to visiting insomniacs. But that job came to an abrupt end when someone on another shift was held up at gunpoint by a robber with a shotgun. He fast came to the conclusion that it wasn't worth getting killed for a few bucks.

At one point he and his friend Stan were clowns performing at kids' parties; Hugh was Coco and Stan played Bozo. They had no tricks, talent or passion for it, although Jackman later learned to juggle. Instead, they would simply jump into dustbins and throw eggs at each other, and were eventually fired after too many children complained. 'At one party, the little birthday girl stood up and shouted out that I was the worse clown she had ever seen,' Hugh revealed. But he wasn't really sorry to get the boot – he reckoned it was the hardest 50 bucks he had ever earned.

He also worked for the National Parks and Wildlife Foundation, handing out leaflets, half the time dressed as a ranger, the other half as Kooey the Koala. Clad in a huge furry suit, he would often pass out from the heat and once, when expected to run the city's annual City to Surf marathon dressed as Kooey, he slipped down a side street and drove to within sight of the finishing line. He came in 600th out of 40,000 runners and still remains the highest-placed marsupial in the marathon's history. 'Dressing up in a koala suit was a real low point in my career. I certainly didn't do that for the art,' he later admitted.

During one of his summer breaks, he participated in a Christian working camp in the Areyonga Aboriginal community on Haasts Bluff in the Western Desert of Central Australia. Something happened to him there in the outback which changed his whole outlook on life. By then, he was nineteen and building homes for Aborigines as part of a Lutheran mission in Areyonga. He met the owner of a general store who lamented that he hadn't had a vacation in half a decade. Hugh told him to take off and said he'd manage the store for a month by himself. 'The locals loved it because I'm sure they were nicking so much stuff, and I had no idea,' he joked later. Yet he discovered a strange, unexpected serenity out in that faraway place. Suddenly all the things that frequently matter to a young man, like ambition and idealism, started to melt away: 'All the things you thought mattered to you just go. It's the land, that feeling of being part of something natural. It felt so right. The Aborigines inspired me. I was inspired by the family, the community, their culture, their togetherness. I'd only seen images of problems in their culture, either drinking or poverty or health issues that's all I knew about the aborigine people.'

He considered staying in Areyonga for good, but his father urged him to go back to college. 'But it was just to finish the course off so I'd get the piece of paper,' Hugh recalled. 'Not that I had my sights set on acting then, but there was enough quiet in my head, I suppose, for me to get an inkling of who I was.'

When he returned for a new term, he enrolled in drama class, mainly to ensure that he had enough credits to pass the course itself. 'When doing my communication degree, I had to do 24 units. I needed an extra two units to be safe so I enrolled reluctantly into drama class because I heard it was quite easy to pass.' That term they were putting on a production of Vaclav Havel's play *The Memorandum*, an absurdist piece, and thanks to a bizarre casting technique Hugh ended up in the lead role, even though he didn't want it.

'My teacher was sort of left-wing. I decided to do this class because everyone said you don't have to do anything; you just turn up. So I turned up, and for the first time in 10 years the teacher decided to do a play, and everyone had to be in it. He cast it in a very egalitarian way: the class list was in alphabetical order and he just drew a line and you played whoever your name was against on the list. I got the lead. And I was like, "I don't have time for this – I'm doing my journal."'

In fact, he found the part daunting and told the teacher that he couldn't manage it, but would be more than happy to get involved backstage or to help out in other ways. But the teacher wouldn't have any of it and said he either had to play the part or leave the class, which meant he wouldn't graduate. Hugh was forced into a corner and had no choice but to attempt the role. He surprised himself by really enjoying it. The show ended up touring around the area and, slowly but surely, he started to fall in love with the stage and acting. It was then that doubts began to creep into his head about what he wanted to do. He realised quite quickly that his real interest wasn't in asking questions or getting stories; it was in playing characters and being part of the narrative itself.

'I soon began to appreciate I didn't have the passion or the skill or the personality to become a journalist. At the start of the course I had big dreams of becoming a great writer, but quickly realised that life wasn't that simple and I would probably be assigned to crappy articles that no one wanted to read. And that you had to do exactly what your editor told you or get fired.'

The final nail in the journalism coffin came during the last few weeks of the course, when Hugh's teacher, Wendy Bacon, talked in detail about some of the less ethical parts of the job. At that time, a very naive Hugh believed investigative journalism was all about touring the world, capturing great stories and nailing deadlines, and so he was shocked when Wendy told the class that the reality of the situation was that in their first few years, they would probably be doing what is called in the trade 'death-knocks'. Hugh would be expected to knock on the doors of bereaved parents or relatives to try and get an interview, or even worse to steal photographs of the deceased from the mantelpiece so they could be printed in the paper. It didn't sound the least bit appealing. In fact, it switched Hugh off so much that he decided that once he got his degree he would turn to his real passion, acting.

He tried out with a local theatre group as a hobby, appearing in an amateur production. However, he knew at the age of twenty-one that if he was serious about becoming an actor it was now or never. He needed to enrol in acting school. The best one around was a year-long programme called The Journey at the Actors Centre in Sydney. The Journey is ACA's (Actors Centre Australia) most prestigious programme, with applicants auditioning from across Australia and New Zealand.

Actors Centre prides itself on a culture of artistic nourishment and freedom of expression. It sounded perfect to Hugh. He applied and the audition went well, but he had one serious problem: the course cost $3,500 Australian dollars – money he didn't have.

It was then that the hand of fate played a pivotal role in his life. 'I got a letter one day telling me I was accepted on to the programme, but sadly it also informed me how much it would cost,' he explained. 'I didn't have the money and I thought that was that. I couldn't ask anyone for the cash and I couldn't get credit from the banks; I was stuck. Then the following day, I got a cheque in the mail from my grandmother's will for $3,500. I thought, "Whoa, that's it! The signs don't get much better than that."'

He subsequently enrolled and found the course to be alternately exhilarating and terrifying. At first he felt as though the world was against him and that the very 'Beckett and Chekhov' – dark and brooding – instructors disliked him for his clean-cut image and his upbeat, friendly personality. He has admitted that the first three months were probably one of the most humiliating and lonely times of his life: 'I was this guy who was not only a bad actor – I also showed none of those signs that budding actors should show. I didn't have a beaten-up leather jacket. I wasn't smoking 60 cigarettes a day, I didn't seem to have all these neuroses, you know, and I just figured, "Damn, I've gotta find some demons in here or I'm gonna get kicked out of the school!" All the other cool guys had all these major dramas and they had this

Brando/Jimmy Dean kind of thing going; and I was just like all cheerful and nice.'

He felt completely exposed; it was the first time in his life that teachers were challenging him, asking him to step up to the mark, telling him straightaway if they thought what he was doing was no good. At times he felt he regarded himself as the class dunce, something that was alien to the former model pupil of Knox Grammar. Feeling vulnerable and overwhelmed, it was as if the whole experience shook him out of what he saw as a gifted child's complacency.

He still remembers the early advice he received from a girl in his class, who approached him one day: 'You're too nice, you'll never make it. If you want to be in this business, you've got to get tougher.'

The reality of the situation whacked him across the face like a baseball bat. He had to change or sink, and so he knuckled down, stepped out of the comfort zone of his middle-class upbringing and started to search for demons inside that he could use to his advantage.

Eventually, the whole acting thing started to fall into place, and it soon became apparent to those around him that there was something special about Hugh Jackman. He had a knack of lighting up a room and making people take notice whenever he performed.

Dean Carey, co-founder and creative director at the centre, explained: 'My first impression was that he was four steps back from a cliff from which he wanted to jump off and fly. He really wanted to know how to take off. You would feed him information, he'd patiently order it in his own mind, and then, when he had it settled, bang! He just combusted.'

The entire year's experience ignited his passion for the craft even more, and the fundamentals he learnt played a huge part in the principles he took into his everyday life.

Ross McGregor, who was the centre's visiting director at the time, commented: 'He was very, very focused. I think he felt responsible to himself or his family, I'm not sure who but he really wanted to achieve something. It was as though he had made a contract, and he'd decided not to renege on it.'

Many years later, in 2007, Hugh proudly accepted the role of Patron of ACA and in his speech to the students and teachers, he announced: 'I am often asked why Australian actors are doing so well on the international stage and my first response is always that the training we receive is world-class. Certainly for me, ACA was a huge part of my development. I really have to thank all the staff at ACA for instilling in me that sense of play, risk-taking and adventure that has made acting for me so fulfilling.'

During his time at ACA, Hugh worked as a receptionist at the university gym to make extra cash. Michael Ryan was an aerobics instructor working there when he first met Hugh, who was taking bookings at the main desk. 'All the girls in my class talked about this guy at the front counter,' recalled Michael. 'Finally, I decided I'd better go take a look for myself and there was Hugh, surrounded by a crowd of women trying to engage him in casual conversation. It was pretty clear he had something going for him even then.'

They soon became friends and Michael couldn't help but notice how skinny the budding actor was. As a joke, he called Hugh 'chicken legs'. 'Pectorally challenged,' was how Hugh described himself. 'That was me when I worked in the gym – I was known as the "before" model. All the others were these buff gym guys. I never understood the gym culture. Why do it? Sitting there, pushing weights, seemed ridiculous. Go to the beach and swim, or go out and run!'

Michael volunteered to help train Hugh, which they both really enjoyed. Indeed, the results were so good that Hugh told his friend that if he ever became a successful actor, he would employ him as a personal trainer. In 2003, completely out of the blue, Michael got a call from Hugh, who simply said: 'Quit your job today, you're coming to Prague as my personal trainer.' Michael dropped everything without a second thought and he is still Hugh's trainer to this day, travelling with him all over the world.

It was also while Hugh was working the front desk of the gym that he had a spooky encounter with a white witch. Annie Semler, the wife of the award-winning Australian cinematographer Dean Semler (*Bruce Almighty*, *Dances with Wolves*), came in for a series of treatments, during which she suddenly stopped and levelled an intense stare at Jackman. 'You're going to be a big star,' she announced. Everyone around them stared at her as if she was insane. 'Don't worry, it's all going to happen so fast. Listen to me, I'm a white witch.' Her last statement only added fuel to the watching audience's thoughts that she was completely crazy. At that moment, Hugh's only concerns were about collecting her money.

It actually turned out the white witch wasn't as mad as they'd thought. The very next day Hugh landed himself an agent, Penny Williams, and then everything began to steamroll quite quickly. Two weeks later he was offered a part on the hugely popular Aussie soap opera *Neighbours*, a show which had provided breakout roles for Russell Crowe, Kylie Minogue, Guy Pearce and Natalie Imbruglia, among others. It was a plum gig, a two-year contract with the allure of easy money and quick fame. Yet he wasn't so sure about the opportunity, feeling it was a little too safe.

However, the big break finally made Hugh realise that he could actually make a living as an actor, so while waiting for the *Neighbours* contract to arrive, he attended an interview with WAAPA, the Western Australia Academy of Performing Arts in Perth.

As the principal of WAAPA, Dr Geoffrey Gibbs had helped to inspire some of Australia's best talent to become actors of international acclaim, but he never forgot the day that a young Hugh strolled into the auditorium, looking like an airline pilot; impossibly handsome, tall, calm and quietly confident: 'I think we all knew instantly that this guy was going to be fantastic.'

It didn't take long for Hugh to win them over so convincingly that for the first time in WAAPA history, the selection panel offered him a place right there on the spot. Unanimous in their agreement, they couldn't believe his incredible capacity to hold their attention. 'I consulted my colleagues,' recalled Gibbs. 'They said, "Get him." Just like that. It was unprecedented to make a decision on the spot. But we thought it was so incredibly brave of him to knock back a lot of money and fame from a successful show like *Neighbours* in order to craft a real future for himself.'

Hugh himself was, of course, over the moon to be offered the position – especially since he had been turned down at around the same time by the National Institute of Dramatic Art. But he now had to make a decision: take the weekly salary and the immediate fame *Neighbours* could offer, or take the risk and spend three years going to acting school?

Already, he had called family and friends to tell them that he had been offered the gig on *Neighbours*. They were all pleased for him, but Hugh being Hugh, he started to have doubts. He thought the TV-show role might be detrimental to his career as an actor. He knew he would learn a lot about handling press and camera techniques if he did *Neighbours*, but he kept asking himself if it would help him audition for the Royal Shakespeare or Sydney Theatre companies. After a lot of soul-searching he had to admit it probably wouldn't, and so he decided to do things the hard way and go to WAAPA. Apparently, his step-sister in England still hasn't forgiven him – *Neighbours* was such a massive hit in the UK that she had phoned all her friends to tell them her brother was going to be a TV star.

Even his friends thought that turning down *Neighbours* was a big mistake, but Hugh headed off to

Perth regardless to study at WAAPA, Edith Cowan University, which was established in 1980. The WAAPA is situated in Mount Lawley, a leafy suburb of Perth. As well as being a friendly, safe and relaxed place, Perth offers all the cosmopolitan attractions of a large, international city. The Western Australian Academy of Performing Arts is recognised nationally and internationally for the quality of its graduates around the world. Many well-known actors, dancers, musicians and music theatre stars including Frances O'Connor, Marcus Graham, Lucy Durack, Rachelle Durkin, Emma Matthews, Jamie Oehlers and Tim Minchin, among others, have called WAAPA home at one point in their life.

Hugh fitted into drama school very well and excelled during the next three years. He worked incredibly hard in a tough, yet enjoyable environment where he was forced to learn quickly and to adapt to change and new challenges: 'When I trained at acting school you did fencing, Shakespeare class, modern dance, circus school, all before lunch.'

Hugh immersed himself in acting; always willing to listen and learn, always prepared to try new roles, to stretch himself, he loved the school and never missed a day. He attended every class, which usually started at nine in the morning and continued through until six in the evening.

Of course there were some doubts along the way, especially when certain teachers at the school confided in him that maybe he should have taken the gig on TV.

Then there was the night when he sat alone in his small, cold flat eating two-minute noodles while watching the character he would have played in *Neighbours* on a small TV set: 'I knew the guy was earning a couple of grand a week, which seemed like a fortune and I thought, "Did I do the right thing?"'

Nevertheless, he stayed focused. He ate, slept, drank and dreamed about acting, and was passionate about the whole experience. It was the most fun he had ever had and in the three years he spent studying, he gained all-round theatre education and experience. He took part in several stage productions including *Tonight We Improvise* and *Barbarians*, *Translations*, as well as director Wayne Harrison's *Romeo and Juliet.*

By his own admission, he only lost his composure on stage once during that time. He was playing Romeo and his father had flown over from Fiji, where he had been working, especially to see his son. They were doing two shows in one day, of about three hours in length. Hugh's dad sat through both performances, even staying put when the house lights came on between shows and people were encouraged to go and get some food: 'Dad didn't move. He sat there for six hours. I was doing Romeo's scene where he finds out that he's been banished. I was crying and emotional. I remember seeing Dad, and he was crying. And I lost it. I lost it completely, to see Dad crying there. Although he has some true British grit qualities, deep down he is actually emotional, very effusive.'

WAAPA was an amazing place to study, regarded as

one of the best institutions in the world and incredibly well supported by the government. 'It was really a turning point in my life. And I also had a great time in Perth as an acting student... an amazing city and a great breeding ground... agents everywhere.'

He had never felt so fulfilled or challenged in his life. Like the ACA course in Sydney, it made him depressed at times, but he liked being pushed to his limits. It was sometimes a lonely place, but the only thing that mattered to Hugh was being on stage, which gave him the opportunity to find out what was underneath the very presentable exterior of Hugh Jackman. During those three years, Hugh grew up.

When he graduated in 1994, all he could think of was getting work as an actor so that he wouldn't have to work another dead-end job. And it wasn't long before he found himself suddenly touted as Australian's next superstar. Within 18 months he had scored a home run in not one, but two major acting fields.

'He reminds me of a young Gregory Peck. There is such maturity in his work. That sense of knowing that Peck has. Unlike most other young actors, Hugh commands attention on stage. Because of his creative integrity, he demands respect for his character. He's also an actor that other professionals like to work with. He gives them a sense that they're all in it together. Some actors, if something goes awry, they worry about themselves and what they're doing. Hugh is always aware of his role as a collaborator

with the play, the director and the other actors. He's always looking for ways to make the whole thing better. People couldn't stop taking notice of him. Everything he does draws special attention to him. He's not allowing himself to go unnoticed.'

Dean Carey (head of acting, WAAPA)

CHAPTER THREE

MORE THAN JUST A SHOPPING MALL HEART-THROB

During his time in Perth, a friend of Hugh's from drama school took him to his first class at the School of Practical Philosophy. The School is a worldwide movement devoted to the study of religious and philosophical ideas drawn from varied sources such as Christianity, Hinduism, ancient Greece and Shakespeare. It teaches how natural laws governing humanity can be applied to everyday life and grew from London's School of Economic Science, founded in 1937 in the wake of the Great Depression. Meditation is central to its practice.

In fact, Hugh's interest started when he noticed a fellow student in drama class who seemed to have a strangely peaceful quality about him. When he asked what his secret was, Hugh was told about the School of Practical Philosophy, so he decided to go along and check it out: 'I'd felt this hole in my life since I had sort of abandoned the strict Christian model, and I felt I needed to replace it, that I needed a path. This made complete sense to me.'

It became a major part of his life, and still is today. Initially, he thought it would help with his acting, but after a few months, he realised it was the other way around: 'It gave me a great grounding and understanding of the world around us. We study great philosophers, thinkers, the scriptures from the East, from the West,' he explained. 'It's not the kind of school where you're actively encouraged to accept or reject any of the information, but to try it out practically in your life, as a way of inquiry. Inquiry comes first, and acting was just another activity that was an extension of it. It's all about personal experience and what helps, what doesn't. You start with working on yourself, then widening that work to helping others around you and the community at large.'

Indeed, wherever he is in the world he attends class every week and has done so for the past 20 years. He believes this has helped him to enjoy the business he is in and stops him from succumbing to the ups and downs that are evident in his profession: 'It's ironic that actors, who can slip in and out of roles, often tend to take their own lives so seriously. It's all a play, after all, and a wonderful one. I think my studies have helped me to put that into perspective and not to dismiss things as trivial or unimportant, but rather to see the rollercoaster quality as part of that inevitable play. I mean, success in this business is very much determined by public opinion and we all know how fickle that can be.'

So while WAAPA gave Hugh the techniques and skills to succeed, the School of Practical Philosophy slowly but surely gave him the inner strength to not only dive head first into the dark, cold river known as acting, but also the confidence to swim against the current.

Following his graduation from drama school in 1994, he did what most Australian film stars have done down the years and entered the world of soaps, mini-series and cop dramas. He was fortunate to land a part in the Australian Broadcasting Corporation (ABC) prison drama *Correlli* in 1995. *Correlli*, which was extensively shot on location in Geelong Gaol, featured Deborra-Lee Furness in the title role as a criminal psychologist named Louisa Correlli. Hugh played Kevin Jones, an intense and charismatic armed robber, who pretends to be brain-damaged to avoid a maximum-security lock-up. Over the course of the 10-episode series, Jones and Correlli have a distinctly dangerous mutual attraction and, in a classic case of life imitating art, Hugh fell in love with Deborra-Lee. The show's scriptwriters couldn't have plotted it any better. A year later, the couple married.

At twenty-seven, *Correlli* was Hugh's first notable casting. Not only did the programme gain good viewing figures, but he personally received very good reviews for his powerful portrayal of the prisoner. On the back of it, he won a small part in *Law of the Land* in 1993, a Channel Nine drama series set in a rural town where the locals had their own way of enforcing the law. It starred

Susan J. Arnold and John Brumpton in the main roles. Hugh played Charles 'Chicka' McCray in one episode only: *Win, Lose and Draw*.

Although not a role that Russell Crowe or Mel Gibson might lose any sleep over, it at least proved that Hugh was slowly getting a firm foothold on the ladder of success. He decided, and not for the last time in his career, that he wanted to try something completely different. Unlike most young actors straight out of drama school with a couple of TV shows under their belt, who would have been more than satisfied with the mark they were making on TV-land, Hugh needed something else. He'd had a taste of the world of theatre from his visits to London and also while at drama school, and now he craved more.

Incorporating the good looks of a leading man and a palpable talent, balanced with unaffected charm, he found his career moving quickly in a new direction as he joined the cast of the Melbourne production of the successful Broadway musical, Walt Disney's *Beauty and the Beast*. It told the story of Belle, a young, beautiful French girl held prisoner by a horrendous beast (who used to be an enchanted prince). The beast must win Belle's love in order to undo his beastly curse. In the Australian musical, Hugh portrayed the handsome but rather superficial Gaston, whose desire to marry Belle turns him from a self-centred but harmless buffoon into a menacing, murderous villain.

'My first audition was for *Beauty and the Beast*. The casting director said, "Why did you sing that song?" I said I'd learned it at drama school. He said, "Never sing that again. It doesn't suit your voice. Go get some lessons and come back in a month." Luckily, I'd read for the part before I sang. I could tell they thought I was good. So when I came back, I got the musical. I may be the only actor in history to have a contract with this clause: "Must take singing lessons every week." I was suddenly doing eight shows a week and taking lessons for an entire year. Who wouldn't get better if you worked that hard?'

The tall and muscular Hugh Jackman wore prosthetic pieces to pull off the exaggerated build of the character, but even with all the added padding, the actor's spot-on portrayal, complete with appropriate pomp and swagger, shone through. Hugh's role as Gaston was the first stage performance for which he received an MO nomination for Best Actor for achievement in a live performance from the Australian entertainment industry. It was also the performance that would be the springboard to parts in *Sunset Boulevard* (directed by Trevor Nunn in 1996) and *Oklahoma!* in 1999.

Despite the huge success of *Beauty and the Beast*, however, he did have one extremely embarrassing experience during the production. The incident in question didn't take place on the opening night, as some have stated. In fact, Hugh has confirmed that it happened three months into the run. It all began when he started getting headaches every day, before and after the show. At first he thought this might be stress-related, but life was good and there was nothing much to worry about. He was told to go and see a naturopath, who instantly diagnosed dehydration: 'You're doing the show, you're working out for the show, and you're just not drinking enough water. You must drink about two litres a day.'

Not one to disobey orders, Hugh did as he was told: 'I drank four litres to make sure. I'd just gone to the bathroom, but waiting in the wings, I was like, bloody hell, I need to go again! I thought, I'll be all right. The number featured Belle and me chasing around the stage, me lifting her up, dragging her, and singing the whole time. Then I realised, no way! I was sucking in air, trying to sing and dance. I picked her up, and I realised I'd peed my pants a little,' he recounted, and went on to explain: 'The very last note was a big-time F-sharp, front and centre. You have to release certain muscles to hit it, the same ones that allow you to hold on when you have to go to the bathroom. I thought, Shit, if I sing this note, I'm going to pee my pants; if I don't, I'm going to be humiliated.'

But the actor inside him took over and in a true 'the show must go on' moment, he continued singing. Meanwhile, down below, nature took its course. As he finished the song, he immediately turned upstage, looking down so that no one could see anything. When he didn't notice a wet spot on his red tights, he thought they must be waterproof.

'I turn upstage. I look down, nothing, absolutely nothing. Of course, I realise these tights are a little bit thick, so I thought, maybe they're like a wetsuit. I thought, I'm gonna end up with a bootful of piss but at least I'm not gonna be humiliated.'

With a cavalier attitude, he carried on the scene. He walked offstage, relieved, only to spot his dresser with a look of sheer horror on her face. Then he looked down – a wet spot had spread right across his groin and thighs. He quickly changed and carried on but it took a long time for him to live down the accident with the rest of the cast and crew.

Somehow, he managed to survive all the humiliation and the 'piss-taking' by the crew to go on and establish himself as an actor who truly could sing. Director Richard Wherrett described him as a 6ft 3in charismatic handsome actor who had a lot going for him in the first place: 'He's a very talented actor who also just happens to have a great singing voice and a great presence on stage.'

Beauty and the Beast was a massive hit and the role propelled him onto his next big stage adventure, a colossal musical production of *Sunset Boulevard* from October 1996 to June 1997.

Andrew Lloyd Webber's Australian production of *Sunset Boulevard* was directed by esteemed theatre stalwart Trevor Nunn from an adaption of the 1950s film version by Billy Wilder, which starred William Holden in the original title role. It saw Hugh as Joe Gillis, a young screenwriter hired by ageing silent star Norma Desmond (played by Debra Byrne) to resurrect her career. In the production their relationship leads to manipulation, madness and death.

When first asked to audition for *Sunset Boulevard*, Hugh had refused because he wanted to move away from musicals for a while after *Beauty and the Beast*: 'It's a medium that I don't believe should be, but is treated as the poorer cousin in the art world,' he said. But all his reservations disappeared when he met director Trevor Nunn, considered one of the best in the world.

The rehearsals were tough. During the first session, Hugh was about to sing when he heard a loud cry from the back of the theatre. 'Stop!' He did as he was told. Trevor Nunn ran up on stage towards him and said, 'Now listen, how many seats are out there?'

'It's about 200,' Hugh replied.

Nunn continued: 'Well, there are 200 people out there who hate you! They *hate* you! You've got three minutes to convince them otherwise or you will lose them.' He pointed to the pit and the music started up again.

Hugh stood there with the rest of the cast all staring at him. Suddenly he felt a rush of nerves and a surge of energy. He belted out the number, his voice reverberating around the empty theatre. It was exactly the response that the director had been hoping for. After that, he never looked back and quite easily made the transition from his larger-than-life character in *Beauty and the Beast* to the cynical Joe Gillis.

It was the year and the performance that singled him out as the most promising new talent in musical theatre, with two major awards for his role. The variety industry's peer-voted Mo Awards and the Variety Club Hearts Awards both voted him Musical Theatre Performer of the Year.

Much later in life, Hugh went on record as saying that

if he could pick the top ten things he had done in his career so far, nine of them would have been on the stage in the theatre. Trevor Nunn became a big fan and described him as a person open to every possibility, an actor who could convert ideas into action instantly: 'The astonishing thing is that he can sing. He can sing magically and he can dance, so you are looking at a diversity of talent that is amazingly rare.'

After the run ended, Hugh went back to TV and appeared in an episode of *Halifax f.p*, another police drama show, where he played detective Eric Ringer, investigating a series of multiple murders at a service station. His career then changed course again for a while as his relaxed and natural presence led him to try his hand as a television host on a fashion show called *In Fashion* in 1997. He hosted the Australian Film Institute Awards in the same year.

Sunset Boulevard had raised Hugh to a new level, however, and he was speechless when asked to sing the Australian National Anthem before 100,000 rugby fans at the Bledisloe Cup match between Australia and their old enemy, New Zealand, at the famous Melbourne Cricket Ground in 1998. He was so nervous, and yet extremely honoured to be part of the whole occasion. Rugby had been his first sporting love and after singing the anthem, he commented that he was so pumped up that he wanted to put on the gold shirt of his homeland team and run out to face up to the infamous men in the black from across the Tasman Sea.

Next came more TV work with guest lead role

appearances in some of Australia's most popular dramas. *Blue Heelers*, a weekly police drama based on a fictional bush town called Mount Thomas, was the most popular local production on television at the time. Hugh played Brady Jackson in the episode 'Just Deserts'.

He then moved on to appear in five episodes of the fourth season of *The Man from Snowy River* (which was called *Snowy River* in the USA and *The McGregor Saga* in the UK), based on Banjo Paterson's poem. It was a hugely popular show following the trials and tribulations of a Western Australian family in the late 1800s. Hugh played the character of Duncan Jones, who shows up while his ship is in dry dock to steal the hearts of teenager Danni McGregor and Rob McGregor's sweetheart Montana. Fortunately for Jones, his childhood friend, Rob (played by Guy Pearce) was away, otherwise the world would surely have been treated to a fight between two future Hollywood stars.

But it wasn't all plain sailing. Hugh did have his critics, including one of his own countrymen, a veteran tabloid reporter, who pronounced him 'too good-looking to be taken seriously'. However, this wasn't going to deter him: he was on a roll and popped up as a guest artist at many events. Hugh did the *Christmas Carols* in Sydney, Melbourne and Wagga Wagga, as well as a Melbourne Midsumma Festival Cabaret production called *Summa Cabaret*. He also sang at the Melbourne Cup and the Hopman Cup, and his voice helped bring in the Chinese New Year, as well as singing at the new model Holden sedan launch at Royal Pines Resort on the Gold Coast. Hugh was quickly becoming the man for all occasions.

Then it was back to treading the boards, but this time to achieve a childhood ambition. Following the success of *Sunset Boulevard*, Hugh was keen to continue his working relationship with the vastly experienced Trevor Nunn, so he wrote to him asking if they might meet up when he and Deborra-Lee arrived in London on holiday in late 1997. Hugh had heard that Nunn was staging a production of the musical *Oklahoma!* and he badly wanted a part in it. There was no reply from the director but Hugh persisted, phoning Nunn's office when he arrived in the capital. He was told that although Nunn was off on holiday the next day, he would see Hugh in the morning and that he should bring along a song and a Shakespeare monologue. He hadn't done Shakespeare since drama school, so Hugh raced to a bookshop, snapped up a Shakespeare play and retired to the Regent's Park Hotel, where Deborra-Lee put him through his paces for four hours.

What he didn't know was Trevor Nunn had been so impressed while working with him in Australia that he wanted Hugh for the lead role of Curly McLain in *Oklahoma!*, the part which Gordon MacRae had played in the screen version. But it was up to the Australian to prove himself to Nunn's demanding colleagues at the National Theatre in London.

The Shakespeare monologue he had selected went well, but it was when he sang 'Oh What a Beautiful Morning' and the entire selection panel sang along with him as though they were in a German beer hall that he knew he was in with a shout.

Although the panel had lined up eight more people to see, Nunn offered him the role on the spot. It was like a dream come true for the boy from Sydney.

The rest of the cast had already been selected and included such illustrious artists as Maureen Lipman, Jimmy Johnston, Josefina Gabrielle, Shuler Hensley, Vicki Simon and Peter Polycarpou. The original *Oklahoma!* from 1943 is still classed as a revolutionary musical in terms of storytelling and broke numerous box office records on its initial opening. It's also regarded as one of the best musicals with some of the finest songs ever written. Rodgers and Hammerstein were renowned for crafting outstanding songs with a perfect blend of intelligence and wit to transport their audiences into another world. Those who had seen the original production of *Oklahoma!* were fearful of seeing the new production because they didn't want to tarnish any of their memories of just how good it had been. Fortunately, because of Nunn's ability to direct and his knack of giving a fantastic feeling of freedom to all the actors, the latest version proved equally successful, and instantly sold out for the opening night.

'The first five weeks of rehearsals we didn't sing a note,' Hugh recalled. 'Trevor made us research everything. He would hang up letters and books and give us copies of the movie to watch. He was determined for us to find what made the musical such a revolution. We all immersed ourselves in all the stuff for weeks. He said

"You think of Oklahoma, you think of people singing", but then he had us do every lyric of every song as dialogue, which when you do "Oh What a Beautiful Morning" it is really tough, because everything's just repeated.' And that's why Hugh loved working with Nunn: no stone was left unturned – he was a true professional with bizarre but unique techniques to get the best out of his actors.

As with most productions of this size, *Oklahoma!* had its fair share of hiccups. There was a scene in the show where a ballerina falls asleep and dreams of dancing with Curly, Hugh's character. On the opening night at the Olivier Theatre in 1998 Hugh was terrified, knowing his limitations when it came to ballet and also aware that Mary Rodgers and guests from the Rodgers & Hammerstein Organization were in the audience. Hugh was supposed to lift the girl, who was an unbelievable dancer, above his head, spin her round and end up with her draped like a swan around his shoulders. But he was so pumped up with adrenaline that as he lifted her she went straight over his back and landed hard on the stage. She was wearing a tutu and her legs were sprawled in the air – not a good look for even the most graceful ballerina! Hugh turned and said, 'Oh shit, sorry,' which boomed out of the microphone to the great amusement of the audience. He made sure it never happened again.

With his strong and energetic performances, Hugh was an instant success. Described by one reviewer as 'virile and melodious', he was proclaimed one of the most promising newcomers to musical theatre. He was nominated for an Olivier Award, but just missed out; he also missed out on a trip to accompany the production on Broadway because at that time, the rules demanded that an American should take the lead role. Jackman understood and was philosophical about it, saying that him playing the *Oklahoma!* lead role in America would be, 'Like having an American do *Crocodile Dundee.*' Yet it didn't concern him that much because he had already set down his marker.

Oklahoma! was more than just a hit with the general public; it became the must-see show for members of the Royal Family in Britain. Every Royal came, with Princess Margaret seeing it nine times and the Queen twice. Hugh was told by the Queen Mother that her daughter, Elizabeth, had seen the original show with Prince Philip when the couple were courting. There was even a rumour that Prince Philip used to sing the song 'People Will Say We're in Love' to Elizabeth when they were alone. The Queen Mother allegedly quipped that she thought Hugh was a much better singer then her son-in-law!

The opportunity also allowed him the opportunity to meet a number of other famous people, although he missed out on the chance to meet former British Prime Minister Tony Blair, who made a special trip to see the show. In fact, the Australian actor had been struck down with a migraine and spent most of the performance rushing off-stage to be sick. The illness also meant the star was confined to the bathroom when he was supposed to be meeting the then Labour Party chief afterwards. 'I remember having a migraine when Tony

Blair came to see *Oklahoma!* I was going into the wings and throwing up whenever I was off-stage. Afterwards, Tony Blair came backstage to meet the cast, and of course I was throwing up.'

Bravely, or maybe foolishly, Hugh invited some mates who were over from Australia on their travels to see the show. He made them promise not to make him laugh or shout out. All the way through the performance he was waiting for them to pipe up and heckle him, so he was surprised when they said nothing. In fact, his performance blew them away. They had been so completely captivated that one friend later said, 'I really didn't realise that was our mate up on the stage. He was a different person, wonderful.'

The musical then transferred to the Lyceum Theatre in London's West End, where *Oklahoma!* had a six-month run.

During his stint in the stage musical *Oklahoma!* Hugh had some time off to travel back to his homeland and the far outback in Queensland, where he pulled on a pair of khaki shorts and dusty boots to star in his first major film, Anthony Bowman's romantic comedy, *Paperback Hero*. Jackman plays Jack Willis, an Australian outback trucker, who in his spare time pens a romantic novel that he submits to a Sydney publisher. Unwilling to give over his masculine reputation and be known as a romantic author, Jack adopts the name of his friend, tomboy crop-duster Ruby Vale, as his pseudonym. When both Ruby and Jack, posing as her manager, are taken on a publicity tour to promote the book, romance blossoms.

Writer/director Anthony Bowman got the original idea for *Paperback Hero* when he was in the US and he read a piece about a Texan truck driver who had written romantic fiction under an assumed name. Hugh was impressed with his latest director's very enthusiastic and spontaneous style and his never-ending good mood, even when things weren't going to script or to plan.

The role was perfectly suited for the open and unpretentious actor, and it earned him even more acclaim and exposed him to an international art-house audience. It also gave him the opportunity to sing 'Crying' by Roy Orbison.

Talking about his role as Jack, Hugh commented that he was attracted to the script by its lovely pace and energy: 'It's a story of Jack eventually coming to terms with what he really is, his feelings and emotions. It's a very Australian thing, and that's what I connected with. He has a great sense of humour, and he's very comfortable with who he is.' Hugh enjoyed making the film and was pleased with the outcome, believing it to be a good showcase in terms of his screen acting.

Claudia Karvan played the other leading role, Ruby. Hugh didn't know her personally before working with her, but he admitted to being a big fan and to have watched her in the movie, *The Big Steal*, four times.

Shooting was tough and very hot work. The temperatures in the town of St George, Queensland, where they were filming, frequently soared to above 40°C. Claudia once fainted because of the heat, and to make matters worse, the air-conditioning in the hotel where they were staying was often broken.

Nevertheless the reviews were good, and especially kind to Jackman. Comments like, '[He] oozes natural charm and charisma' and 'His voice is terrific' abounded. *Paperback Hero* didn't rock the world of cinema, but it was a diverting and amusing way to spend an afternoon on the sofa with a box of chocolates. For the ladies there was the added pleasure of watching a young Hugh Jackman in shorts and a vest.

It was his performance in *Paperback Hero* and the reviews of *Oklahoma!* that led to him signing with Creative Artists Agency (CAA) in the US, a move that most actors would have given their right arm to achieve.

After the film was in the can, Hugh squeezed in another Royal appointment and performed at the Royal Command Charity Performance in London, before returning to continue in the role of Curly in the West End. It was another example how this relatively young man from Australia was fast becoming a superstar. As he himself said, 'It was really weird to be sitting in the Queensland outback, and then to sing in front of the Queen a few weeks later.'

On his return to Australia after the stage show in London had finished, Hugh moved onto his next film role in a movie titled *Erskineville Kings*. This was actually filmed after *Paperback Hero*, but it was released first, in 1999, and is thus often thought of as his first movie role.

Erskineville Kings was written by Marty Denniss who, incidentally, was one of Hugh's good friends from drama school. Denniss was considered by many at the school to be quite brilliant but he was also slightly argumentative. The school let him go after his first year. It turned out that during his stint, Marty had been writing plays and he had turned one of them into the screenplay for *Erskineville Kings*.

The drama was about two brothers reunited by their father's death after years apart. Australian director Alan White created a very bleak, but gorgeously photographed urban drama about life in Sydney's seedy inner suburbs. Hoping to escape his father's drunken and abusive behaviour, Barky (played by Denniss) runs away from home to cut cane in the north of the country. Two years later, he returns to his down-and-out hometown to attend his father's funeral and to make amends with his brother Wace (Hugh Jackman's character), with whom he had a falling-out. As he meets up with old friends and his ex-girlfriend Lanny, Barky reveals more and more about the enigmatic workings of his mind and the grim circumstances of his upbringing. Shot on a very low budget, the film nonetheless creates a compelling portrait of a gritty, oppressive land. The movie was filmed in the streets of Newtown and Erskineville in Sydney and the title of the movie refers to the King's Hotel, a fictional hotel in which most of the action takes place. It was screened at the 1999 Montreal Film Festival and launched to international buyers at the American Film Market prior to an Australian release later in the year.

Alan White, the director, didn't have a problem in casting Hugh: 'When I talked to people about who I was casting in the film, I'd say I've found this great actor Hugh Jackman and they'd go, "Isn't he the song and dance guy?" And I'd go, "No, he's a great actor." And I think that's what Hugh is all about. He has this wonderful chameleon quality.'

Hugh believed at the time that this was one of the most challenging and possibly best pieces of work he had done. He felt there was a level of truth and rawness to the movie that required an intensity of acting he hadn't been asked to do before. It was an emotional and challenging role for an actor so new to the art of film. He invested his heart and soul in the production and it made him feel fantastic as an actor: 'It really did, and I probably exorcised a few demons. Maybe some I didn't realise were there. And read into that as you will in terms of the parallels with my own life.' For his performance, he won the 2000 Film Critics Circle Australia (FCCA) award for Best Male Actor and was also nominated for the 1999 Best Actor by the Australian Film Institute.

'There is no star system in Australia. Everyone is more equal there and maybe that makes Australian actors a little cooler and not as snobby as many in Hollywood. I've done lots of musicals, and so had Russell Crowe.

'Many of us have acted in more or less terrible soaps. But that's all part of being an actor, you take what you get and don't try to make big films and be "hot" all the time. I also think that it's important not to take on a project just for the money, you have to like what you do as well.'

Hugh Jackman

CHAPTER FOUR

EARLY BRITISH GANGS

Hugh met his wife, Deborra-Lee Furness, while on the set of his first notable role in television on the popular show *Correlli* in 1995. Unlike the young Jackman, 35-year-old Deborra-Lee was already a big name in Australia. Winner of the Film Critics' Circle Best Actress Award for the movie *Shane*, she had also acted alongside Meryl Streep in *A Cry in the Dark*, as well as with Patrick Bergin in *Act of Betrayal*. In addition, like most female Australian actors at the time, she also made an appearance in the now cult TV show *Prisoner Cell Block H*. She also appeared onstage in LA alongside Ed Harris in *Scar* too and scored a major part in the cop drama *Street Legal*, with Brian Dennehy and Bill Paxton. Just before Deborra-Lee starred in *Correlli*, she again hit it big when she starred in the TV series *Fire*, Australia's version of the UK hit, *London's Burning*.

Correlli, though, was the show that ultimately changed her life. 'I was playing a prison psychiatrist,' she said, 'and Hugh was my crim that I had to sort out, and within the script there was meant to be a chemistry between us, and I remember when we first started working together that he was such an exciting actor to work with. We developed this wonderful repartee with each other and I really enjoyed working with him. I don't think it was love at first sight; it was just a respect, I think, for the work.'

Deborra-Lee's upbringing in many ways mirrored Hugh's, except that while he spent most of his early life living in leafy suburbia, she was on the road. Like Hugh, her own childhood was turned inside out by the loss of a parent, but in her case, the loss was accidental, with the death of her father in a car accident when she was eight years old. Despite the tragic loss at such a young age, Deb described her own childhood, raised alone by a working mother, as a happy one, but with one abiding feeling: 'I think I always felt different because I wasn't conventional. I didn't have a father and I didn't have brothers and sisters and, you know, I always remember everyone had a brown paper bag with a Vegemite sandwich. I always had lunch money, because my mother worked, but I always wanted a brown paper bag.'

She was schooled early in a gypsy kind of lifestyle as she constantly moved with her mum who was building a working life to make ends meet. Deborra-Lee had attended 12 different schools by the time she graduated, which must have been tough on someone so young: 'I moved around a lot. I think on a kid it is hard because you come into a new environment and you're the new person, and there's all these groups set up.'

In spite of being a reasonably confident and creative child, Deborra-Lee often went out of her way to perform in the classroom to make friends and wrestle the attention in her direction: 'I was sort of the class clown. I was always the new kid because I went to a lot of schools, so I had to be funny. And I thought, oh, people laugh at this, maybe I'll just make a living out of it, become an actress. It was a very flippant thing.'

Her mother, Fay Duncan, who re-married when Deb was 11, was a strong and determined woman who went on to become director of the Bone Marrow Donor Institute in Melbourne (of which Hugh and Deborra-Lee later both became patrons). It was Fay, Deb said, who instilled in her the no-nonsense confidence she exudes: 'She made me believe I could do anything I wanted. My healthy self-esteem definitely comes from her. So I grew up with the idea that women can be movers and shakers in the male dominated world.'

She also credits her mother with the generosity of spirit that Hugh later said was one of the things he loved about Deb: 'I'm the daughter of a single mum, and in Australia at that time it was very much a macho male-dominated society, but the way I grew up, my mum was the boss, and it means you don't need to rely on a hunter-gatherer. You go and hunter-gather yourself and create your own autonomy. Mum worked in business: she wasn't burning her bra, she was just doing it, running the show, and so I guess that's where I saw that strength.'

Deborra-Lee had wanted to be an actress ever since she could remember, but taking on board advice from her mother about having a back-up plan, she started out working as a secretary in the news department at Channel Nine. She then moved onto a current affairs programme and then, very much like Hugh, considered becoming a journalist until the acting bug took over.

An independent and successful spirit, by her late teens, Deborra-Lee travelled to London and by the age of twenty was at the American Academy of Dramatic Arts in New York studying acting: 'It just seemed the most exciting place to be.' The drama school had trained Kim Cattrall, Lauren Bacall and Katharine Hepburn. 'I became immersed in creativity and learning. Drama school was so much about empowering the person and giving them the tools and techniques and confidence to do what they wanted to do; I didn't stop working.' There, she was briefly married but has stated it was just a quickie to get her green card, and she doesn't talk about it much. She was a rare creature in the Big Apple, and at that time most Americans knew very little about Australia. They would often say to her on hearing her accent, 'Oh, you speak English so well,' as if Australia was not an English-speaking country.

After four years she returned to Australia where she worked non-stop, typically cast in 'tough cookie' roles until a car crash in 1985 put her out of action for nine months. 'It was interesting because it was like, right when I was just sort of back from drama school, and I just had so many films lined up and there was a lot going on, and then bang – I had a broken ankle, a compound fracture and I had skin grafts and it really set me back. It was the first time in my life that I had a sort of real reality check, and it just stopped me dead. I didn't know if I was going to walk again, never mind work as an actress, and my face was crap and my head was aching. I looked like Elephant Woman.'

Determined and on crutches, she auditioned for her landmark cinema role in the 1988 Australian film *Shame*, in which she played a feisty lawyer riding a motorbike through the outback. 'That was probably my most favourite job, and I think the experience of me having to sit for nine months waiting to recover from the accident added to the depth of that character.'

When the film was released in the US, she returned to join the other Aussie hopefuls battling to make it in Tinseltown. She spent five years bouncing between Los Angeles and her homeland. In LA she lived with actor Tom Burlinson, and had a 'blast', amusing herself by reading scripts by the pool of his Bel Air mansion. 'Very Hollywood,' she said. Yet she decided to return home when her breakthrough role in California never came and she became concerned about her lifestyle: 'There were kids in Africa starving and I was worried about the size of my butt.'

She returned to Australia for the role that would change her life, personally and professionally: *Correlli*. 'A psychic told me that if I go back to Australia everything will work out, and she was right,' she said. 'I met the man of my dreams.' And Deborra-Lee got to work with that man on the set of the prison drama. As she mentioned, though, she didn't believe it was love at first sight, although Hugh definitely thought it was: 'Yes, and it happened to me. I was twenty-seven, single and not expecting to get married. Then I met Deb. She was very cool and I had a huge crush on her.'

His first abiding memory of her was the initial morning when a car picked him up to go to rehearsals. Deborra-Lee was in the front seat. 'I thought, that's cool, I like a person who sits in the front seat. And all I knew of her was from her work, and that she was a big star and she was my leading lady. She kind of took off her seat belt, swung around, pulled down her sunglasses, looked me straight in the eye and said, "Deborra-Lee Furness" and I said, "Hi, Hugh Jackman."'

On the second morning, the same driver picked up Hugh, but this time Deborra-Lee wasn't in the car. The driver, who must have seen the disappointment on his face, blurted out, 'Oh sorry, Mr Jackman, I was given instructions to pick her up second.' Hugh smiled to himself as they drove to her home, thinking how on that first day, he had been blown away by her forthright, down-to-earth manner, but underneath it all she had a little bit of a star in her as well. He really liked that and said, 'I found that sexy.'

The sexual tension between Deb's character and Hugh's was evident to all during the series and it didn't take long for this to bubble over into real life. 'I had a crush on Deb almost from the moment we met. I was embarrassed because I didn't think my feelings would be reciprocated. Here I was, a fresh-out-of-college twenty-seven-year-old actor. Her New Year's resolution that year was "no actors and no one under thirty." I was Deb's worst nightmare.' For this reason, he deliberately didn't go near her for a while, trying hard to give her space even though he was very attracted to her.

Deborra-Lee confessed she did have the 'no actors and no one under thirty' rule, but it was due to the fact that she was busy working and she wasn't looking for a relationship. She quickly broke that rule when she met the most extraordinary man ever. There was a connection, a meeting of hearts and minds. 'To be honest, I never thought I would end up with a younger man, but Hugh was more mature and worldly than most forty-year-old men I know.'

They became good mates, spending a lot of time giggling like two school kids at the back of the class, but Hugh continued to hold back his private feelings because he wasn't sure if she felt the same way towards him. After a while, he decided to go for broke and hatched a plan to woo the woman he had fallen so much in love with. He organised a dinner party at his house for about ten people from *Correlli* and invited Deborra-Lee. His father, a great cook, gave him the recipes for a good old-fashioned 'how to impress a girl' meal. The menu consisted of pumpkin soup, snapper and for dessert his old man's signature dish, *crêpes Suzette*. All day, Hugh slaved away, getting everything prepared and creating just the right atmosphere. The hopeless romantic didn't leave anything to chance.

All in all, it turned out to be a strange but rewarding night. Just before he was about to serve the *crêpes*, Deb's mobile phone rang. It was one of her very famous friends, who informed her that he was outside Hugh's house in a limo with Mick Jagger, and Mick was requesting she came down to party.

Inwardly, of course, Hugh was gutted that the girl of his dreams was about to get whisked away by one of the most famous front men in the world. However, he put a brave face on it and went to get Deb's coat. Unbelievably, she told him she wanted to stay. He was stunned. 'But Mick Jagger is outside my house on Beaconsfield Place in Melbourne, waiting for you. What are you doing here? Go with him, enjoy yourself.'

But Deb had made up her mind about who she wanted to party with, and it wasn't the ageing singer. She replied to the invitation: 'Tell Mick I'm having dinner with Hugh Jackman,' then she hung up.

Hugh's legs went to jelly. He thought, wow, how cool is this woman? He went into the kitchen to calm down and get the desserts ready. After a few minutes, she came in to give him a hand. He finally got up the courage to tell her how he felt; he just sort of blurted it out. And to his great relief, she told him she felt the same way. It was as if they had both met each other at the perfect time and were meant to be together.

Instantly, they became an item and went everywhere together. They formed an invisible bond, a rare thing that would deepen and endure as they embarked on what would become a grand odyssey for them both – 'When I met Debs, I just felt I could be myself completely. When you really meet someone that brings out the best in you, it is a really joyous thing.'

Their relationship shifted quickly from best friends, to lovers, to soul mates. Deb proved to be the perfect match for Hugh. He was naive at times, new to the business, while she had an intoxicating can-do attitude and a knack for making people laugh and feel at ease. 'She's pure passion; she has more fun than everyone on the planet. She's brought out a lot of the confidence to be who I am. She looked a lot like Kim Novak, but she's definitely from the Ethel Merman school with her humour. I'm a little behind in the wit department, and she's always saying, "Come on, Hugh, keep up, keep up!"'

As their romance became more serious, Deb took Hugh home to meet her mother for the first time. Fay nearly died because Hugh was covered in fake tattoos and was sporting the mullet haircut of his character in *Correlli*. Yet after 30 minutes of interrogating him, Fay completely changed her mind. She knew this good-looking young man was the one to make her only daughter the happiest woman in the world.

'This is no act either,' said Fay. 'They have the most wonderful and genuine relationship. They see the world through the same eyes. If I had to design a perfect son-in-law, husband and father, he would be Hugh Jackman.'

People in the street began to take notice too as their relationship became public. On one occasion the pair were shopping together in a supermarket, walking around arm in arm. When the check-out girl looked up and saw them, she blurted out to her colleague, 'I knew it was too good to be acting!' with reference to their on-screen romance in *Correlli*.

A few months later, Hugh showed another huge leap of faith when he proposed to Deb: 'No matter how much I thought I knew 100 per cent, you never really know until the moment you ask. I'm an actor so I like to exaggerate things and I was determined that the proposal was going to be good enough that I wouldn't have to exaggerate it. I was working in a show in Melbourne and I had Mondays off so I suggested we go for a walk in the Botanical Gardens. There is a café there where I decided to do it two weeks earlier. So I was nervous and had a mate of mine set up a table with a tablecloth and roses and champagne and breakfast and everything was beautiful so that when we turned the corner right by the lake with the backdrop of Melbourne, she saw the table and said, "wow, they must be doing a Vogue Living shoot or something" and I said "surprise!" She started to cry, which was not in my plan so I knew I had to ask her right away and I did. It turns out there were 40 schoolgirls hiding behind a tree because my friend had seen them coming and made them wait so they wouldn't interrupt us. They finally come out and say "what's happened?" and Deb got on the table and shouts, "I said yes" and they all applauded. That was probably the most romantic thing I've ever done and I just felt a complete sense of relief and joy; it was the best feeling in the world. From that moment on, I felt like I had gotten all that dating crap out of the way and we could get on with our lives.'

Hugh designed the engagement ring himself. He was nervous and didn't really have a clue about jewellery or diamonds, but he knew that he wanted the ring to mirror Deb's personality. He told the jeweller that he didn't know what he was doing or looking for, so he just sat the guy down and explained in detail every nuance of his future wife's personality. It took an hour and a half and he later admitted that he must have bored the guy stupid, but in the end the man said, 'Yeah okay, here's the ring, here's the diamond.'

The couple planned to get married in the spring of 1996. 'You know, there is a fair amount of thinking before you get married, like who is going to be my team-mate on this trip? And then I met Deb and I thought, oh, this is it. I've never met a woman like her. She was a force of nature. I can't tell you how blessed I am to be with her. She makes me laugh. I'm totally inspired by her.'

On their wedding rings they jointly agreed to have matching inscriptions in ancient Sanskrit: *Om paramar mainamar*, which translates as 'we dedicate our union to a greater source'.

Hugh explained the idea behind the inscription, which was very close to both their hearts. 'Deb and I studied at the School of Philosophy in Melbourne and we both believed in the concept of serving others. We had this idea that nothing, no person, no union of two people, no country, is greater than the Absolute. That our life should be dedicated to the service of the absolute, the service of truth, the service of God.'

Their union itself became recognised as the Wedding of

the Year in Melbourne in 1996, and it was reported that a famous women's magazine paid 30,000 Australian dollars for the privilege of publishing the couple's photos from the happy day. The ceremony took place on Saturday, 11 April at St John's church in Melbourne. The reception, held in the historic Rippon Lea Estate in the same city, was a lavish event with all Hugh's family present. Xen Pardoe-Miles, the organiser and calming factor behind some of the biggest weddings in Australia, commented that even to this day, it was one of the best weddings he has ever done.

After Hugh and Deb got hitched, their life turned into one big rollercoaster ride, but the pace of change didn't alter their attitude towards each other. If anything it made them stronger. In fact Hugh said it was ten times better than any single life he could have conjured up for himself. 'To me it was a no-brainer that we should be together. She is the first person in my life I feel 100 per cent comfortable with. If I've done something or feel something that I'm ashamed of doing or feeling, I can tell her and there's no judgment.'

Deborra-Lee, on the other hand, being a free spirit and an only child, had to quickly learn to adapt to having a live-in relationship with Hugh who had been one of five children. 'You have to navigate together and see where you both side on everything, from politics to religion to child-rearing. In a relationship, you're standing there, stark naked, going, "Here you go, warts and all", and you're showing the person you care about and respect the most all your goods, bads and uglies.'

They were savvy enough to realise that if their relationship was to survive in the bizarre world of show business, where celebrity marriages often crash head first and burst into flames at the first bend, they needed to protect and respect each other. 'She'd seen so many relationships go awry, particularly on location when people were away for months on end,' Hugh explained. 'Absence doesn't necessarily make the heart grow fonder; it makes it wander.' They decided to make a pact never to spend more than two weeks apart, which became the backbone of their relationship. Even though they have worked worlds apart, they have never broken that promise.

They use the short times they are apart to spice up their romance. 'My wife loves the idea of me coming home in costume because it makes her feel like she's having an affair, but in a good way. When we met, I was cast as a prisoner with tattoos and she'd say, "Don't take your tattoos off tonight!" and I'd be like, "All right!"' However, Hugh admits it is his stockbroker look and his sexy dance moves that Deb secretly loves the most.

And over the years, he has had lots of opportunities to dress up for Deborra-Lee as his own career went from strength to strength, while she on the other hand suddenly became known in many quarters as 'The Wife'. It was a hard lesson for her at first. She explained, 'I was an actress and all of a sudden, I'm Mrs Jackman. And when I'd go to the bank, the bank manager would talk to Hugh, and I'm like, "*Hello*! What *is* this? Is this the 1950s?" There'd be moments like that, when it was like

I had a new costume, a new character, a role I was playing, so I had to navigate around how that felt.'

According to Deborra-Lee, there was certainly a change of attitude towards her from the press and fans almost immediately after the wedding. She had always been seen as a kick-arse heroine, but all that changed after she said 'I do'. 'When Hugh and I got together the alchemy changed, and I got the wrath. There was a time I felt this rush of negative energy and I thought, what happened? I was a chick's chick and I was, like, the popular kid at school, and all of a sudden there were nasty comments in the magazines being made at me, that I was older than Hugh and playing the role of not working, and being married, and wanting a family.'

The way she was treated at times, by certain people, hurt them both, but it was especially hard on Deb. When they first went to Hollywood, people would rudely ignore her. She'd call it the 'chopped liver syndrome' – she would literally be knocked out of the way by women clamouring for her husband's attention.

Halle Berry, who starred with Hugh in several films, saw this first-hand: 'Hugh is sexy beyond belief. Waves of women were always coming on to him while we were shooting and poor Hugh would always just politely turn them down.'

Hugh continues to maintain that his wife has nothing to worry about at all; he is well aware that all the attention has nothing to do with him and everything to do with his status in Hollywood, and credits his relationship with Deb as keeping his feet firmly on the ground and keeping him humble. On one occasion, when he was leaving for the opening night performance of *Sunset Boulevard*, he turned and told his wife he was off. She said, 'Oh, don't forget to take out the garbage.'

Hugh loves the honesty and humour that Deb puts into everything she does, and although she can be brutal at times, he wouldn't have it any other way. Over the years, Hugh has worked with many beautiful women and he always insists on taking the actresses out for dinner with his wife. 'Invariably, they always like Deb more than me and quite often say, "Your wife is amazing. She's so interesting, a lot more interesting than you." Every person I've ever worked with has ended up liking Deb more than they like me. I remember working with Meg Ryan on *Kate & Leopold* and it was our wedding anniversary. Deb and I planned on going to the Rainbow Room but I had to work. So Meg took Deb out for our anniversary instead.'

Deborra-Lee is quite clearly secure in their relationship, and is confident in what they have together. She accepts all the attention Hugh gets in public and no longer minds as long as he gives her all of his attention when they are alone at home. He often talks about her being the rock in his life, the one giving him the encouragement and support when he needs it most. It was his wife who was the first person he looked for when in 2009 he walked out on stage to present the Oscars, and he was so pleased when she gave him a little nod: 'I knew I could completely die on my ass there. One mistake and the entire film industry could fall out of love with me, or whatever, and everything could fall apart. But when you know there's a rock there, that goes a long way, particularly in this business.'

He came clean later when he said that he was lucky she had actually stayed awake during the ceremony. Apparently Deborra-Lee has a habit of falling asleep at the drop of a hat – especially when she goes to see Hugh's films. 'She's fallen asleep during every movie I've ever done. At one première, this big-time producer, who is known for growling, growled down the row to me, "Wake your wife up, Jackman!"'

The only thing that ever caused Hugh any concern whatsoever about their marriage was when his father uncovered something that he feared would prove there might be an incestuous relationship between himself and Deb. When three of his five children decided to attempt a career on the stage, Hugh's father decided to research his family to see if there was an acting connection among his ancestors. But the investigation dug up a familial problem, which prompted Hugh to beg his dad not to pry further.

Hugh said, 'He found out that two of his great aunts were on the stage in Britain and their maiden name was Furness. My wife's name is Furness as well, and it's a particularly weird spelling of the name. We discovered her ancestors from two generations back were also from the north of England. I started thinking, "My wife is my sister, maybe cousin at best," but we thought, "We've consummated the marriage, what the hell!"'

Even though it turned out to be a bit of a red herring,

it proved to be a great after-dinner story when entertaining guests.

'I believe that we do have, you know, soul mates or partners in this life and when I met Hugh there was just a click and it wasn't, you know, love at first sight, like the second I looked at him and it was just I knew. There was a knowingness and he sort of felt like he got me and it was, he was cute, but it wasn't just about that; it was there was something that just gelled... and I looked at him then and thought this man will be in my life as a friend, and then it developed into something else.'

Deborra-Lee Furness

CHAPTER FIVE

JACKMAN GOES MUTANT

It was October 1999 in Toronto, Canada, and filming had already started on a new big-screen movie based on the cult Marvel comic books, *X-Men*. It promised an all-star cast, an original storyline and spectacular special effects. Everything was in place – the equipment, the crew, the backdrops, the make-up artists, and the main cast. Well, almost all of the main cast. There was one major issue: the man pencilled in to play the reluctant mutant hero, Wolverine, was missing in action.

Dougray Scott, the Scottish actor who cut his teeth in the cult British movie *Twin Town* before moving on to Hollywood, had been selected to play the role. But he was still in New Zealand filming *Mission Impossible 2*, which was running several months behind schedule. This left the movers and shakers at Twentieth Century Fox with a massive headache since Wolverine, the comic strip's shaggy, steel-clawed mutant character, was at the centre of its story.

Director Bryan Singer, who had directed critical favourites such as *The Usual Suspects* (1995) and *Apt Pupil* (1998), waited for his original choice of leading man for as long as he could. At one stage there was a glimmer of hope that Scott would be released early from the filming of *M:I-2* by rival studio Paramount to take his place as Wolverine. When that hope soon disappeared, it became obvious that they needed a new actor urgently or the production would run into serious problems. But who could play the pivotal role and, just as importantly, would they be available at such short notice?

Singer himself had initially turned down the opportunity to direct the *X-Men* blockbuster twice, but changed his mind after reading most of the old comics and watching all 70 episodes of the *X-Men* animated series. Since its 1963 debut as a Marvel Comic, the X-Men had amassed a huge amount of devoted followers and according to Marvel, the series was the most popular comic-book franchise of all time. Like Superman and Batman, two other characters that had leapt from pulp pages and onto the big screen, it was only a matter of time until the mutants came to life onscreen, too. The underlying storyline concerned a band of unique-power possessing mutants living on earth, where they were hated and persecuted by humans. Under the guidance of their leader, Professor Charles Xavier, the X-Men strived for a world where humans and mutants could peacefully co-exist, battling with the radical mutants

(Brotherhood of Mutants), who wanted to exterminate the human race.

Singer and producer Tom DeSanto sent an outline of the film to Fox which had a very serious theme, apparently comparing the conflict between the two leaders in the story, Xavier and Magneto, to the power struggle between Martin Luther King and Malcolm X. Fox liked it and put up a budget of around $60 million for the project.

Bryan Singer started casting the film back in the spring of 1999 and he had already put together a strong and headlining team of actors. He approached Patrick Stewart to play Professor Xavier, a telepathic mutant confined to a wheelchair, who ran a school for gifted mutant kids. Stewart, already renowned for his *Star Trek* work, was hesitant about playing yet another fearless leader, but once he read the script and realised it was a modern movie with a serious theme, he happily accepted the role. Next was Halle Berry, cast to portray Storm, a mutant who could manipulate the weather. Anna Paquin's Rogue character absorbed the power of anyone she touched and Famke Janssen was cast to play a telepathic Jean Grey.

Of course, any action flick worth its special-effects wizardry has to have a worthy villain and *X-Men* had Sir Ian McKellen to play Magneto, one of the most powerful mutants around. His sidekicks included the eerily creepy Ray Park as Mortimer Toynbee/Toad, a very agile fighter with a menacing streak and a long, prehensile tongue. Sabretooth would be played by wrestler Tyler Mane and the shape-shifting Mystique by Rebecca Romijn-Stamos.

However, for Singer, time was fast running out for him to get a replacement for Scott, so the director spent days trawling through the list of other possible candidates who had gone through a set of rigorous interviews, some 10 months prior. Hugh Jackman's name was near the top of the pile marked as strong candidates, which was ironic considering it was an interview that he almost didn't go through with in the first place. Not being a comic-book fan himself, he had never even heard of the X-Men or the hugely popular character, Wolverine. In fact, he thought the audition was for a movie about an Australian pop band of the 1980s called the Uncanny X-Men! And his wife, who had accidentally glanced at the pages of the script, wasn't at all impressed.

'I got four pages of the script,' recalled Hugh. 'I think almost every actor my age in the world got those same four pages. And it started off with...it said, "The mutant Wolverine's claws come out of his hands," and then it had the stage direction "Shook!" with an exclamation mark. "S-H-O-O-K!"'

'Deb got no further than that and said, "Put it down! You're not doing this. It's ridiculous. There you are at the National Theatre working with Trevor Nunn and you're gonna go play a mutant with claws that go "Shook"?'

Hugh didn't know what to think but decided to audition anyway, which caused quite a stir when he turned up with his outrageously unfashionable hairstyle. 'I was doing the musical in London at the time, playing

Curly in *Oklahoma!*, so I had a perm in my hair. I put a hat on to do the audition and about halfway through the casting director was like, "That was great, could you do one without the hat? I can't really see Wolverine wearing a baseball cap."' So Hugh took off the hat and started to read the lines when she jumped in again after two lines and shouted, 'Cut, put the hat on now and can you do it less like a cowboy!' Hugh hadn't been able to help but speak with a bit of the American accent that he had picked up from playing Curly every night for the past few months.

Nonetheless, even with the bad hair day and the fake accent, he must have impressed someone because they planned to fly him to New York on Concorde to meet up with Bryan Singer and do a final test. They even arranged to have him sign a contract upfront in case he got the job. Unfortunately, it all fell through when the makers were told Scott, who was their original choice anyway, had agreed to do the movie straight after *Mission Impossible 2*.

Slightly upset, but as always philosophical about life, Hugh said that if he was honest with himself he was more disappointed that he didn't get to travel on Concorde than the fact that he didn't get the job. And, of course, Deb was over the moon that she didn't have to watch him in a film in which his claws 'shook'. Hugh moved on and finished the stage show in London and later returned home to Australia where he was named Australian Star of 1999 at the Australian Movie Convention, before he headed off to the States for more important business.

So, with Hugh Jackman now popping up towards the top of the possible candidates list, Bryan Singer wondered if the Australian actor was still available, and whether he would still be interested after they had overlooked him in the first place.

Hugh was in LA at the time and about to start adoption proceedings for his son, Oscar. The call, 10 months after the original audition, came as quite a surprise. 'Dougray Scott was doing *M:I-2* and it was going over, and *X-Men* had already started four days earlier. I was asked if I was interested in a second audition. I think I must be in the record books for the longest times between auditions in history. It was like 10 months.'

This time, he didn't hesitate. There was something about the role that felt right to him. He packed up and headed to Canada, only to be stopped by officials because he didn't have a work visa: 'What I did have was a printed sheet with my lines from the script on them. So basically, I'm begging them, "Look, man, I'm having a meeting with the director of *X-Men*."'

The border guard was unimpressed. He yawned and asked Hugh if he was one of the animators. Hugh informed him that he was possibly going to be Wolverine. All of a sudden, the customs guy started screaming out to his colleagues, 'It's Wolverine!' Minutes later, Hugh was signing autographs, before he even got his paws on the job.

However, he blew Bryan Singer away in the second audition, landing the role of the mutant and having his steel claws fitted the very next day. It was official: he was now Wolverine, the feral, hot-headed mutant with a steel skeleton frame, razor claws and mutant lamb chop sideburns.

He still didn't appreciate just how big a deal it really was until he walked into the Creative Artists Agency (CAA) office in LA with Deb to sign the contract and have a glass of champagne with his agent. The whole CAA staff stood up and started yelling down the hallway at him, 'Go, Wolverine, go!'

Deb, who still couldn't picture her husband donning claws and an Elvis hairstyle, muttered, 'I think this is bigger than we ever expected. This is huge.' Later she joked that telling him not to take the role was the one time in her life she had been wrong.

After a short celebration and just enough time to purchase a plane ticket, Hugh was back in Toronto with a suitcase full of sandals and shorts in temperatures of minus one. He was thrown into hair and make-up tests, moulds were made of his hands, and his body quickly transformed into the Wolverine character.

One thing Jackman wasn't quite prepared for was the backlash from the hardened comic-book fans who were not only stunned, but extremely vitriolic in their displeasure at the fact that this unknown actor from Down Under, who was better known for prancing about on the stage, was about to step into the angry boots of Wolverine. They voiced their outrage in letters and emails posted to Marvel and Twentieth Century Fox complaining about their choice. 'But luckily, no one really knew anything else about me, so the jury was out until they saw the movie. After that I think they were happy. I'm sure I would have heard if they weren't,' Hugh remarked.

One of the main complaints from *X-Men* fans about Hugh was the small fact of his size. At 6ft 3in tall, Hugh was an entire foot taller than the comic book hero Wolverine. To get over the size difference the filmmakers were frequently forced to shoot him from unusual angles or only from the waist up. On occasion, Jackman would open his legs wider than usual to make him appear shorter than he actually was.

'The character I play is actually only 1.6m [5ft 3in]. Before I had any kind of acting profile I was encouraged to lie about my height. I was told to say I was about 6ft [1.83m] tall. I was worried about it when I first had my audition because pleasing fans of the franchise was important.'

In fact, the subject of his height came up in discussions on the internet; fans didn't think it was right. A lot of people who saw the film and had never met him thought he was very short: 'James Marsden, who played Cyclops, who is only 10cm [4 in] shorter than me, was put on boxes and platforms in our scenes together. You'll notice that every character in *X-Men* looked taller than me,' Hugh explained.

Aside from the height issue, the director and Hugh both knew that the look of the character was ultimately important. He needed to look real, stylish and cool, yet recognisable to fans. The last thing they wanted was another comical Dick Tracy character. Hugh had three weeks of hair and make-up tests, and at one point had 14 people around his chair in the trailer checking out his mane. Until he could grow a beard, they had to add hair extensions, and they used a ton of hairspray to get the big-haired look of Wolverine.

They also gave him a set of dangerous 9in claws, which were extremely tough to get used to wearing. The first pair he wore were made of steel. Hugh said, 'These looked great, but I couldn't fight with them. I punctured myself. I hit myself with them and cut my head open. I was fighting with one of the stunt women and something happened and one of the claws went straight into her. And I stopped and looked at her arm and it was bleeding badly. She screamed out. "Yes, I've been stabbed by Wolverine!"' Everyone stood around shaking their heads at the joy which was evident in the girl's face. 'But that's stunt people for you,' Hugh added.

On the other hand (or the other claw!), they had some fun with them too. Between takes, Hugh would often stick marshmallows on his claws and roast them over the fire, while the crew jokingly fabricated him new 'claws' – one hand featured a pair of scissors, another had a magnifying glass taped to it.

Around 700 pairs of Wolverine claws were constructed for the original *X-Men* film. They were made of metal for close-ups, plastic for longer shots and rubber for stunts. Each pair was specially fitted for Jackman or his stuntman. The special-effects crew also made an incredible replica of the star's arm so they could film the claws physically popping out without using digital effects, which proved extremely expensive as it was only used once.

Hugh confessed he had never read any of the comics, dubbed in many quarters as the 'thinking man's comic book', but he soon found out there were thousands who did – in Australia, and everywhere else, for that matter. In fact, people were extremely passionate about the books, especially the Wolverine character. Hugh believed that playing someone who was still alive, like Will Smith did when he played Muhammad Ali, was a high-pressure job, but in a way, playing a fictional character who is larger than life in so many people's minds, and an idol to so many grown men, was even tougher. At Halloween, hundreds of kids want to be Wolverine; forty-year-old men get their favourite *X-Men* character tattooed on their backs. Some even name their dogs Logan (Wolverine's civilian name) after the rebellious mutant.

Mutton chops and big hair aside, being thrown into the role a week into filming didn't leave Hugh any time to get to understand or grasp the inner workings of his character. Even though Bryan Singer didn't want his cast to look at the old comic books, as he wanted the actors to bring their own personalities to the roles, Hugh secretly read the comic strips, falling in love with the artwork: 'I feel like a lot of what's in the comic books informed me in the way I approached the role physically. For instance, a battle in a comic book might take four pages, but you're only shown sixteen images or so of a character. In that space the reader is conveyed all the physical and emotional ups and downs of a big battle. It's amazing how compacted it was.' He tried to incorporate the images that stuck in his head into Wolverine's fighting stances and techniques.

One of the hardest things for him to capture was Logan's aggression, an emotion that he had sometimes failed to achieve during his time at acting school. He knew there must be a beast inside him dying to get out; he just needed to find some inspiration to unleash it. And so he called on his favourite play in drama school, *The Bacchae*, a gruesome Greek tragedy about a king who literally gets eaten alive by a group of women in a kind of orgy. 'I loved that idea of animalistic chaos and following our own desires. I think Wolverine represents that in its most allegorical sense. He's a man who battles between the animal and the human, between the chaos in him and the self-control he must have. We all deal with this to some extent. At which point should we let go and do what we want to do? And when should we submit to rules? Coming to terms with our true natures and who we really are has always been a fascination to humans. I know it fascinates me.'

And he even studied how wolves react in the wild, a technique he had learnt while in drama school. He visited a science museum, where they had a section on wolves on a 3D dome movie screen. As he sat there and watched, he was mesmerised by the way the wolves kept their noses close to the ground. One of Wolverine's characteristics is his extra-sensitive sense of smell, and

Hugh tried to incorporate these animal-like actions into his film character.

The Wolverine character is ultimately a good guy who is very angry inside, so he also took inspiration from two famous characters. Jean-Pierre Rives, a good-looking, blonde-haired French international rugby player and captain, is one of Hugh's sporting heroes. He remembered growing up and seeing Rives running around like a mad terrier with blood pouring down his face in almost every game. It was an image that stuck with most kids who watched the sport at that time: 'And then I get a role like this and I think I am that terrier, I am Jean-Pierre Rives.' The other was a young Mike Tyson. Hugh drew on the boxer's habit of prowling the ring, all-powerful and compact, before the opening bell.

He used the images to instigate controlled aggression within himself, but the significant turning point came one icy morning in the middle of winter in Toronto, where they were shooting: Hugh took a cold shower by mistake. His wife was sleeping in the next room and so he couldn't scream. He stood there for a minute holding all the emotion in and suddenly realised this was exactly the way Logan must have felt – he wanted to yell and punch someone's head in, but couldn't. From then on, every morning before Hugh went on set, he took a cold shower to remind himself of what he needed to do.

However, sometimes getting pumped up too much caused some problems that ended up being quite painful for the star. In one scene he got into character and while leaping off a 6ft wall, thinking he was invincible, he caught his testicles and ended up rolling around in agony. After that particular incident, he decided to leave the more dangerous stunts to his double, Steve, which also pleased the studio and the insurance company.

It was only after he started to master the inner character and take comfort in what he was trying to achieve that Hugh really started to take notice of the powerful meaning behind the script – people isolated from society, treated with hatred and suspicion because of special gifts they possessed. The story explored how the superheroes coped with the gifts that made them powerful and respected, yet weak and misunderstood. In a strange way it brought back memories for Hugh of his parents' split and the way people had treated him like some kind of misfit or outsider. He found the story easy to relate to.

When filming started, he felt as if he was stepping into a completely different world, a world unlike anything else he had been used to. It was the biggest movie he had ever done. The budget for *Erskineville Kings* had been under one million dollars, while *Paperback Hero* was considerably less than that. And now, here he was starring in something where the budget ran into tens of millions of dollars.

The first night of filming summed up just how bizarre it really was. An outdoor sequence was being filmed at the train station and Hugh went along to watch. 'I remember pulling up and it was like going to a Rolling Stones concert. There must have been about 400 people there, cast, crew and extras. There were these big balloons on which they hung the lights, way up in the sky, which lit up the entire area. It was a surreal feeling.' Someone showed him to his trailer, which was so big that it was the size of the pub back home, and a while later, when he was sitting in there, someone else popped their head in to apologise about the size of the trailer and said that the real one would be coming in on Monday.

Another thing that took Hugh 'a while to get used to' was the amount of time it took to get him ready for each scene, even though this was nothing compared to what some of the other actors had to endure. He still has an enormous respect for Rebecca Romijn-Stamos, who played Mystique. Her elaborate blue cosmetic coating alone took eight hours daily to apply to her naked skin and an additional two hours to remove. And that wasn't the worst of it: during that time she couldn't drink wine, use skin creams or fly the day before filming because the change in body chemistry would cause the 100 prosthetic pieces to fall off. In between takes, she was kept isolated in a windowless room to ensure her look remained secret. To celebrate her last day on set, Rebecca brought in a bottle of tequila and did shots with her fellow cast and crew members during a break in filming. Unfortunately, that day she happened to be filming the Wolverine versus Mystique fight scene (which she did in her birthday suit). Later, she threw up blue-coloured vomit from all the chemicals in her make-up – all over Hugh.

Aside from the huge boost in his career, another massive bonus for Hugh was the opportunity to work alongside, in his eyes, two of the greatest actors alive today; Patrick Stewart and Sir Ian McKellen. He described them as the English versions of Robert De Niro and Al Pacino. It was more than an honour; working with the Shakespearean actors from years ago was like a dream come true. Ian McKellen was a hero of Hugh's and he had watched him on stage years before playing Macbeth. 'To actually work with them, I had to kind of forget that I was a little bit in awe and remember that as Wolverine, I couldn't give a stuff who they were. We have this design of them as doyens of the theatre, but both of them love acting and are also surprisingly silly and childlike.'

The scenes between the two great actors fascinated and excited Hugh. Both had a very English way of acting, which is more about what the character doesn't say than what it actually does: 'They had a beautiful way of playing that. There was so much going on underneath the surface and in the pauses, and when they just stopped to listen. It is an English tradition, particularly with the last generation of actors, which you see in Ben Kingsley, Michael Gambon, Ian McKellen and Patrick Stewart; it's their ability to be irreverent and playful, and emotionally full and open, yet intellectually rigorous. I think their intellectual rigor is extraordinary, the way they attack the text.'

Despite all the positives associated with the production, the journey to get the movie into the cinemas was troubled. The release date, originally scheduled for Christmas 2000, was brought forward to the main summer slot due to a rescheduling of some of Fox's other films that year. It caused a race against time, and director Singer barely completed it in time for its release date, prompting Fox to cancel a June press junket to promote *X-Men*.

However, the buzz over the *X-Men* film spread from coast to coast in the states and then quickly spread around the world without the extra promotion. Despite the sceptics, and the advice given to Hugh to book another gig before the film came out in the event of it being a flop, there were massive crowds of fans camped out in front of Los Angeles theatres to buy tickets on opening night. Indeed, the gamble to bring the comic books to life paid off handsomely: *X-Men* brought in $57 million in its opening weekend, breaking a box-office debut record for non-sequel films. Hugh remarked, 'I think the studio was nervous leading up to the release. No one expected the opening we had on the first *X-Men*. I think it really shocked a lot of people. It became a phenomenon overnight.' The film eventually grossed $157 million and was the ninth highest-grossing movie of 2000. It was also great news for *Marvel*, not only in comic book sales but also for the potential of bringing other *Marvel* hero characters like Spiderman, Captain America and Ghost Rider to life.

Even the most hardened of Wolverine fans melted when they witnessed how Hugh brought the comic book Wolverine, an edgy and conflicted character, to vivid life, lending his considerable presence to the role. He effortlessly stepped into the character's big shoes and didn't once look out of place, bringing a rock-solid performance, smouldering temperament and a confused sensitivity to the complex Wolverine. In so doing, he won over both general audiences and fans of the cult hit comic book character alike.

'Only after the film came out, and the fans came out, did I realise that if I'd done a bad job, not only would it have been the end of my career, but I would've been spat on in the street, you know? Because I met people who have their entire back tattooed with Wolverine. I mean, they are serious, trust me!'

Despite spending much of the film's 104 minutes hidden behind some seriously bizarre hair, Hugh's popularity and Australian heart-throb profile immediately started to grow. He had to quickly learn how to deal with notoriety in the United States. Before the movie he was relatively unknown there and didn't mind the anonymity. Suddenly he found himself, and his much-photographed face, a hot commodity in Hollywood: 'I was sort of thrilled, in a way, that I got the chance to play the character before I became famous. Once you start doing talk shows and people start to see your personality, it gets harder and harder to get away from that. So the fact that this was my first blockbuster film meant I got a role that I probably never would have if I'd been known for something else.'

Like Mel Gibson coming to life as *Mad Max*, or the cigar-smoking Clint Eastwood in the *Fistful of Dollars* spaghetti westerns, or John Travolta strutting his stuff in tight-fitting trousers in *Saturday Night Fever*, Wolverine was Hugh's very own defining moment.

With the film's success, he started to get a taste of what it was like to be an 'X-Man'. Obsessed fans followed him around town, popping up at odd times and places. 'I kind of keep wanting to say, "How the hell do you know where I am all the time? I don't even know where I'm going. What's going on here?"'

It was all quite overwhelming and it took a while for him to appreciate just how successful the film was. 'If you'd asked me to play a game of, "Okay, you're going to have a Hollywood career. What movie would be the one that would break you?" This would be a million miles away from what I would choose. I never in a million years would have guessed it would be this. I knew it was a great role once I read the script, and I was into it. I knew nothing about the comic book, but I'm like, "This is *Dirty Harry*, and this is kind of the Han Solo anti-hero thing that I kind of grew up with. I get, I think I'm onto a great role here."'

Part of that role included going to the *X-Men* conventions held throughout the US, where whole displays were set up of all the *X-Men* paraphernalia. Hugh commented, 'It was the closest thing to being a rock star.'

At one show, his wife couldn't quite resist telling a five-year-old boy that the man she was with was Wolverine. The little kid looked up and stared at Hugh. In complete awe, his father said, 'You're Wolverine! So tell me about it! When's the movie coming out? My son's been waiting for so long!' Hugh focused on the kid: '"So you watch *X-Men*?" He goes, "Yeah." I said, "Who's your favourite character?" The child's response? "Cyclops."'

The entire merchandising around the film freaked Hugh out. There were dolls, pillowcases, rulers, magnets, wallpaper, towels and even a blow-up voice-activated punchbag, which he later got for his son. 'At first I couldn't believe I was doing a movie where I was going to be a doll, but when I saw them I thought it was kind of funny.'

He harked back to the day on set when the guy who had been designing the dolls came out with the prototype clay heads and all the leading actors had to look at them and give their approval. Ian McKellen loved his, saying it looked young and nothing like him: 'I love it, you can do it!' he said. Hugh thought the same; he didn't want his to look completely like him – 'I don't know why. People might start sticking forks into it or sticking it in the freezer, or even feeding it to the squids! There was even one figure that talked with my voice. How weird is that?'

As for encountering mobs of comic-book fans, he had no complaints. At first, he didn't get mobbed because he wasn't recognised but he still had the odd weird encounter with fans. The incident with Vinnie at Bobby's restaurant in New York is one of his favourite anecdotes; he explained why: 'The restaurant is owned by De Niro, so actors go there all the time, and Vinnie's the manager. The waiter came up and said, "Are you the guy who plays Wolverine?" This is about the fourth time I've been there. I said, "Yeah, I am." He said, "Oh my God, Vinnie's a huge fan and really wants to see you. He's over there, behind the counter."

'I look over, and there's Vinnie, ducking behind his little booth, literally, ducking underneath. Ten minutes it took him to come and see me. And he came over in a sweat, sweating. I said, "Nice to meet you, Vinnie. Are you a fan?" He looked at me, he goes, "Am I a fan?" Then there was a silence. He took his shirt off, in the middle of his restaurant, he turned around, and he had a full colour tattoo of Wolverine on his back. He goes, "Am I a fan? Of Wolverine?" He got down on his knees, he was sweating, he said, "Thank you for doing the film! I loved the film! It's fantastic!" My wife pulled out a camera and said, "Vinnie, do you want a few shots?" Well, Vinnie was doing the poses. He had his arm around me, he turned round and was flexing his back with the muscles. We took a whole roll of film for Vinnie and sent them to him. I think I ate there for free.'

A few months later, Hugh was at a launch of a film at Fox Studios along with Nicole Kidman, Cate Blanchett and Tom Cruise. They were standing around when he saw Dougray Scott, who was waving to him. The two men started chatting and Dougray told Hugh that he'd seen the movie and that he thought Hugh was fantastic in it. Hugh simply said he was sorry; he didn't know what else to say, but the Scotsman shrugged his shoulders and simply replied, 'Ah, that's Hollywood, these things happen.'

'I offered Hugh the role on the spot. Usually, you think about it or you make a call, or you call an agent. It's the first time I've ever offered a role to an actor on the spot since I offered Kevin Spacey The Usual Suspects. *Jackman was really extraordinary.'*
Bryan Singer, director of *X-Men*

CHAPTER SIX

SOMEONE LIKES HUGH

Suddenly, Hugh Jackman found himself catapulted from near-obscurity, especially in the USA, to immediate worldwide superstardom following the success of *X-Men*. His popularity grew to unimaginable heights within the film industry and his agent company (CAA) were bombarded with more scripts and offers than they could handle. Wisely, he wanted to avoid being typecast in the Wolverine-type action hero role for the time being, but he was keen to flex his acting muscles. Due to the amount and range of offers available, he was now able to carefully select characters that were far removed from the brooding, anti-authority Logan. It proved to be a busy and fruitful time for the man from Oz.

Not averse to doing a spot of comedy – he had done a little on stage and on TV, back in Australia – Hugh took the role of an incorrigible womaniser in the 2001 bitter-sweet, romantic comedy *Someone Like You* alongside Greg Kinnear and Ashley Judd. The screenplay had been adapted from the novel *Animal Husbandry* by Laura Zigman, which was actually titled *Animal Attraction* on its release in the UK.

The story tells of how, after a series of ill-fated relationships, Jane (Ashley) finally meets Mr Right, Ray (Kinnear) who is emotionally available and not afraid of commitment. Six weeks into their blissful courtship, Ray asks Jane to move in with him and they start looking at apartments. But little by little, Ray starts to pull away and Jane realises that once again she's been dumped. Her womanising co-worker, Eddie (Hugh), just happens to be looking for a roommate and so Jane reluctantly moves in.

Desperate to understand what happened and to get over Ray, she comes up with a theory of interpreting male-female relations by observing the behaviours of wild animals. She shares the idea with a friend who works at a men's magazine and is given an anonymous editorial column devoted solely to her thoughts on the matter. But no one could have predicted the chord she would strike among women with her theory, and the column's wild success makes Jane start to question her conclusions and open her eyes to what might be right in front of her.

The very contemporary, funny and insightful film about male-female relationships helped the handsome Jackman to show off his charming side as Jane's serial-dating co-worker. Hugh found it very liberating to play someone like Eddie, the kind of guy who can just say whatever is on his mind and get away with it. He half-joked that it was the way all men would love to act if they could get away with it.

The significance behind the storyline made him look back to the time when he was single and still on the market: 'If I think back to the people I dated or went out with, not one was like the other. I was not one of those guys that went for the same type of woman all the time. And I never understood why, when a guy is going to get together with a woman, they would want the woman to come back to their place! I always think what a waste when you could go back to her place, see inside her home, see how she does things. Coming back to your own place seemed kind of boring to me, especially when you're living with four other guys in a silly little place in Chippendale.'

Like most Hollywood romantic comedies, the film ended with Hugh and Ashley sharing a freeze-frame kiss. Commenting on the clichéd lovey-dovey ending, Hugh shrugged his shoulders and said, 'It's Hollywood. What can you say? They don't finish with the argument or when, three weeks later, they're giving each other the shits and saying, "This is not going to work out." Also, that damn song is never playing in the background, either. When you're kissing, you're thinking the baby's going to wake up, or it's when the phone rings.'

Their kiss on film, like most on-screen smooches, wasn't as romantic as it seemed. The pleasure at these moments is usually lost with the pressure of the camera crew milling around and the director shouting instructions: 'You have people telling you, "Just open your mouth a little more, but don't use your tongue. We don't want the tongue, because close up it really looks ugly on film, but we really want it to look passionate. Come in for a slow kiss, make it more romantic, etc."' Hugh also commented that at the end of the scene, Ashley's face looked a bit like Ronald McDonald's, thanks to his two-day-old stubble!

Someone Like You did fairly well at the box office, with most of the critics giving it the thumbs-up, and it gave Hugh the opportunity to work with two of the industry's funniest men: experienced director and natural comedian Tony Goldwyn and Greg Kinnear, who was known in the business as one of the funniest guys on the planet.

With the romantic comedy under his belt, Hugh was on a roll and nothing could slow him down. Reuniting with Halle Berry, he then accepted a part in the hacker-heist movie from Warner Brothers called *Swordfish*, produced by Joel Silver, who had also produced *The Matrix.* In *Swordfish,* Hugh plays a jaded super-hacker who is recruited by an outrageously wealthy and charismatic criminal genius (John Travolta) to write a program set to steal $9.5 billion from the US Government. It's a mix of espionage, thriller, suspense and action, all thrown into one.

'Professionally, my life changed a lot after *X-Men,* like, amazingly. The scripts, they started to come in, and all of a sudden I was acting opposite John Travolta in this Joel Silver picture. I was like, "Whoa, hold the phone!"'

Hugh apparently met the producers by accident at LAX airport on his way to New York when they were in the middle of scouting for talent to cast in the film. They raced up to the first-class lounge and sat down with him to talk about it. Hugh was impressed with the idea, so they handed him the script to read on the plane. He thought the first three pages included one of the best monologues he had seen in a long time for John Travolta's character. Hugh turned to his wife and said, 'I'm doing it,' and she challenged him by commenting that he was only on page three. But he added, 'Even if it goes to shit from here, it's brilliant!' Words that probably came back to haunt him after the film was released.

John Cusack and Val Kilmer were also considered for the part of Stanley, Hugh's character, but ultimately, director Dominic Sena opted for Jackman because he felt the actor was less typecast than Cusack or Kilmer. It was rumoured that John Travolta had turned down the part of Gabriel Shear a total of six times before changing his mind when he heard director Dominic Sena was on board, and that the leading man would receive a reported $20 million for his troubles.

Hugh signed up prior to Berry, and was ecstatic when he found out that she was being considered for the role. 'I wanted to email her the whole time and say, "Please do it," but I didn't want to put pressure on her.' The two actors had worked together on X-Men, where they'd forged an on-set friendship. 'The moment I heard she was doing it, I was like "Yes!" because I couldn't think of any actor who could have that presence the role requires, as well as the acting chops. So of course I was so thrilled. And of course Halle and I, it seems like we work together at least once a year, so we don't want to break that rule.'

Along with the pleasure of working alongside film veteran John Travolta, Hugh also got to share an outdoor scene with the beautiful Berry which features her topless. When asked how he handled the scenario, aside from claiming his eyes never left her face, he said, 'To be honest I was probably more embarrassed than she was. But it was one of those scenes that took place over three days. The first day we were scheduled to do it in the morning, there were sun and clouds. Halle decided to sit there on the chaise longue the whole time, waiting for the conditions to improve. But it was postponed for the day.'

The next day wasn't any better. In fact, the weather got worse. Even though they were shooting in Los Angeles, it was almost zero degrees. Even with the heaters set up by the crew to keep her warm, Berry was still freezing cold and covered in goosebumps. Filming stretched out into the third day and by that time no one really cared if she was topless or not; they all just wanted to wrap it up and move on. 'So by the time we were shooting on the third day, I mean she was practically arriving in the car naked,' recounts Hugh.

Berry remembers the time vividly: 'He's one of the kindest men I've ever met. I was very nervous and Hugh was more concerned about me than I was. He wasn't just sitting around waiting for me to take off my shirt; he was the one who called for the set to be closed and he told a guy who didn't need to be there to beat it. I had to shoot that scene three times, and thanks to Hugh it wasn't stressful.'

During another sexy scene, she was clad in skimpy lingerie. John Travolta entered through a door and was supposed to say the short line, 'This is friendly.' Instead he blurted out, 'OH MY GOD, just look at that body on that girl! Can we applaud that, please?' Everyone looked at him in amazement, mouths wide open. He simply turned and added, 'What? She has... It's perfect!'

The spontaneous reaction from the superstar broke the ice for everyone on the set caught in the embarrassing situation, and reduced them all to fits of giggles.

But not all scenes featured Berry half-clad. Another scene, between Hugh and Halle, was for some reason virtually identical to one that they shared in *X-Men*. After meeting Gabriel for the first time, Stanley (Hugh) is seen throwing water on his face while Ginger (Halle) watches over his left shoulder in the background. It was a carbon copy of the scene at the train station in the original *X-Men* film where Hugh (as Wolverine) is seen throwing water on his face while Berry (as Storm) watches over his left shoulder in the background. No one would comment on whether this was by accident or design.

In yet another scene, Deborra-Lee turned up unannounced on set, only to find her husband filming a scene in which a beautiful young actress is performing oral sex on him – 'There was a scene in *Swordfish* where I had a gun to my head, I'm trying to crack a code and a girl under the table is giving me a blow-job, all at once.'

They had been shooting on and off for two days and to

make it seem real, Hugh told the girl to occasionally pinch his inner thigh hard so that his facial expressions would be convincing. After the scene was finished, his wife strolled up to the girl and said, 'Hi, I'm Deborra-Lee, Hugh's wife, and I think you're giving my husband a blow-job.' The actress went bright red and apologised, but Deborra just added, 'Oh, don't worry. You're getting paid to do it, so enjoy it!' Luckily for Hugh, it is one of the advantages of having a wife with a sense of humour who also happens to be in the business.

He also got to add stunt-driving to his list of expertise in *Swordfish*: 'Stunt driving was a lot of fun to do. I went along for the class and the first thing you do in the car is get in with the instructor, and you're up on two wheels, doing reverse one-eighties, and sliding into parking spaces. Within an hour, you're doing all the stuff you thought you'd never do, or thought wasn't possible.'

In addition to driving like a maniac on-screen, he also had to learn about the world of computer hacking. And in true Jackman style, he went all out in his preparation, spending time with real-life hackers rather than reading books on the subject. Like many people, he had a stereotype of what hackers were like, but found most of them to be racier, tougher and more edgy than he had imagined. Indeed, lots of them were into amphetamines and the whole rave scene: 'I saw it as a very adrenaline kind of culture, very subversive, powerful, a kind of idealistic and rebellious kind of group.'

The actor was so determined to be just like a true, grungy computer hacker that he turned up on set the first day with a nose-ring, which took producer Joel Silver completely by surprise. He looked at it for about five minutes and all of a sudden Hugh could feel about 15 other people, including the director, staring at his piece of jewellery. Then Silver shouted, 'No, I don't want it. That nose-ring would be 40ft on the screen and I can't deal with that!' The nose ring was subsequently removed, never to return.

But the star did come clean on the fact that he may not have been the perfect fit for the role of a hacker as he was no good at all on computers and rarely, if ever, even surfed the internet. As a matter of fact, when Hugh first came to Hollywood, his lack of computer skills nearly drove his agent insane because the rising star refused to use his PC to research all the important people he would be dealing with. 'When my agent called me to see how I was getting on with the research, there would be a long silence and I could hear him whispering "fucking idiot" on the other end.' In the end the agent just gave up and did the research himself, handing the results to Hugh in person.

While *Swordfish* had a great cast and one of the most complicated and visually stunning opening scenes in Warner Brothers' history, it did poorly at the box office and even worse with the critics. Some of them even went so far as to say it was one of the worst films ever made. It was then withdrawn from cinemas shortly after the terrorist attacks on New York City and Washington DC on 11 September 2001, due to a scene which involved a building exploding.

To Hugh's credit, he was saved from receiving too

much flak about his own performance. Poor reviews aside, it was time to move on and like most romantic types at heart, he had always fancied playing the dashing gentleman in an English period drama. So when filmmakers were having difficulty in finding a believable Leopold, he jumped at the chance when asked to take on the role of the charming Third Duke of Albany for the movie *Kate & Leopold*. Commenting on the casting, director James Mangold said, 'Hugh is an amazing actor and entirely unique in this day and age. He just has the essence of great movie stars of the past. There are times that you can see Errol Flynn or Cary Grant in him.'

Kate & Leopold was a romantic comedy fable, which also starred the wonderful and talented Meg Ryan. Two strangers from different times meet in New York City. Leopold, an impoverished English baron living in New York at the end of the 19th century, needs to marry a rich lady to help recover his family position. Kate, a successful businesswoman, also lives in New York, but in the year 2001. When Leopold falls into a mysterious time portal and awakens in the modern era, he and Kate meet and fall in love.

Before filming began, Hugh was nervous about getting the accent just right and not offending anyone back home in Australia: 'Upper-class English men are never portrayed as the likeable leading man. They're usually something else. I won't go into it, but, growing up, that was my experience,' he said. 'The accent wasn't that hard for me to do because my father's English, from Cambridge, and my mother's English. I'd been in

England a lot. So, I got the sound right, but my dialogue coach said I also sounded as if I had a carrot up my you-know-what, as if I was *judging* the character, which I *was*. So I stayed with the accent, not the character, for about two weeks at home. It drove my kid crazy because I was reading him stories in that voice. It certainly drove my wife crazy.'

He worked with an etiquette coach, the same one who had assisted other actors on *Sense and Sensibility*, to ensure he got the character's mannerisms just right. The aim was to have him appear poised and intelligent, while at the same time trying to look relaxed. He had sessions twice a day for weeks, where the coach would literally slap his hands when he gesticulated. She'd say, 'Oh, that's a dead giveaway, you're *so* middle-class, Hugh.' Eventually, Hugh learned to sit on his hands to stop them from waving about. The aim of this was to slow his mind and keep him calm. In fact, he discovered that gesticulating was seen as un-aristocratic in 19th-century England for just that reason – it signified a busy, cluttered mind, which was not considered becoming in the upper classes.

Hugh also wanted to find out about the people from that period, and so he did some extensive research to learn all about the rules and the customs. In the 19th century, individuals actually practised looking effortless in order to make the person they were with feel more relaxed and comfortable. When someone spoke, people would truly listen. Whenever anyone entered a room, everyone would stand up. And when someone sat down, another person would pull out their chair so as to make it easier for them to join the group and feel welcome. The objective behind it all was to take care of the other person first.

And his wife benefited, as Hugh learned to appreciate others more. 'My wife likes it. She's getting a few more flowers these days, but she still yells from the bathroom, "Put that toilet seat down, Leopold!"'

Hugh really liked playing the role of Leopold, and he enjoyed the way he and his character developed throughout the film. 'But let's be clear here, I'm certainly no Leopold in life,' he quipped. 'I mean, I grew up with English parents and my father being very English in terms of manners at the table, and there were lots of rules. I kind of revolted against it. And now here I am, doing this movie, and etiquette coaching really made me understand it all. It's an art form, a system of treating the other person as more important than yourself. It's the opposite of what I thought. I thought manners were all about shutting you up and keeping you quiet.'

While on set, he had the chance to get to know Meg Ryan for the first time. Like most, he was aware she was a brilliant comedian and a wonderful actress, but he didn't appreciate just how extraordinarily generous, warm-hearted and down-to-earth she was. 'Two minutes with Meg and you realise she's a very special lady. One day while we were rehearsing on the sound stage and there was no one else there; I asked my driver to go and pick up some sushi. Meg came up and said "Sushi, I love sushi – where did you get that from?" I told her I got my driver to go and get it and she said, "You can just go and ask your driver to get your lunch?" I said, "Well, yeah.

Hello? Meg, you're a major motion picture star. You can ask your driver, who is waiting outside 24 hours a day, to get it." And she said, "I always forget things like that. I'm not a very good star. I've got to get better at that.'"

The two became great friends, even to the point where Meg felt inclined to help him out of a very personal dilemma one night. 'I was working on the night of my fifth wedding anniversary and so Meg phoned my wife and took her out to dinner instead of me. My leading lady took my wife out for my wedding anniversary! Kind of odd.'

As well as taking etiquette lessons, he also studied ballroom dancing and trained to ride a horse for *Kate & Leopold*. It was the latter that made him look a bit of a fool in front of his leading lady. During filming, he had given her the impression he could ride. On the day they were going to shoot Meg on the back of the horse that Hugh was riding, the director started by shooting a scene where Hugh was riding towards her on his own. 'So Meg came on the set to watch. First take, I went straight past, through the shot, everything was fine except the horse decided to put on the brakes because it saw a light and I went straight over the top, landing on my arse. And, of course, it hurt like hell, but the first thing I did was look up and there was Meg shaking her head and going, "Oh no! I'm getting on that horse in two hours with this guy."'

A red-faced Hugh knew deep down that he needed to get straight back on the horse or Meg would never ride with him. And so he did, and luckily Meg joined him, which he believed was a truly heroic thing to do after watching him fall off so ungracefully. During one scene, they had to gallop through Central Park. Both were very nervous because they thought they were going to crash into all the filmmaking instruments and crew around them. They held on for dear life. When Hugh dismounted, he joked that he needed a few days off to recover because he felt like he had suffered three broken ribs from Meg holding on so tightly.

Later on that afternoon, the two were asked to rock backwards and forwards on a punchbag suspended on ropes to simulate a shot of them on horseback riding through a stack of trees. Hugh thought that this would turn out to be the most ridiculous scene ever, but was pleasantly surprised when he saw it on film: 'But now, if you watch the movie back that looks real and the one that was real looked fake.'

With Meg being so easy to work with and Jim Mangold, the director, making the atmosphere so enjoyable, Hugh commented that *Kate & Leopold* was probably one of the most fun films that he had ever worked on. And it seemed to pay off for the actor because his charming English manner and upright moral stance created the perfect romantic lead actor. For his performance, he received a Golden Globe nomination for Best Performance by an Actor in a Motion Picture.

Another huge bonus for Hugh, and everyone else involved with the movie, was that singing superstar Sting wrote the title song, 'Until'. Sting had seen an unedited version of the film and liked it. 'I thought it was romantic, and very, very funny,' he remarked. 'It was just what I needed to watch at the time. There were still all kinds of mayhem going on in the world. So, I thought this film was a perfect antidote and it's very easy to get inspired to write a song in a similar vein.' The song was nominated and won many awards, including the Golden Globe Award for Best Song and a nomination for the Academy Award for Best Song in a Film.

The reviews were good, with some calling it a perfect date movie and others saying that even though it was strictly a 'chick flick', it was one that men could relate to. Hugh reckoned that personally he learned a lot from playing the character of Leopold. It taught him to try and do everything with grace and presence, and to always try to do something romantic and unpredictable for the woman he loved. 'Unfortunately, I could become the most hated guy in films if the characters I play are so romantic, and while watching the movie a girl said to her date, "Why don't you do things like that for me?" So my advice to any bloke is that before you go and see the movie, do something unexpected for her. Then, when you watch the movie, she'll turn to you and say, "You're just like this guy."'

All things considered, it turned out to be an eventful year for Hugh as far as films and playing alongside great actors and actresses went. 'Deb and I often stop and go, "Oh my God!" It's a bit weird when you walk in to do a rehearsal with John Travolta. Your heart skips a beat a little bit because you grow up with them a huge idol for you, then you get to meet them. It's a little odd.' He went on to further explain how unreal it all seemed. 'Then while shooting *Kate & Leopold*, I was sitting watching dailies with one of the other actors and my character was about to come on at the end of the scene, so there I was one minute watching Meg do a scene then all of a sudden I got to walk on, and it was like one of those moments where I'm watching a Meg Ryan movie and all of a sudden I walk on! I could never have dreamed of all the wonderful things I've gotten to do and the people I've worked with, so I feel very blessed.'

When *Kate & Leopold* finished, Hugh went back to the gym to bulk up his muscles for the second instalment of *X-Men*. It was less yoga and etiquette lessons, and more Neanderthal grunting and sharpening of claws. Logan was about to return!

But not just yet. With everything Hugh had going on he still managed to fit in some other activities in 2002. He put on his tuxedo to be part of a large celebrity cast asked to present the 74th Annual Academy Awards broadcasted live from the Kodak Theater in Hollywood. Those presenting included Woody Allen, Halle Berry, Russell Crowe, Tom Cruise, Denzel Washington, Will Smith and a host of others. Although he had a small presenting role, Hugh admitted that it was the most nerve-racking moment of his life. He said of the experience, 'I slept for about an hour and I had a little bit of sushi to come down. There'll be a lot of drunken parties back home and people betting on the winner, and that's usually what I'm doing, so getting up there in a suit and talking for a little bit is kind of bizarre.' Yet it all went off very well. He was also a presenter on the 59th Annual Golden Globe Awards.

In June of the same year, Jackman briefly returned to the stage when he sang the role of Billy Bigelow, opposite Audra McDonald, in a special concert performance of *Carousel* at Carnegie Hall.

It was also in that same year that he made possibly one of his poorer decisions when he turned down the chance to play the role of Billy Flynn in the movie adaptation of the musical *Chicago*. The part eventually went to Richard Gere, and the movie went on to snatch six Academy Awards. Hugh maintained, and still does, that he was too young for that role: 'You have some thirty-four-year-old guy up against Catherine Zeta-Jones and Renée Zellweger, and it becomes a different movie. At one point, Harvey was telling me they were thinking of Kevin Spacey, and I told him, "That's exactly right. You should hire him." Then I was in New York when the movie opened and the queue was around the block. I sat down and thought that I had probably made the biggest mistake. Yet I still honestly think that it was the right thing to do. I still think I was too young for that part.'

To finish off the year in style, he hosted the Christmas edition of *Saturday Night Live* with musical guest Mick Jagger. He had never seen a single show until the producers sent him tapes so that he could understand the format, but he revelled in the opportunity and played a series of sketches and different characters throughout the show, including a German male model and a doll designer, while singing several songs including a heartfelt rendition of 'Have Yourself a Merry Little Christmas', backed up by the females in the cast. Hugh is terribly short-sighted and has extremely blurry vision when not wearing his contact lenses, so he actually had to memorise everything because he couldn't read the cue cards.

The show finished with Hugh in a skit about what his Christmases were like in Australia, where a boxing kangaroo would visit each year, with Jackman's dad, portrayed by Will Ferrell, failing to beat a kangaroo in a bout and the beast taking unfair advantage in a rather rude way. Eventually, the young Hugh and his sister wonder if their dad isn't purposely letting the kangaroo win. 'I got more reaction from *Saturday Night Live* than from any movie I've ever done. I mean, I had no idea how many people watched it. I didn't grow up with *Saturday Night Live* but I did know all the comedians who came from there; it was one of the most fun weeks I've ever had. I'm dying to go back there if they'll have me.

'The only problem was Will Ferrell. There were three skits that were so funny, and I ruined them because at the rehearsal I couldn't get through them without laughing. Three of his skits got cut, which was such a shame. And during the Christmas kangaroo skit at the end, I couldn't look at the monitor, which had me being sodomised by a kangaroo. It was out of control. I loved it. It was a real highlight and, as I said, I didn't know how many people watched it. I'm glad I didn't know.'

'Hugh's a stitch. He was funny and sweet and acerbic and hilarious in his role. When we first met, he was so prepared. I felt like a big dope, hanging out in rehearsal to cruise for snacks.'

Ashley Judd, Hugh's co-star in *Someone Like You*

CHAPTER SEVEN

HERE COMES THEIR SUNSHINE

To people looking in, Hugh and Deborra-Lee appeared to have everything going for them: money, fame, happiness and the classic Hollywood lifestyle. But what most didn't see or appreciate was the unhappiness behind the smiles; the heartache that prodded away at them behind closed doors.

The couple had tried for years to have a child of their own. Their original plan was to have two kids biologically and then adopt another one later. Hugh recalled how difficult it was for them: 'It was unexpected. I got married in my mid-twenties, and before that it had been all about not getting pregnant. My wife is very headstrong; she'd gotten pretty much everything she wanted in life, except this.'

The emotional strain took its toll on both of them, but the couple were determined to do everything they possibly could to achieve their dream. They approached a specialist, who suggested trying IVF treatment. 'I remember going to our doctor, who gave us the figures about childbirth through in vitro fertilisation (IVF). The chances reduced by 14 per cent each time you have a go. I hope Deb doesn't mind my saying, but that was a tough, tough time. Physically, you go through a lot with IVF. I was giving Deb injections every day and hormonally she was all over the place. There's anxiety. Your mind centres on when you're going to do it. You become obsessive.'

It was around 1998 and Hugh was playing Curly in *Oklahoma!*, rehearsing all day and performing on stage each night, yet he still had to find time in his exhausting schedule for performing in a very different sort of way. 'We'd been told by a naturopath that you've got to make love every day for a ten-day period. I never thought I'd get to the point where I was like, "Deb, can I have a break?"'

After three long years of near-misses and mental torture, Deborra-Lee decided that for the sake of their own sanity, enough was enough. 'Well it's not really a happy period. We were obviously upset when we didn't get pregnant and had some miscarriages and we tried, but it must have been something in the water, or *not* in the water! We did the IVF and that didn't work. We always wanted to have a child first and adopt a child. So it just sort of changed the plans a bit. And then when we started to consider adoption first, then it was like, what are we worried about, it's no big deal.'

The moment they agreed to change direction and go down the adoption route, all the years of hurt and desire to give birth to their own children began to fade. They could finally see the light at the end of a very long tunnel. Or so they thought.

They weren't aware of how difficult it was to adopt a child, especially in their homeland of Australia. It was a real struggle, even for a couple in their privileged position. It is hard to believe what they, and many other people, had to go through to adopt. They experienced first hand the miles and miles of red tape, and became completely overwhelmed by the hurdles and obstacles that got in their way. In the end they opted to adopt a child from the USA because the system was a lot more straightforward there.

The whole experience lit a spark in Deborra-Lee, which at first turned into a raging fire of anger and frustration. 'The adoption laws in Australia are too restrictive. Of course, checks need to be made, but they had a very negative approach. It was like they were trying to discourage you. There are 130 million orphans in the world! Who is looking after them? If you are a citizen of the world, on some level they are all our responsibility. And if you have got parents who want to adopt and there are children who need a home, it seems like a no-brainer. There are not that many children in Australia who need adopting, so we looked internationally, and that is what is difficult.'

She eventually turned her outrage into something more positive and is now a vigorous advocate of the right to adopt, heading a campaign against what she sees as Australia's 'anti-adoption' laws. She came across so many women who had been through the same struggles, and she knew she had to do something about it. Her crusade is to help couples with their own horror stories of futile attempts to make an unwanted child their own. 'I'm fortunate,' she said. 'I now have two beautiful children and that's why people come to me and say, "Deb can you help me?" I tell them it will be long, expensive and may not happen.'

The aim of the campaign is to put significant pressure on the government to simplify the process of overseas adoptions and speed up the adoption of needy orphans from Asia and Africa. Australia ranks last in inter-country adoption throughout the world, and Deborra-Lee thinks the Federal Government is still fostering an anti-adoption culture that thwarts thousands of childless couples from adopting overseas babies. Deb strongly believes that she and her celebrity husband could have been childless today because of the red tape and bureaucracy that forced them to return to the US to adopt. She's pushing for a government body to be established immediately to take sole responsibility for adoptions.

In the US, the adoption process took less than a year. Neither of the children that Hugh and Deborra-Lee adopted were orphans, and both are mixed race. According to Hugh, Oscar was a bit of everything – African-American, Caucasian, Hawaiian and Cherokee. 'We specifically requested a bi-racial child because there was more of a need. People will wait 18 months to adopt a little blonde girl; meanwhile, bi-racial children are turned away. The same was true for Ava: she was half-Mexican, half-German.'

It was also true that there was a general reluctance and fear among white couples to adopt a mixed-race baby. 'Our lawyer brought the form back to us and said, "This is not the time to be politically correct. Are you sure this is what you want?" We were definite about it,' said Hugh. 'Adoption is about taking a baby into your home, and your heart. It's the best thing we've ever done.'

Oscar Maximillian Jackman was adopted on May 2000 and their daughter, Ava Eliot Jackman, came along five years later, in July 2005.

Oscar's adoption was an open arrangement, which meant personal details were shared between the biological and adoptive parents. Right from the start, Deb knew Oscar was the one for them. She recalled, 'I kept saying to Hugh when we were in discussions early on with the mother from Iowa, that I was waiting for some kind of message, some kind of sign.' That sign came when she was on a flight from Los Angeles to Toronto, where Hugh was shooting *X-Men*. 'I looked out the window and there was this incredible electric storm outside and it was so beautiful. I was just staring at it and I said to the guy sitting next to me, "Wow, look at that, it's amazing! Where are we?" and he said, "I think we're somewhere over Iowa." And I knew that was where the birth mother I had been speaking to was from. I grabbed the stewardess and I said, "Do you know where we are?" and she said, "Oh, come up here," and took me up to the pilot's cabin. It was before September 11. And I went in there and I said, "Where are we?" And he said, "See down there, there's Cedar Rapids," and tears started to roll down my face and I knew that was my message.'

Hugh and Deb are not ashamed to admit they flouted the rules by becoming friends with the birth mother, the young woman from Iowa. She even lived with the couple for a short time before Oscar was born. The young girl was twenty-two at the time and pregnant with her fourth child. She was scared of being in Los Angeles so she stayed with Hugh and Deb, along with her fourteen-month-old child. This is not typically allowed, yet here was a young woman willing to give them the greatest gift of their lives; they just wanted to look after her. Deb recalled, 'I think people don't stay in touch because of fear, and I had nothing to be scared of. What, there's no fear, he's my son, and so... I don't call her every week, I mean, but once a year I'll sort of be in touch and see how she's doing. And this is a young girl, who at twenty-two was having her fourth baby.'

They stretched the rules even more by attending Oscar's delivery, at the mother's invitation. 'Hugh and I were there in the room when he was being born. The doctor said, "You know, here he comes," and I'm like with the camera taking photos, and there were tears and photos, and Hugh cut the cord and he was put straight into my arms.'

Hugh also recalled what the experience was like. 'The first time I held him, the first time I picked him up and held him in my arms and saw that little face, well, any anguish or pain or heartache we had over not conceiving just stopped. It just stopped, right there, right then and we never thought about it again. I remember the guy who delivered him said, "Congratulations, but don't drop the baby", then he walked out. To this day, whenever I get asked advice about fatherhood, that's what I say: "Just don't drop the baby."'

He was amazed what a generous and loving thing it is for these young girls to give their babies up for adoption: 'They know they can't take care of their own baby, whether it be physically, mentally, emotionally or financially. They know it, and they give their child to someone who can. What a strong thing to do.'

Deb originally wanted to name their son Balthazar. She thought it would sound cute, especially when shortened to ZarZar. But Hugh said that a boy named Balthazar would just get beaten up at school. Deb confessed later that everyone hated the name except for her. Then again, she didn't care what he was called as long as he was fit, healthy and theirs. In the end she conceded, and they opted for the more practical Oscar.

The new mum's life changed overnight, and Deb now felt complete. She couldn't wait to show Oscar off. She'd had years of pain, looking at photos of friends' children, and now it was time to show the world her own little Oscar: 'I'm one of those people on a plane who would turn around and boast to perfect strangers about how my son was a genius.'

For the first few years, Oscar was not the easiest of babies and it was a shock to the system: the crying, early wake-ups, and everything else that surrounds a newborn.

The couple jokingly said it was one of the reasons they waited five years before adopting their second child, Ava, who they both agreed was a dream of a baby.

In Ava's case, the adoption process was closed; they didn't get to see her until she was four days old. Despite their strong family life and the stable home the couple had to offer, Ava's adoption also held a series of problems. Hugh and Deb had already been refused permission to adopt a little girl before Ava came along. 'I think the perception of Hollywood, of actors and actresses, is so distorted that the idea that two people can be in a conventional marriage that works is just something some people find hard to believe,' Hugh said. 'When we were adopting Ava, we were actually in discussions with another girl, but her mum refused to let her daughter adopt to us because we were a "Hollywood" couple. She was trying to protect the child, which is right and good, but Deb and I are so far away from a "Hollywood" couple, it's just not funny.'

And their kids were not going to be spoiled, either. 'I mean, I didn't own one thing that hadn't been owned before by one of my brothers or sisters until I was twelve years old. My whole life was hand-me-downs, from clothes to hats to toys. I remember when I was turning twelve, my dad said I could have a present, anything I wanted, and I said "shoes", a pair of brand-new shoes no one else had worn. That was my big dream. I'm not complaining about those days at all, I'm just saying Deb and I know where we come from.'

The incident proved that despite the popular belief that

A-list stars get preferential treatment in the adoption process, the suspicion that celebrities might be wanting to adopt as some sort of publicity stunt can actually make it even more difficult for them. 'It's totally unreasonable. Anyone who has kids knows it's a hell of a lot of work and no publicity stunt. No doubt it comes from a desire that should be praised, not criticised. These were places and situations that seemed hopeless for the children, and here is an opportunity for them all. I say good for them.'

With the red tape behind them, they officially adopted baby daughter Ava Eliot in May 2006 after an adoption process lasting almost a year. The hearing was a joyful experience for everyone including the judge, who was happy to be handling such a positive case. Hugh and Deb, of course, cried the entire time, while Ava flirted with the judge, crawling all over his desk.

There was five-year difference between Oscar and his new sibling, but any worries Hugh and Deborra-Lee might have had about jealousy proved unfounded. He was old enough to really look forward to having a sister, and even suggested names for her – fortunately, the couple didn't think 'Staten Island' was a fitting name for their new daughter. They told Oscar what was happening every step of the way and the moment Hugh and Deb arrived home with Ava, they thought big brother Oscar was going to cry with happiness. From day one he was always sticking up for Ava and protecting her. If someone leant forward, he would jump up and yell, 'Don't touch her, that's my sister!'

Hugh is disarmingly modest when he describes his

children and often gets teary-eyed when asked about them in interviews. 'We're very blessed. Oscar is an amazing kid and Ava is just perfect. It has nothing to do with us; it's just the way she came out of the box. She's the happiest little kid. You put her down for a nap and she wakes up smiling. She's always smiling. I love my work but every time I come in the front door, I turn to mush. For me, no matter what's going on in my life, the most important thing is my family and my connection to them. They ground me, give me focus about what's important in life.'

Although the children are both mixed race, the couple haven't encountered any real prejudice towards their children. Deb admitted, however, that sometimes in the earlier days when she and Oscar were in the park, other mums would question whether she was Oscar's mother. When she said yes, of course, they would say, 'Oh, is he adopted then?' And she knew they knew he was, but she didn't care. Hugh and Deb have both talked to Oscar about what being adopted means and he doesn't have a problem with it.

Of course having children changes everyone's lives, and Hugh and Deb are no different. Deb remembers little things like the fact that, although she was never a big wine drinker, she suddenly found herself watching her drinking and trying to become more grown-up and responsible. 'You know, it was hilarious, because Hugh and I were two sort of wild kids and all of a sudden he turned into his father and I turned into my mother, and we both said no, you do it this way, not like this. And we were trying to be perfect and responsible, and it was frightening, but amazing how it just comes so naturally.'

Hugh enjoys all the added responsibility that comes along with fatherhood as it makes him question himself, and ultimately, makes him feel more of a man. It brings out elements of his character that he believes were already there, but needed releasing. Even getting up for the 3am feeds and nappy changes has its good side. 'Becoming a father, I think it inevitably changes your perspective of life. I didn't get nearly enough sleep. I can understand being hesitant about getting dragged up at ungodly hours throughout the night. But all I can liken it to is that period of falling in love, when everything is ecstatic and the girl calls you at four in the morning because she's awake and she just loves you. She wants to tell you you're the best guy she's ever met. A year later you think, four o'clock in the fucking morning? What *is* she doing? It's been a year! It is a bit like that. At times I don't want to get up and I think, Deb, can you do it? But the moment you're there, it's fantastic.'

Even today, he still gets emotional where his children are concerned. When Ava calls out his name after a long day at the office, or when he attends his son's school plays and is asked to say a few words, only to look down and see his smiling son giving him the thumbs up, Hugh's legs go to jelly.

Obviously being recognised and worshipped by movie fans and the like does have its disadvantages. Unlike most people, who are allowed to escape and enjoy time off with their family, being a Hollywood superstar is not that simple. There is a public fixation to delve into the private lives of celebrities and packs of paparazzi are always sniffing around for that magical picture.

Hugh is usually philosophical about it all; he realises it's all part of the big mean machine called fame. And although he does his best to protect his family, he finds it a relatively minor distraction. If he's at the beach with his children and his private moments are being photographed by some guy hiding behind a tree, he politely informs the paparazzo that he can take all the shots he wants as long as the kids don't know they're being photographed. He doesn't want either of them to be self-conscious or uncomfortable in public: 'People on-screen are put on a pedestal and the public wants to know about them. No one dives into acting without realising, "Hey, if I get what I wish for, if I'm successful, I'll have to deal with all that."' He tells his children the truth: people see him in movies and want to know what he does at the weekend. 'They don't really love me, I tell Oscar. Real love is what you and I have and will never go. The interest in me, the fame, and the magazines will one day disappear. I don't know when, but that means it's not real.' It's that kind of detachment that keeps him so level-headed – a detachment cultivated from 15 years of daily meditation.

The kids are finally starting to understand the world in which they find themselves. When they were younger, Hugh had difficulty trying to fully explain what he did for a living. He used to tell them that when he was going to work, he would play pretend. On one occasion Oscar turned and said, 'Daddy, I don't want you to go to work any more, I don't want you to be a lizard.'

Although a devoted father, Hugh is the disciplinarian of the family, which is perhaps a throwback to his old man's ways. And he's not afraid to handle the awkward parts of parenthood either. He's already had the infamous father and son talk about the birds and the bees. 'It's not awkward,' he says. 'In fact, it was welcome. My dad never ever did it with me so I was very adamant that I was going to do it with my son.' He doesn't back down when it comes to talking to Oscar about the opposite sex either, but believes his best advice sometimes falls on deaf young ears. On one occasion, he and Oscar were shopping when his son pulled on his father's arm. 'Dad, look two o'clock, hot chick.' Oscar then quickly made his way over to the girl in question and said: 'Hey, my dad's Wolverine.' And then he brought the girl and her friends over to Hugh. 'Hey Dad, can we have a few autographs for the girls?'

However, if there's one thing Hugh hopes to pass on to both of his children, it's a passion for life, because he feels that passion sustains life itself. He believes that if they are lucky enough in their lives to find and do something that they really love, they will have discovered their holy grail.

Even though they have two beautiful children, Hugh and Deb have no plans to adopt any more. Jackman, the youngest of five, himself said, 'For Deb and me, our family is the most important thing to us, but we travel so much we fear that if we have more kids, it'll be too much. Also, every time we get on a plane with our two kids and are all crammed in together, we think maybe we will leave it at what we have.'

'I see why people have more and more kids because it kind of brings out more of yourself. I imagine, every kid you have, it makes your capacity for love even greater. When you fall in love and you get married, it's such a relief. You're like, "Oh, this feels so right and this woman is just so great and I love her." And then you have a kid and it kind of just gets even bigger. And it's frustrating and it's tiring and all those things but your sense of, like, living life becomes so much bigger.'

Hugh Jackman

'I love watching my children laugh, grow and evolve.'

Deborra-Lee Furness

CHAPTER EIGHT

HOWLING AT THE MOON... AGAIN!

In June 2002, when Bryan Singer called on his ensemble cast to follow him to Canada to play a gang of mutant misfits for the second time, none of them had to think twice about it.

Like most action movies destined to be followed by a sequel, the development phase for X2 began shortly after the original X-Men film premièred. David Hayter and Zak Penn wrote separate scripts and combined what they felt to be the best elements of both into one screenplay. Michael Dougherty and Dan Harris were later hired to rewrite some of the script, changing the characterisations of some of the new recruits and deleting several scenes because of budget cuts. It took 20 different draft versions to get to the final script, and there were rumours that some of the rewrites had been commissioned specifically to give Halle Berry more screen time – her popularity had risen substantially since winning the Academy Award for Best Actress in *Monster's Ball*.

The concept they finally decided on for the second movie, called *X2: X-Men United*, was similar to the first, but with a more complex storyline. It also featured several new characters, including a new villain, William Stryker (Brian Cox). The plot, inspired by the Marvel graphic novel *God Loves, Man Kills*, pitted the X-Men and their enemies, the Brotherhood, against the evil Colonel William Stryker, who leads an assault on Professor Xavier's school in an attempt to build his own version of the mutant-tracking computer, Cerebro.

Hugh had been glad to have a break from the Wolverine role after the first film: 'It gave me a little break between one and two, and it gave my wife a bit of time with a clean-shaven husband. It's nice kissing my kid, too, without all that facial hair.' But by the time the sequel started filming in 2002 he was eager to get the claws out again.

And this time, die-hard comic book fans were itching to see Hugh bring their hero to life. He had gone from enemy number one, for even having the audacity to attempt to step into Wolverine's boots, to being their new superhero. And with the huge financial success of *X-Men*, the entire cast and the same director had come back to work together again. Hugh couldn't have been happier; he knew the sequel would be bigger than the first in every way. In his eyes, it explored the characters and the story in a deeper way. Bryan Singer had scored even more money from Fox this time around to improve the special effects and action sequences, although some of this budget was cut later on. There was even a little extra humour in parts of the script.

More importantly, this time Hugh was given more opportunity to get prepared, mentally and physically, for the demands of the role, rather than being thrown in after filming had already started. 'Yeah, from day one, I felt really good,' he said. 'I was physically in better shape because in the first one I had no chance to get ready. I literally had come off a three-week holiday in Sicily so I wasn't in the best of shape. And on this one, they gave me a trainer to get into shape.' It was the same trainer who trained Angelina Jolie for the title role in *Tomb Raider*. He even had a nutritionist: 'I think they thought that an Australian's idea of a diet was to have only six beers instead of ten or something, but I'll tell you I learnt a bit. That nutritionist, man, it was brutal. There was no bread, there was no sugar, it was kind of wild.'

Part of his punishing workout requirements included bench and leg presses. At one point he was benching 314lb and leg-pressing 1,000. He laughed when asked about rumours that he took steroids to get his body into shape, denying it with an excellent riposte: 'No, I worked out with a natural bodybuilder and although I love acting, nothing is worth having testicles the size of raisins for!'

His workout meant spending an hour and a half in the gym every day, going through different routines that changed every few weeks. He went from heavy weights with a long rest period between sets, to lighter weights with slower reps, and back to fast explosive lifts. But he pigged out, consuming around 1,000 extra calories a day to fuel his workout. It often meant eating a lot of small portions, starting at a bizarre hour of the morning. He really pushed himself hard while mentally running through the character he was going to play.

Hugh got into the right shape and the right mindset to step back into the arena, but there was one thing he needed to put right: the one criticism fans had had of the first film was that he hadn't been tough or unpredictable enough, and he himself agreed. He'd been talking to fans and they'd said, 'You don't kick enough ass. Let's see that berserker rage!' And he realised they were right: 'When I went back to *X-Men 1*, there really wasn't a lot there. I had a huge fight scene with Mystique, where I ended up on my back, knocked out, and there was a bit at the beginning, but other than that he was quite tame. So, when I read the new script, I thought the relationships were better, I thought it was funnier, I thought there was more action, but I still said, we've got to get even more action. I kind of fought for a little bit more in the mansion scene sequence, particularly. That was a little more berserker rage there than was originally written.'

Filming was due to start in March 2002, but because of some issues it didn't begin until late June. It ended that November, with most of the filming taking place at the Vancouver Film Studios, the largest soundstage in North America, where more than 64 different sets were used in 38 locations. The sets themselves were big. Stryker's underground lair, for example, was built in an old warehouse and was the largest set in North America. It involved over 60 miles of cable and was so large that the cast and crew members had to use bicycles to get to and from the bathroom as quickly as possible. Even then, the production area only used about half the space in the warehouse. Everything on the sets was incredibly detailed, too; the replica of the President's desk in the Oval Office was so intricate that it took two months to build. Filming did relocate from Vancouver to Kananaskis, near Calgary, for a series of climactic shoots requiring winter weather. But as luck would have it, there was no snow so they had to bring in snow-making machinery to help create tons of the stuff for the scene. The actors didn't seem to mind, though, because while they waited for the manmade snow to pile up, they used the local Delta Lodge for some pampering treatments like herbal wraps and hot stone massages.

The final scene in Xavier's mansion with Cyclops, Wolverine and Professor X was actually shot at Shepperton Studios in London, simply because Hugh was shooting *Van Helsing* at the time and the producers released him for only one day to do the final shooting of *X-Men*. This explains why his hair looks higher than usual in that scene – he had to wear the Wolverine wig over Van Helsing's long hair!

He found being Wolverine a lot easier the second time around. 'I think almost everything ran smoother. I mean, the process of hair and make-up was the same, hanging me by my feet and spraying three cans of hairspray on my hair. If they didn't do that I'd look more like Moe from the Three Stooges. It's all just exactly the same length.' He added, 'In every part of it, it was easier. I think everyone in the studio was given more leeway to do what we wanted. I felt like I owned the character more. I can go back to the original *X-Men* and see the scenes where I'm sort of there, but it's not fully in focus for me.'

The only source of concern from Fox was the rating. In the end the film was edited to bring its US R rating (meaning audience members under 17 would have to be accompanied by an adult) down to a PG-13. Director Bryan Singer talked a bit about the changes. 'Originally we got an R rating, and then just a few minor things about intensity that were trimmed. But very little. I was very pleased. There's very little blood in the movie. There's some intensity in it, but it's not a gory picture by any means and we kind of solved those problems in the story, and it's kind of fun and the audience realises it is not a terrifying threat, and this is not a massacre.'

The fight between Hugh and the character Yuriko Oyama (Kelly Hu), which actually took three weeks of shooting, was one that got slashed quite a bit in the final cut. In spite of this, the fight scene itself became extremely intense during filming. 'I got a bit of a concussion during one scene, and Hu is such a pro, man.' Hugh recalled. 'If she'd hit me, it would just touch me. It would look like she'd whacked me, but she's a black belt, so she knew how to do it.'

Not so Hugh himself. In one scene, he was on the ground when Hu ran up to him. He was supposed to turn and punch her in the stomach. 'She kept saying, "Harder,

harder, harder, harder. I can take it,"' and I said, "Okay, but just do me a favour. Will you wear a pad there?" So she put on a black pad, and he turned around and banged her straight in the breast. He couldn't believe it – he had done four takes without the pad and each had been perfect, and as soon as she gave him the target, he missed and hit her full force. He stopped and asked, 'Did I get you?' Grimacing, she whispered, 'Yep. Next time just a little lower. Thanks, Hugh.'

There were lighter moments on the set as well. While they were shooting quite an intense scene in a tunnel, Hugh came out in a G-string and flip-flops. Jokingly, he yelled to Lee, the assistant director, 'Lee, this is a disgrace – I want a closed set!' Lee replied, 'I'm very sorry, Mr Jackman, when we're ready to go everyone will be gone.' And so, at the end of first take, Hugh ran through the tunnel and as he rounded the corner, 30 women from the set, including Jimmy Marsden's mum, were waiting for him. They all stood there, wearing huge grins and waving five-dollar notes. Although Hugh found it funny, it proved a real dilemma for him as he tried to cover himself up while wearing a set of fake claws.

Other lighter moments included several gags played on Bryan Singer, the director. One included Hugh pretending to be a gay Wolverine character: 'It was the moment where I walk into Cerebro. I walked in and went, "Oh I love what you've done with Cerebro! It's fantastic!" and I sat in Patrick Stewart's lap and of course, he got right into it and we played out the whole thing, and then I walked off. Bryan's face was ashen for about two hours.

It was like, "If this gets out, Wolverine's absolutely gone." And then, of course, for weeks after he proceeded to tell everyone who came on set, "You've got to see Hugh doing Wolverine as a gay guy!" I doubt it will be on the out-takes.'

Any rumours of tension on the set of the *X-men* sequel were certainly unfounded. Everyone agreed that this time around, it was definitely more relaxed, including Singer himself. With the success of the first instalment, Fox alleviated the pressure they had applied. 'Let's have a little more fun with it, let's have a little more fun with the characters and the making of the movie,' Singer kept saying, and Hugh remembered how the director got the fans involved, too. 'There were always fans wherever we were, and he'd go out almost every day, pick a fan and say, "Do you want to come and have a look on the set?" then take them around. There we were, going from our trailers and trying to hide from paparazzi, and Bryan's just taking people through: "Come have a look. Welcome to our set."'

Singer also believed that the additional pressure of making the sequel was alleviated due to the hardcore fan support. 'There was more time and money this time around, and I had a better sense of what I was doing, because I'd already established these characters and already cut my teeth in the genre. So, I felt a little less pressure and actually a little more freedom, and it was great to bring in new characters. They all knew that with the first film, they were stepping into the unknown. "Do people really know *X-Men*? How big is the fan base?"

Then when it opened, it was so huge. I think everyone in the film is proud of it; I think everyone was really into it and loved it. We generally all got on well together.'

Singer was very intuitive, which Hugh didn't mind, although this sometimes drove the rest of the studio mad because it often led to delays in shooting. What Hugh liked about his director was that he didn't have an ego and was open to change: 'Bryan is nervous about things being cheesy, which is why he makes such good movies and why he's such a great director for this kind of film. It's great as an actor because even if you feel you have some dialogue that's a little on the nose, it'll either get cut or it'll come off fine or he'll change it. I think he's found a good balance in this movie. I think he did a great job.'

And the respect was mutual. The two became close; close enough for the director to talk honestly to him about how he could improve his performance. 'I'll always respect him for that,' said Hugh. 'I think that it was that talk that kind of really woke me up and took me out of this whirlwind of, "I'm in Hollywood and it's all new and everything." I just got back into the acting to find it, and I think that's when I really found the character and he kind of had faith in me, so we've always had a good relationship.'

So much so that Hugh began to get involved in changes to the script if he felt he could add something to it. 'By the time we got back to X2, it was my sixth film in America. So, I was a little more used to it and I was not afraid to say, "Listen, I think that this in the script needs to be changed." I wasn't thinking, "Oh, I'm gonna get fired." Or I wasn't thinking so much that I've got to please the director. When you first start, you just feel like, please don't fire me, but then your confidence gets better.'

'That stuff in the mansion, I loved all that stuff,' he said, referring to a scene at the Xavier School for Gifted Youngsters. 'I like the whole idea of Wolverine being the reluctant babysitter and having 50 people coming. In this one there was more of an example of his berserker rage, which was one thing I think was missing from the first.'

Most of the other actors were also encouraged to get more involved and expected to ad-lib, unlike the first film. Ian McKellen, for example, actually worked with screenwriters to make the scene in which Bobby Drake (who plays Iceman) tells his parents that he is a mutant look more like a gay 'coming-out' scene.

When the movie wrapped and the director was asked if he would work on any more *X-Men* films, Singer said he wasn't sure. He had established ideas and elements in the sequel that would lend themselves to future pictures but at the same time, he stressed, he would probably like to do something in between. 'I don't know if it's to get back to my roots, smaller films, or go and make another event picture. I'm not sure yet. I'm developing things.'

X2: X-Men United was released in the US on 2 May 2003, accumulating $85 million in its opening weekend. The film grossed $214 million in North America alone, while earning another $192 million worldwide, coming at a total of $406 million. *X2* was a financial success since it recouped its production budget three times over. It debuted simultaneously in 93 countries, the largest

North American and international opening ever at the time. In addition, it was the fifth highest grossing film based on a *Marvel* comic, and was the sixth highest of 2003, also earning $107 million in its first five days of DVD release. It entered *The Guinness Book of World Records* as the Widest Film Release, having opened on 3,741 screens on the same day. The film was considered by most critics to be even better than the original, with Hugh again being given a lot of the credit even though he was just one of an ensemble cast.

X2 won the Saturn Award for Best Science Fiction Film. In addition, Bryan Singer (direction), Dan Harris and Michael Dougherty (writing) and John Ottman (music) all received nominations. It also received other nominations, with its costumes, make-up, special effects and DVD release coming to a total of eight altogether. The Political Film Society honoured X2 in categories of Human Rights and Peace, while the movie was nominated for the Hugo Award for Best Dramatic Presentation (Long Form).

A successful video game was also released shortly after the film. 'I don't know if they've used my voice or not, they probably have,' Hugh remarked. 'I did a lot of recordings on the first movie for dolls and videogames, so they probably just used the same stuff.'

'Hugh's a down-to-earth guy, a well-grounded guy, a zero-ego guy, with none of the bullshit that a lot of people have in this town.'

Tom DeSanto, executive producer
of *X2: X-Men United*

CHAPTER NINE

THE 'QUEEN'
OF NEW YORK

W hat does a relatively new, but very successful, actor from Down Under who's just finished filming the second in the series of one of the biggest action-movie franchise hits of the century do for an encore? Does he find a similar role quickly? Wait for the next instalment, which is bound to come? Take the money and relax in the sun? Or spend long hours in the gym to build up his already hard body even more?

The answer is none of the above. Instead, Hugh traded in his tight-fitting white vest, retractable steel claws and side-burns for a pair of tight-fitting trousers, a set of maracas and a floral shirt to transform himself into the flamboyant Peter Allen in the Broadway musical, *The Boy From Oz*.

The sensational hit told the dazzling, funny and heart-breaking story of the great entertainer, Peter Allen, from humble beginnings growing up in the Australian outback, through his meteoric rise to fame as an international star, selling out week-long engagements at Radio City Music Hall.

Singing in the country pubs from the age of eleven, Peter Richard Woolnough survived family tragedy to become a local TV star at sixteen. Later discovered by Judy Garland, went on to marry her daughter Liza Minnelli, he became a well-loved performer plus Oscar-winning songwriter. He also appeared in New York City with the Rockettes. However, he was infamous for burning the candle at both ends and as time progressed, he developed a homosexual relationship and his marriage subsequently ended. He passed away in 1992 due to AIDS-related throat cancer soon after being diagnosed.

Peter Allen had an amazing life and his story made for one hell of a show. It had already been a massive triumph in Australia, where it was first performed in 1998 at Her Majesty's Theatre in Sydney. *The Boy From Oz* became so successful that it played to packed houses across the country and ran for a total of 766 performances over two years, starring Todd McKenney in the lead role.

It was almost inevitable that the one-man show portraying the life of the flamboyant, openly gay Peter would eventually make its way to Broadway. On 16 September 2003 it previewed at the Imperial Theatre in New York, officially opening a month later and running up until Hugh's contract ended on 12 September 2004. Over that time period, the show played 32 previews and 365 performances. Directed by Philip William McKinley, with choreography by Joey McKneely, it starred Hugh as Allen and Isabel Keating as Judy Garland. Stephanie J Block played Liza Minnelli, Beth Fowler was Marion Woolnough, Jarrod Emick starred as Peter's AIDS-stricken lover Greg Connell, while John Hill was Mark Herron (Judy's husband).

Hugh spoke about the show when it opened on Broadway: 'For those of you who didn't know, Peter Allen first became famous in America for marrying Liza Minnelli. He used to be the opening act for Judy Garland, who he met drunk in a club in Hong Kong many years before. He then became kind of a prolific songwriter. He won an Oscar for "Arthur's Theme" and he wrote many hit songs that you would know, but his life story was truly amazing.

'This boy from the outback in Australia was the polar opposite of Wolverine, and I'm really not exaggerating. He was very flamboyant, was our Peter. Famous for his Hawaiian shirts, gold tap-dancing shoes, jumping on top of the piano, making out with pretty much anyone and everyone who stepped across his path, and dancing with the Rockettes. He was a pretty outrageous character. He was great.'

When Hugh signed up to do the show, there were those who thought the star from *X-Men* had gone insane to even consider giving up the bright lights of Hollywood at such a lucrative stage in his career to take a gamble on such a controversial show.

'So when I was first offered *The Boy from Oz*, I turned it down. I said to my wife, "Deb, this sounds like a great idea. But I want to do movies." So I went off and did movies. The show was a big hit in Australia, and I went to see it. That's when I turned to Deb and said, "I made a big mistake. I should've done the show." Later, when my agent rang me and said, "There's something for *The Boy from Oz* on Broadway," I said, "I'm doing it." I didn't care what part.'

It was still a big gamble for the rising star. 'Aside from the fact that it was a gay character who was not that famous, not the greatest singer, piano player or dancer in the world, I was going to take 12 months out of my film career and I was in mid-30s. Some may have said I made a bad decision,' Hugh observed. However, Hugh knew that playing Tenterfield in New South Wales's most famous export in New York was not only going to be extremely challenging and would stretch him to the limit, but it would also be the role of a lifetime, fulfilling another of his personal ambitions to perform on Broadway. He said, 'Peter was the consummate showman and his music was so honest. When he sang "Tenterfield Saddler", he would break your heart.'

Conversely, it wasn't as though Hugh was turning his back on the film world entirely. There was a new film coming out the same year called *Van Helsing*, which he hoped would keep him in the Hollywood spotlight until he re-emerged.

Interestingly, the decision to move from movie set to centre stage actually helped to boost his career later on down the line, with priceless exposure to several directors who came to see the performance. Darren Aronofsky was one such director; he thought Hugh would be great for a role in his movie, *The Fountain*. He went backstage after the show and gave Hugh the script to read, as did Christopher Nolan, who directed Jackman in the 2006 film *The Prestige*, a drama about two 19th-century rival magicians. Allegedly, people representing Woody Allen also saw the show, which later led to him being cast in *Scoop*. His performance was also key to him being selected to host the Oscars later on, when Steven Spielberg apparently put his name forward.

Aside from the career opportunities, the prospect of spending time living and working in the Big Apple excited both Hugh and his wife. 'I think it's the best city in the world. As far as cities go, everything's there. I think it's so vibrant. I love the people. I think they're honest, in your face. If they don't like you, they'll say, "Get out of my way!" If they like you, they'll slap you on the back and support you. It's a very intoxicating environment to be in. In terms of theatre, there's not a more supportive theatre community than in New York. It's really kind of a real thrill to go there. I mean, don't forget, I'm a boy from the suburbs of Sydney, so getting to New York is a huge, huge thrill,' he said.

As for his transition from film back to stage work, he didn't seem to miss a single beat. His aim was never to be off the stage for more than five years. He didn't know if his agent was particularly thrilled about the 12-month contract he had just signed, but it was still exhilarating for him. It was a dream to star in the first Australian musical ever to be performed on Broadway and to play a character for whom he had such great admiration.

Indeed, his growing reputation as a Hollywood superstar in the making proved to be a real bonus. His fame attracted a lot of people who didn't typically frequent the bright lights of Broadway, boosting sales considerably for the show itself and other productions on the famous strip. And he must have realised he was hitting the right notes because he was even immortalised as a caricature at New York's famous restaurant, Sardi's – a big honour in the city that never sleeps.

Hugh had never seen Peter perform live but had watched footage of the star on television and listened to his music while growing up. To prepare for his role as the star performer, Hugh watched all the Peter Allen videos and read everything he could get his hands on. He also spent hours talking to people about what the man himself, an icon in his homeland, was really like: 'He was an incredible performer for one thing, and he's written some songs that are very loved by Australians. But his story really struck a chord with me. He was incredibly brave as a performer. He had a go at everything. His ambitions were limitless, and he had the courage to match it. He had this sort of *joie de vivre* throughout all the ups and downs in his life and he just lit up the stage. He was one of those rare individuals who could have the audience in the palm of his hand from the moment he walked onstage.'

In September 2003, Hugh took on the extravagant new persona of Allen, singing, dancing and bounding out into the audience to flirt with both men and women. His performance lit up the stage, and he revelled in all the showmanship and glitz. He sang 21 songs per show, eight shows per week. 'Yeah, I'm sure I should have been a showgirl!' he said, laughing out loud at the thought.

Portraying Peter was a daunting task, especially as he hadn't so far played a real person in either stage or film before. Peter Allen was not a fictitious figure and Hugh knew there would be extreme pressure to portray the character exactly as he was in real life. And he did an amazing job of overcoming all doubts or expectations.

Being a true professional, Hugh tried his hardest to get his portrayal of Allen exactly right and after a few weeks of rehearsals he thought he had cracked it. However the director, Philip McKinley, was more concerned with capturing Allen's spirit and less interested in capturing his physical mannerisms: 'Around the fifth week, I thought I had found out who Peter was and the next thing was to put on the outer crust and walk and talk and all that. As I began doing that I noticed Phillip was getting a little perturbed. Finally, he said to me, "You know, it's strange, the effect is not as strong as before. It actually works better if you give little hints of Allen and incorporate his signature moves rather than give a literal impersonation of him." And he was right. People who knew Peter came up to me after the first few performances and said, "Oh, my God, I thought that was Peter up there onstage!"'

Peter's friends and family members came to see the show. One woman who particularly touched Hugh was the mother of Peter's long-term lover Greg, who had also died of AIDS. He found it very sobering to have people in the audience who knew the characters so intimately.

Generally, they seemed thrilled that Peter was being remembered on Broadway because Broadway, in many ways, was his great love and his dream. The fact that *Legs Diamond*, the 1988 musical starring and written by Allen, didn't work there was one of the greatest disappointments of his life, and so *The Boy From Oz* was a fitting tribute to the showman. The people who were closest to Peter appreciated Hugh's uncanny and amazing depiction of the exuberant showman.

The resemblance was particularly noticeable when Hugh, like Peter, interacted with his audience. And the great thing about playing Peter Allen was that the character gave him permission to do things he wouldn't normally do. Hugh's strict, Catholic upbringing ensured he was polite and respectful to people, but he did things in the show that he still can't believe he could actually do, never mind get away with: 'Peter was pretty brave as a performer and it brought out the outrageous side of me that I was too nervous to do in the beginning, and then I began to relish it, and really look forward to doing it.'

At first, he was a little nervous of ad-libbing and interacting with the audience as Peter Allen had done. He knew New Yorkers could be quite brutal and was afraid that he might be heckled by someone in the audience and that it would leave him stumped for a response. Still, after a while he realised it didn't matter – the audience loved the personal interaction, funny or not.

Within no time at all, he started to pull off the impromptu act quite brilliantly. Something happened in one of the first performances. Peter Allen was famous for dancing on top of the piano: he treated it like the vault in gymnastics, jumped all over it. Hugh would dive across the top of the long grand piano, finishing in a position where he'd be lying across it, going 'ta-dah!' He'd been doing it for a month, and one night as he slid across, he knew he was going too fast. It was a really slippery surface and he ended up on the floor. He got up, laughing hysterically; the audience absolutely loved it. But he wasn't content to leave it there.

'I stopped the band and said, in character, "Okay, I don't know what they're mixing with the cleaning fluid. Jason, get out here!" Jason was from the stage crew, and he was terrified. I said, "Jason, mate, you're cute, but listen, I almost broke a bone. What did you clean this with?" He said, "I cleaned it with water" and I said, "Bullshit, show me!" I made him take off his little tool belt and take a run at it. He went right off the piano, and the audience went nuts. That was the beginning for me, as Peter Allen, of breaking down the fourth wall with the audience.'

He built it into the show, later pulling Sarah Jessica Parker, Sean Combs, Eric Clapton and Steven Spielberg up onstage. Another time, he dragged Matt Damon and Barbara Walters on stage and while she sat there frightened, Matt and Hugh gave her a very sexy lap dance.

He would also stop the show if interrupted by latecomers and force the offenders to stand up while he playfully ripped them to shreds or just chatted with them. One group of women who were late because they had been shopping were forced to stand up and show off the new fake Kate Spade handbags they had bought in Chinatown.

However, Hugh was also on the receiving end sometimes, mainly from women. 'I've had some pretty full-on ones,' he admitted. 'Once, a woman ran down to the front of the stage and said, "Hugh, I've always wanted to do this," and lifted her top. She had these massive tits. I just pissed myself laughing and said, "I'm glad you got that off your chest!"' Another time a woman in the middle of the show yelled out, 'I want to bite your ass!' Hugh thought he would silence her by calling her bluff. So he hung his butt over the edge of the orchestra pit, but instead of sitting back down she raced down and bit his derrière. Some even threw their underwear onto the stage as he became the 'Tom Jones' of Broadway. 'It's a little strange when you're on stage and people fling underwear at you,' he smiled, sheepishly. 'By the way, I made the ultimate error the first time it was done. I said, "Oh, is that for me?" and I put them on. From that moment on, in every show something flew my way.'

During his conquering run, Dr Gibbs from WAAPA and wife Carole flew to New York to see their protégé. Hugh memorably dragged Gibbs on stage to accompany him in one of the song-and-dance routines. 'It's the only time I have ever seen him quiet,' Hugh recounted. 'I said, "Thanks for not upstaging me, Geoff," and he just went red and tried to rush off.'

His interaction with the audience was one of the best parts of the show but a flippant comment nearly landed him in deep trouble when he performed in a one-off for the opening of Wynn's Casino in Las Vegas. Hugh pulled Elaine Wynn, the owner's lovely-looking wife, on stage. While he danced with her, he said out loud, 'You know, darling, underneath that wonderful gown you are wearing, you are just G-string trash.' As soon as he said it he thought, 'Oh God, I'm going to be buried in the Nevada Desert in less than three hours!' But when he looked down into the audience, her husband was howling with laughter. At that moment, Hugh knew that under the guise of Peter, he had a free ticket to do and say whatever he wanted.

Phil McKinley, the Australian director of the show, described Hugh as a dream to work with and predicted great things for his leading man: 'When an actor ad-libs, it can be a disaster, but Hugh did it so well. He's going to have this amazing career where he truly will be an all-around superstar performer.'

Hugh's performance came as a massive shock for many fans, especially the Wolverine ones who arrived to see the macho Logan and were presented with a very different persona, particularly in the scene where he kisses another man. There was one famous performance when someone stood up and shouted as Hugh was about to lock lips with the other male actor, 'Wolverine... no, don't do it!' The producer and Jackman knew they could never have written that sort of reaction or made up the resulting publicity that it generated. For weeks after, the story was splashed all over the entertainment pages of the newspapers.

Contrary to what one might think about the physical requirements of playing a gay showman, Hugh was in the best shape of his life. He had to be, in order to sing and dance his way through the rigorous regime of 21 songs per show, eight shows per week. And he never missed an appearance, even with a broken foot. He described it as one of the most satisfying stage experiences of his career but admitted that he had really had to work hard for it: 'The show was pretty full-on for me. It was a tribute to Peter Allen, and frankly, I don't know how this guy lived his life, given the energy he put out. He used to do two shows a night! He just wanted to live life at Mach Five all the time. I really had a ball, but it was like jumping into the deep end every night.'

The healthy regime he followed to help him through the demands of the role was the modern equivalent of living the life of a monk. That year, Hugh said he didn't do much outside the show except sleep, eat and rest. They nicknamed him 'Grandpa' around home because he was always in his slippers and napping. The upside of the gig was that he was home during the day to pick up Oscar, who had just started nursery school, leaving him the opportunity to sleep in and spend some time playing with his son before going to the theatre.

To get into character, Hugh would often dance and sing the show songs at home. At the time, his then three-year-old son Oscar liked seeing his dad dancing while he made breakfast. In fact, the little boy enjoyed it so much he often asked his dad to do an encore: 'Oscar loved dancing with me. When I first started rehearsing Peter's songs, he seemed to pick up on their emotional impact very early. Sometimes when I was singing, while I was getting breakfast he'd tune in immediately. He called them "Daddy's sad songs". He would come over and give me a hug, and say, "Daddy is so sad."' To show him everything was alright, Hugh would knot his tie around his chest and dance around singing 'I Go to Rio' which, of course was 'Daddy's happy song'.

The show, which fully embraced Peter's homosexuality, turned Hugh into something of an icon, and the gay community championed him as their new pin-up. 'I've never been threatened by playing a gay character, although ultimately, I find it a pretty boring way to describe someone. Peter wasn't defined by his sexuality; he was a performer. The key to playing him was not playing him gay, but like a little kid, because he was up there. Fearless,' he observed.

Although Hugh denied being gay, by the end of the show's run a fairly substantial rumour was circulating about his own sexuality. 'I only know that because my wife told me. Every time Deb would go to the ladies she'd hear people saying, "Is he or isn't he?" She'd yell out, "He isn't!"' He let out a deep, chesty laugh. 'I just took it as a compliment to be honest. Maybe I'm doing a good job of it.'

Openly, he admitted that playing a gay man didn't really make him more sensitive towards gay issues in politics. Being in show business, he has had many gay friends and he's never really made a huge distinction based on someone's sexuality. In fact, he deliberately tried not to play Peter too gay. He knew Allen was camp and had fun, but it was also a part of his joie de vivre; he was like a kid in a candy store. And Peter was quite deliberately non-political because he believed he was an entertainer and that once he crossed the line into the political arena it would hurt him. Even in his controversial time, with the Stonewall riots and everything that was going on in the gay community, the gay movement was really calling for poster people. Yet Peter consistently refused.

In making such a choice to attempt to play someone like Allen, Jackman stepped aside from his peers and showed himself to be one of the world's most unusual and potentially important superstars. As *The New York Times* put it: 'In Hollywood, where typecasting remains very much a force, Mr Jackman retains a slight stigma.' In the film industry, straight men often shy away from playing gay characters, while stars who are actually gay often keep their sexuality under wraps rather than admit to it. Paranoia rules, along with the fear that fame and fortune will suddenly be snatched away if an actor is tarred with the wrong brush. So for Hugh to take the role on Broadway and embrace it in all its glory proved that he was not only talented, but courageous enough to ignore Hollywood's common bigotry. Which was plain to see when the executives at Fox Studios LA worked hard after the production finished to reposition him into his macho image, calling him a younger, rough-hewn Clint Eastwood.

Even today, when asked to name the biggest three

rumours about him, Hugh simply replies. 'Gay, gay and gay.' However, he is starting to tire of the Chinese whispers. 'I just think the whole idea of judging someone based on their sexuality is ridiculous. In Australia, we're much easier on all those fronts. I was playing a gay guy. I actually took it as a compliment. I'd be happy to go and deny it, because I'm not. But by denying it, I'm saying there is something shameful about it, and there isn't anything shameful. The questions about sexuality are asked more here in America than anywhere else, because it's a big hang-up and defines what people think about themselves and others. It's not a big issue in Australia.'

However, Hugh did have the courage to confess that at one point in his life he had pretended to be gay to pick up girls: 'I probably shouldn't be saying this, but I remember when I was about nineteen, me and my mate used to go to these dance parties which were 80 per cent gay guys, and where the girls were sick of heterosexual guys hitting on them. We would go there until two in the morning, and by then the girls were really drunk and they would wish the guys weren't gay, and that's when my mates and I would swoop in like vultures.'

Gay rumours or not, the show played to packed houses every night for the entire year. And although critics were not particularly kind, Hugh received the highest marks for his demanding role. He also generated an enormous following. A group of devoted fans, who called themselves the Ozalots, went to see him perform some 20 or 30 times in a row. By June of 2004, he had created such a stir that it came as no surprise when he won the Tony Award for Best Leading Actor in a Musical.

On 10 May 2004, he woke up to find out that his new film, *Van Helsing*, was the No. 1 movie in America *and* he had received his first Tony nomination as Best Actor for *The Boy From Oz*. 'My wife walked in and said, "The studio's on the phone. You just got nominated for a Tony and your movie's made over $50 million." I just thought, I should record this and put it on an alarm clock and I'll wake up to this every day.' Indeed, it was a Groundhog Day any actor would die for.

As a matter of fact, the opening weekend of *Van Helsing* had ten times the viewing audience of the entire run of *The Boy From Oz*. 'And that's a year's work,' observed a stunned Hugh.

The night of the 2004 Tony Awards saw the biggest stars of Hollywood and Broadway come out to celebrate and by then it seemed everyone was rooting for one man, Mr Hugh Jackman. He was also host, as he had been in 2003, and later in 2005. Fellow Aussie Nicole Kidman had been given the honour to announce the winner for Best Leading Actor in a Musical. Hugh was up against strong competition including John Tartaglia in *Avenue Q*, Alfred Molina in *Fiddler on the Roof*, Hunter Foster in *Little Shop of Horrors* and Euan Morton in *Taboo*.

'As Nicole was reading the names, I couldn't hear her. I was literally like a lip reader. My wife had been so confident that I would win that she promised she would run naked down Broadway if I didn't. I thought, that could be kind of cool. I wouldn't mind seeing my wife run down Broadway with nothing on.'

Ultimately, Deb was saved from an embarrassing moment in her life as Nicole called out her husband's name and Hugh received a standing ovation as he walked up to accept the award. He also won the Drama Desk Award for Outstanding Actor in a Musical in that year. Isabel Keating won the Drama Desk Award for Outstanding Featured Actress in a Musical, while the show itself received nominations for four other Tony Awards, including Best Musical.

The experience of performing in the show night after night taught Hugh so much about himself. 'Acting had always been a kind of way to play someone else. Like to play someone else was easier to play yourself. And even though I'm playing Peter Allen, it has made me more comfortable with things like hosting the Tony Awards, just being on the stage without a script, just interacting and connecting with the audience. And also in a way it made me a little homesick for Australia.'

When the show ended, he traded in his maracas to spend time playing dad to Oscar. 'As soon as I finished with *The Boy from Oz*, I just hung out with Oscar. It was great. You know, the publicity people always say, don't tell people this, but for me, hanging out with Oscar, meant gardening and stuff. I love gardening; I love cooking. I was in heaven. I suppose I was meant to say bungee jumping and all that.'

He did dip into the closet to bring out the floral shirt yet again in 2006, however, to transform back into The

Boy from Oz when the production went back to Australia for a series of special arena shows in his home country from 3 August 2006 to September of the same year. The arena show starred Chrissie Amphlett as Judy Garland, Angela Toohey as Liza Minnelli, while Colleen Hewett played Peter's mother, Marion Woolnough. It was an extravaganza with a capital E, in the style Peter would have wanted. During the song 'I Still Call Australia Home', sung by Hugh, hundreds of kids were racing down the aisles, and with 'Rio' there were dancers as you'd find at the Carnival in Rio de Janeiro. There was a cast of 160 and an arena that held up to 15,000 people: 'It was all my rock-star fantasies come true, except I was in sequins, which is not exactly how I'd imagined it. *The Boy From Oz* was a celebration of not only a great Australian, but of what it means to be Australian, and it was great to celebrate Peter Allen's life in a thrilling tour with a great Australian cast.'

'*I have been going to the theatre for some 60 years. I was there for Brando in* Streetcar. *But nothing prepared me for Hugh Jackman in* The Boy from Oz.'
William Goldman, renowned screenwriter

CHAPTER TEN

VAN THE MAN

While Hugh was still strutting his stuff on stage in New York, a few films that he had completed prior to becoming the infamous Peter Allen were released in the same year.

The first two were short art-house movies, which were seen by a much smaller and different kind of audience than he had become accustomed to. *Standing Room Only* was a short silent film written and directed by his wife, Deborra-Lee. It was her directorial debut and focused on a kaleidoscope of people queuing up outside a box office and waiting to get tickets for a sell-out show. The idea came to Furness six years earlier while she and her husband had themselves waited in line to get tickets to an Al Pacino performance (it was, of course, before they became rich and famous).

Deborra-Lee recalled how it all came about: 'We were

in New York and Al Pacino was doing a one-man show and we wanted to go and see it, so three mornings in a row we got up earlier to get there to get in line to get tickets. And on the third day we got in line and we were among the first eight people there.'

For the next few hours the incongruous group, which included a plumber and his wife from Jersey, Hugh and Deb from Australia and a woman from Spain, talked, joked and formed an invisible bond that got stronger the longer they stood in line. Eventually, they got the tickets and the strangers disappeared from each other's lives. On the night of the actual performance by the great man himself, Al Pacino, Deb was so tired from getting up so early for three mornings on the trot that she actually fell fast asleep on Hugh's shoulder throughout most of the show.

Yet it was the entire experience, not just the show itself, which left its mark on her, and ultimately got her creative juices flowing: 'I said to Hugh at the time, I said this would be a great short film, such a metaphor. We were so result orientated, that you know that was all about seeing the show, like getting the tickets and doing that, and the actual journey of getting there was far, infinitely, more interesting, meeting these amazing people.'

She quickly wrote a story loosely based around their experiences that morning, and then more by accident than design, got money from Sting's wife, Trudie Styler, to help fund the production after talking to her at a party. 'I told her about the idea at this party and she wrote a cheque right there on the spot and gave it to me.'

Miramax Films' kingpin Harvey Weinstein topped up the remainder of the budget of $250,000 while they were attending a ceremony in Los Angeles. He told Deb: 'Kid, you're making a movie, and if people think I'm only giving you the money because your husband is Hugh Jackman, just tell them it's called using whatever advantage you have.'

It wasn't long before the film began to come to life. Shot on a cold March morning in front of one of the theatres in central London's Covent Garden, the cast of principally British stars assembled was very impressive: Michael Gambon, Will Ash, Mary Elizabeth Mastrantonio, Andy Serkis, Sophie Dahl, Alan Rickman, Joanna Lumley, Lindsey Marshal, Nick Audsley, the wonderful Maureen Lipman, and of course Hugh, who Deb joked, 'Had to sleep with me to get the part.'

It turned out to be a very accomplished piece, shot almost entirely as a 12-minute silent movie with minimal dialogue and rounded off by an emotive score from Australian composer David Hirshfelder. *Standing Room Only* proved a major success at film festivals and was shown on TV. It gave Deb the confidence to follow her ambition and sparked the idea to start their own production company in 2005.

Many years later, they were both so thrilled when one of the couples they had met on that day, seven years prior, came to see Hugh in *The Boy from Oz* and brought along with them a few snapshots of everyone standing in line waiting for tickets. For Deb, this was a moment that seemed to complete the whole experience.

After that, Hugh showed up briefly in another short film, this time little more than three minutes long. *Making the Grade*, written and directed by high-school student director Corey Smith, was produced for a segment of MTV's *Total Request Live* and was shot at Nutley High in Nutley, New York. It was about two female students, both madly in love with their hot teacher, Mr Slattery (Hugh). But when the time came to take the final exam, which would determine whether the students passed the course, a drastic move by one of the two students resulted in an interesting twist of plot.

Corey revealed that it took three hours of brainstorming at Starbucks with the two leading actresses to decide on the right actor for the role, and unbelievably they got the man they wanted. Hugh, in his blazer, tie and jeans, perfectly fitted the image of the maths teacher. Corey shot an hour and a half sequence with Hugh and the girls, and then shot another scene without him. Unexpectedly, it earned Jackman a nomination for the Best Actor award for the short film category at the New York Independent Film and Video Festival.

After dipping his toe into the world of art-house movies, it was time for another biggie from Hugh, which came in the shape of yet another huge summer blockbuster, *Van Helsing*. This time instead of fighting rebellious mutants, he found himself donning a Clint Eastwood-style hat, adding hair extensions and pitting his wits against a set of legendary monsters including Dracula, Frankenstein and the Wolf Man.

The action-packed film saw Hugh in the title role as Gabriel Van Helsing, the arch-enemy of Dracula and a character that had appeared in Bram Stoker's original version of the Dracula story. It was a role that had previously been played on film by Anthony Hopkins and Laurence Olivier, although never as the protagonist. Originally, filming was planned for 1994 as a direct sequel to the 1992 version of *Dracula*, with Anthony Hopkins reprising the title role. In fact, the proposed film was put on hold for many years, during which time numerous elements of the story were changed. In the revised version, *Van Helsing* was younger, more adventurous and worked for the Catholic Church to get rid of any souls they regarded as unredeemable.

In his Vatican-commissioned mission to take care of Dracula, the hero comes into contact with the hugely iconic Frankenstein and the Wolf Man. Even though classed as the good guy, straight out of the Logan school of democracy, Van Helsing is a very enigmatic character. Like the Wolverine character, he enjoys the heat of battle but is troubled by the emptiness he feels in killing demons that he knows still possess human souls.

According to writer/director Stephen Sommers, the role of the monster-killer demanded an actor who should look like a fearless demon-slayer but still play to the hearts of female audiences. He needed to be tough and romantic; someone women would love and guys would trust. Sommers knew that Hugh had the necessary combination of skills, looks and talent. As the director put it, it was an easy choice to select the Australian: 'He's 6ft 3 and 210 pounds of solid steel. We were adamant about getting Hugh Jackman from the start. He was the only guy we ever wanted. How many guys out there are that good-looking and that talented? It had to be a man; it couldn't be a boy. A lot of younger actors are really good but Van Helsing was kind of worldly, he'd been around. He had to have some weight to him, yet he was not of Harrison Ford's age. There are not that many great-looking, super-talented guys in their early thirties. Hugh was the perfect and only choice.'

Happy as they were to cast Hugh in the lead role, playing another comic-book adventure hero wasn't really on Jackman's radar: he was in the middle of the *X-Men* franchise and he didn't think he needed to get wrapped up in another. In the end, the compelling script changed his mind, and he was glad that he went ahead: 'I read this script and the movie and characters were very different. My only reluctance about doing it was that after *X2*, I wanted to do a smaller independent movie with Darren Aronofsky called *The Fountain*, so I was a bit reluctant to be in another big franchise-type summer popcorn movie in a way. I feared to go down that road.'

He also knew that making such movies took a long time, a year of his life: 'Then I knew I was coming to Broadway for a year, so do I really want to be doing that? Then of course there could be *X-Men 3*, then *Van Helsing 2*; that could be my film life. It could be a bit of a

know that *Van Helsing* is going to be
ne character and Stephen Sommers told me
robably the only actor to worry about being in
essful franchises.'

other major influence in his choice to take the lead
s that most of the cast were from his homeland. The
Aussie mafia' as they became known included Richard
Roxburgh, who was in *Moulin Rouge*, David Wenham
from *Lord of the Rings* and Shuler Hensley, who played
Frankenstein. Shuler happened to be a great friend of
Hugh after they starred together in *Oklahoma!* back in
London. Backstage the old mates, often in full costume,
would entertain the other cast and crew members by
singing duets between takes.

As for his leading lady, Stephen Sommers always
wanted the stunning Kate Beckinsale for the role of Anna
but feared she would find it too similar in tone to the
vampire/werewolf film *Underworld* in which she had
starred in 2003. Eventually her agent got Sommers to
send the script, and Beckinsale immediately signed on.
She was the last member to be cast in the dark, romantic
adventure story.

Hugh had never worked with the actress before, and
although she is extremely beautiful he found her to be a
lot tougher than she looked: 'Occasionally Kate would
pull the English rose thing, but then as soon as the action
started she was tougher than all of us.' He described one
stunt that he was particularly nervous about when they
were on wire 50ft above ground: 'We were supposed to
land on a mat with Kate astride of me and her knees on

either side of my head. I did it once with the stunt double and she nearly landed on my shoulder. Then Kate took over and I thought, just a few more inches and I am going to get a knee in the face. We did it three times and Kate got it right every time like an Olympic gymnast, like bang, bang, bang. She's very athletic.'

Kate herself remembered the stunt and mischievously commented on Hugh's reaction: 'If you tell an English girl you want a crotch in the face, you're going to get a crotch in the face.' Conversely, if she had one complaint about doing the film it concerned how long it took her to be made up before each scene: 'I was in make-up for three hours a day. It was a nightmare. The boots took 25 minutes to get on. Every tiny curl took so long.'

Universal Pictures gave director Sommers $150 million to spend on resurrecting the legendary band of bloodsuckers. Not surprisingly, the special effects took a huge bite out of his budget. It was the first movie, other than the *Lord of the Rings* trilogy, to use the MASSIVE software program. Effects artists at Lucas Digital's Industrial Light & Magic created a three-dimensional bust of Jackman's head that would be superimposed into action sequences too dangerous for live actors. In order to pull it off, Hugh had to sit completely still and then they would animate the action sequence without moving his body. So, someone would be yelling out, 'Alright, Hugh. So, you're going to jump off a cliff and then you're going to be taken by a vampire. Alright, here, Hugh, cut! We really need it bigger, man. It's got to be a lot bigger.'

For the first three months, filming took place in the countryside outside Prague. The crew created amazing outdoor sets that minimised the time actors had to work in front of blue-screen sets and the work they did was unbelievable. Indeed, the village created was actually left standing for some time afterwards in the anticipation that a second film or a TV series based on the character would be commissioned. The proposed spin-off series called *Transylvania* was pitched to NBC. It featured a wild-west sheriff taken to Europe to battle monsters, with occasional guest appearances from Hugh as Gabriel Van Helsing. However, the series idea was stillborn, partly because make-up, effects and location shooting in Romania would have been too expensive, and partly because the film's opening weekend box-office takings were far below expectations (which also meant the proposed sequel to the film was doomed).

All the interior shots were done in LA because they needed such huge sets. In fact, one set proved so big they couldn't find a studio anywhere in the world where it would fit, so they built it in a car park in Downey, California. It was the biggest thing Hugh had ever seen, even bigger than the *X-Men* sets.

Sommers, one of the old-fashioned kind of directors, set the tone and professionalism of the movie right from the start. He ended each day at 7.30pm with the same energy he had in the morning; he never went a minute past 7.30, but in that time he gave 100 per cent. Each day, he would pop his head into Hugh's make-up trailer to see if the star had any issues or questions. 'Trust me,'

Hugh insisted, 'that doesn't always happen. He made it really easy. It was almost frighteningly free of tension and there were no breakdowns whatsoever.'

The star from Oz also found his director to be an incredible filmmaker. Hugh didn't believe there were many individuals around who could handle a film as big as *Van Helsing*, but Sommers created an epic adventure from start to finish. 'I had every confidence in what I could do with the role but not for a second could I pull off all the special effects work. The more I know about it, the more miraculous it was when I saw what Steve had done with it. It was a step up for me because my name was above the title and I was playing the lead character, and that was the first time I had done that. It was a deliberate choice and I would have only done it with someone like Steve.'

Just as he did in his other movies, Hugh insisted on performing as many of his own stunts as possible, although this got him into trouble when he accidentally knocked over a group of innocent Czech Republic extras who happened to be from a homeless shelter and hired for the shoot. Due to the booming film industry in the country, they had suddenly found themselves with 40 or 50 days of work a year, which was a lot of money to them. The extras would do anything and everything on the set to ensure they didn't get fired. 'They are brilliant actors,' recalled Hugh. 'In the movie, the turn-of-the-century peasants looked incredibly real, by the way. And there was one scene where the brides were attacking and there was this big mêlée going on in the village, and I was running forward to grab onto the legs of Kate Beckinsale, who was being dragged off by a wire. So it was very important for me to stay focused. But this extra ran in front of me.'

The unfortunate extra must have been no more than 5ft tall. Hugh put his hand in front of him and felt him crumple: 'It's what Jonah Lomu [the massive New Zealand rugby player] must have felt like whenever someone came to tackle him. This guy just went tumbling and as I continued on with the take I was thinking, I think that guy's in a bad way. I think he must have broken at least something. So I went to try and find him, and the poor guy was running away from me. I mean, he was terrified that the big Hollywood star was going to come and fire him and he would lose his job. I just wanted to apologise to him. And he ended up with a broken arm. In fact, in the course of that day I knocked over some old women and children as well as breaking this poor guy's hand. And I said to Steve, the director, "You know what? If you cut this the right way, you could make me the most unlikeable hero in movie history."'

While in the middle of filming *Van Helsing*, Jackman was also beginning to prepare for his role as the flamboyant song-and-dance man, Peter Allen. The traits of the two characters couldn't have been further apart, and for a while this created quite an identity crisis for him: 'It was strange because Van Helsing had this kind of mask. He was sort of mysterious. He had this reputation with lots of testosterone flying around. But he was a guarded and reluctant hero. And you know, it's the polar opposite of Peter Allen. Peter would've loved him, you know.'

He was also unprepared in other ways: 'I hadn't done

any tap dancing really in my life. So I had to learn to tap. I was in my trailer and had this wooden slab made for me by carpenters. And I was in my Van Helsing costume with tap shoes on tapping away in between set-ups. And I feel this presence behind me. And I turn around. And there's Steve peering his head in the door then and muttering, "Do not tell a soul about this. No one."'

On its release, *Van Helsing* grossed $200 million worldwide and brought in $52 million during its opening weekend. The DVD sales alone were $65 million in the first week in North America, which when put in context, is more than half the revenue from all the theatre runs on Broadway. In spite of its viewing success, the film itself wasn't at all popular with most of the critics and earned Hugh his first-ever nominated Razzie Award for Worst Actor in a Movie. Luckily for him, he didn't win!

'Hugh arrived with this Nicest Guy in Hollywood label. I had to hope all the cast were like these nasty English people and Australian people, who wanted to find out what was going on here with him, because something must certainly be going on, because you never hear anything nasty about him. They're like, "Does he like women's underwear? Does he have anything to do with animals?" We hoped this guy was a complete phony. We kept peering into his trailer and saying, "Hey! We just popped in!" And, I mean, there was nothing.'

Kate Beckinsale, actress and co-star in *Van Helsing*

CHAPTER ELEVEN

SINGER'S LAST STAND

The year 2006 witnessed the *X-Men* roadshow yet again rumble into towns and theatres across the globe. Except this time, the road trip wasn't such a smooth journey. In fact, given the troubled history surrounding the third instalment, *X-Men: The Last Stand*, it was somewhat amazing that it actually made it to town at all.

Things got off to a bad start when franchise director Bryan Singer jumped ship even before the movie had started its engine. Originally, he was committed to doing a three-film deal with Fox, which began with *X-Men 2*, but he and Fox were unable to agree on terms. During the stand-off, rival production company Warner Brothers offered him the chance to direct *Superman Returns*. Singer informed Fox that he was going to take Warner Brothers up on the opportunity, but wanted to return to direct *X-Men 3* when he had finished. Fox representatives were allegedly outraged and as a consequence, his deal was terminated and British director Matthew Vaughn was hired to take over. Later, in a 2009 interview, Bryan Singer divulged that he regretted his decision to direct *Superman Returns* over *X3*. He went on to confess that he realised his mistake long before he watched the third film, while he watched it and after watching it.

Things became worse when just six weeks before filming was to begin, Vaughn, too, left for personal reasons. It was rumoured that he had cited the huge amount of pressure put on him to deliver the film in a very short amount of time, a script he felt was flawed, and a large amount of interference from various parties as his reasons. Though he was only with the production for a short time, his work contributed to *X3*'s later success: he was instrumental in the addition of several key scenes and in signing Kelsey Grammer and ex-football hardman Vinnie Jones to the cast.

Subsequently, Brett Ratner, director of the *Rush Hour* series and the Hannibal Lector prequel *Red Dragon*, found himself sitting firmly in the cursed director's chair. Nevertheless, Ratner wasn't at all fazed about being third choice. He brought with him a clear idea of what he wanted to achieve: he had spent time studying the script and the previous *X-Men* movies, highlighting all the things he liked about them and the things he thought needed improvement. Ratner identified three major changes: he wanted to make the new *X-Men* funnier, sexier and more emotional. The result was a film that provided a bigger slice of emotional engagement than the first two, yet still provided enough crowd-pleasing moments to be a success with the fans.

The storyline for the latest epic was loosely based on two X-Men comic-book stories, *Dark Phoenix Saga* and *Gifted*. It evolved around the events taking place after a private-led government-supported laboratory discovered that by using the DNA of a powerful boy, they could transform mutants into human beings. There was only one real option for the mutants – accept the cure, give up their powers and become human. But Magneto insisted on retaining his powers and set up a strong force to fight against the government and destroy the boy. Predictably, it was up to the X-Men to stop Magneto and his cronies.

Obviously, Hugh and the other original cast members were extremely concerned about the game of musical director chairs and he commented: 'I was upset that Bryan wasn't coming back to direct X3. It was so long before we started shooting the movie and for me at that point, I hadn't committed to it. I committed to looking at the script.' He instinctually knew that regardless of who was directing, they had to have a great script. 'And by the way, Matthew Vaughn needs to be credited because he helped to develop that script and he did a great job in terms of a starting script. And Brett did a great job and smartly didn't try to recreate the wheel. I don't think people who are not very au fait with film will really be able to tell the difference stylistically. And yet Brett's a really emotional guy, a real passionate guy. In some ways

Bryan was more cerebral, where Brett was a little bit more suited to this script, which was more emotional and, even by the end, more melodramatic.'

With all the dark clouds hanging over the head of the sequel, however, there was at least some good news when Halle Berry, who had originally turned down the film, citing lack of character development in the previous two instalments and a tense relationship with director Bryan Singer as her reasons, changed her mind. Some speculated that her change of heart came not just with Singer's departure but also with the major box-office flop of her movie *Catwoman* in 2004. She only agreed to return on the condition that her role was expanded. Consequently, her character served as leader of the X-Men, which actually was in keeping with the original comic books.

Hugh didn't mind the change at all, believing the real strength of the movie to be in the evolution of the characters, in particular the roles he and Halle played. So while Berry's character, Storm, got ready for motivational speeches, he tried hard to take Logan to another level. Simon Crane, stunt coordinator for *Mr & Mrs. Smith*, *Troy* and both the *Tomb Raider* films, helped him remove the Mike Tyson, knock-'em-out-with-one-punch street-fighter attitude and instead incorporated more art into his fighting style, something more akin to the artwork in the comics.

The script also provided Logan with greater scope as a team player as well as more interaction with the other characters throughout the motion picture. Hugh's

Above left: Hugh Jackman with co-stars Maureen Lipman and Josefina Gabrielle at the *Oklahoma!* opening night at London's National Theatre.   © *Getty Images*

Above right: Having a laugh: Hugh backstage with Howard Keel at the *Oklahoma!* production. (1991).   © *Getty Images*

Below: Hugh showing a lighter side on the set of *Kate & Leopold* in New York's Central Park. (2001).   © *Getty Images*

Above left: Striking the famous Wolverine pose at the US première of *X-Men 2*.

© *Getty/WireImage*

Above right: Hugh at the 2006 ShoWest Awards, where he picked up the gong for Best Male Star.

© *Getty/FilmMagic*

Below: With *X-Men 3* co-stars Rebecca Romjin Stamos, Halle Berry and Famke Janssen at the 2006 Cannes Film Festival.

© *Getty/WireImage*

Above: The leading man on horseback during the filming of *Australia*.

Below: With legendary director Baz Luhrmann and Nicole Kidman at the *Australia* première.

Above left: Hugh shows off his toned body on the beach in St Tropez. He puts in a lot of work in the gym for the *X-Men* films, building the muscle needed to play Wolverine.
© *Getty/FilmMagic*

Above right: Family man: Hugh gives Ava a piggyback outside Grauman's Chinese Theater in April 2009.
© *Getty/FilmMagic*

Below: Hollywood Walk of Fame: Hugh makes his mark in the famous Grauman's cement.
© *Getty/WireImage*

Above: Hugh promoting the Australian production of *The Boy From Oz*.
He won rave reviews for his portrayal of Peter Allen.
© Getty/AFP

Bottom left: Performing a flamboyant musical number as Peter Allen. *© Getty/AFP*

Bottom right: Hugh and the love of his life, Deborra-Lee, at the Worldwide
Orphans Foundation benefit gala in 2009. Deb is the founder of Orphan Angels
in Australia.
© Getty

Above: 'Lookin' good!' Hugh flexes during a gym workout as he undergoes the Wolverine transformation once more. © *Getty Images*

Below: ...and puts his new muscles to the test against TV host Jimmy Fallon on *Late Night with Jimmy Fallon*. © *Getty Images*

Above left: 'You're gonna need some bigger claws!' Hugh at *The Wolverine* première in Leicester Square.

© *Getty Images*

Above right: Hugh and Anne Hathaway make a striking pair in Berlin, promoting *Les Misérables*.

© *Getty Images*

Below: The duo pick up a gong at the Annual Screen Actors Guild Awards with *Les Misérables* director Tom Hooper.

© *Getty Images*

The dapper actor
shows off the fruits
of his hard work – a
coveted Golden
Globe statuette.

© Getty Images

character was still a composed, leather jacketed, cigarette-smoking-in-the-school-corridor type of guy, but his loner image started to slip a little: 'I wouldn't say he was a card-carrying X-Man, or that he had a permanent suite at the mansion, but really in this movie his journey was more about what role he would take. He had to take on more responsibility which went against his grain but with which he coped.'

Although happy with the new development for Wolverine, he made a clean breast of it by saying that if he could have changed one more thing about his character, it would definitely have been the hairstyle. Not only did it make him look like an uncool Elvis Presley, the half a can of hairspray required to keep it in place put a hole in the ozone layer the size of Mars!

Although the hairstyle couldn't change, there were other improvements to the movie, including the addition of new cast members. He was more than impressed with Brett's casting brilliance, which included hiring Ellen Page in the role as Kitty Pryde, an appointment which he described as inspired. He was also impressed with the acting of Cameron Bright as Leech: 'The little boy that played Leech, Cameron Bright, was so brilliant. I didn't actually work with him but I saw him on set and he was just perfect for that role. It's quite haunting. I saw him in *Birth* and he was great in that. In this movie you can't get him out of your head. I also thought Ben Foster was terrific as the Angel. It was a tough role to pull off and I really believed his dilemma. I would've liked for him to have more to do.'

Kelsey Grammer, who played the role of Dr Frasier Crane in the TV hit *Frasier* for too many years to mention, and ex-football star Vinnie Jones also joined the group of actors as Dr Henry 'Hank' McCoy and the muscle-bound villain named Juggernaut respectively. Hugh recalled, 'The truth of the matter is he [Kelsey] made me laugh so much that there was more footage on the cutting-room floor of me laughing because of Kelsey than actually good film. He just had a look in his eye that was so wicked. I really loved working with Kelsey.'

Vinnie, the hard man from the soccer field who made his violent debut as a rough, tough criminal in the British classic, *Lock, Stock and Two Smoking Barrels*, was an old friend of Hugh's. Alongside Halle Berry, he had worked with Jones on the film *Swordfish* several years before. 'I remember on *Swordfish* Vinnie found a blow-up punching-bag doll of Wolverine and tied a noose around his neck above his trailer and proceeded to kick it around'. On the first morning of *X-Men 3*, Hugh thought he would have his revenge and so he turned up in full Wolverine gear, all muscle and mutton chops and said, 'Okay, mate, this is your chance. Now you can really have a go at it for real.' Vinnie stared at him for several moments before they both burst out laughing.

One night, when the pair were reminiscing, Vinnie informed Hugh that he had done about 27 films since *Swordfish*. Hugh couldn't believe it. 'Twenty-seven films?' he commented, 'I think I've done maybe five or six!' Vinnie frowned at him and spoke slowly in his cockney accent,

'Yeah, and you've made more in one fucking movie than I've made in all 27 put together!'

Their friendship grew even stronger off-camera with some friendly banter and rivalry as the Australian and English cricket teams battled it out back in England for the right to win the Ashes (the cricketing equivalent of the World Cup as far as both countries were concerned). Hugh reckoned that when he turned up on set after England lost, Vinnie had never watched cricket in his life: 'Then all of a sudden he became a mad cricket fan, especially when England won the Ashes. I went over to my seat on the set one day and Vinnie had erected this tent which had the Union Jack on the top and an urn with ashes inside.' He raised a smile before adding, 'Vinnie, as normal, was so much fun to have around. He was great. He really popped in the film too. Oh, and by the way, no matter what he tells everyone, those muscles he had in the film, were all fake. Computer generated.'

Senior actors Patrick Stewart and Sir Ian McKellen also benefited from some computer-generation wizardry. In the opening flashback scene, their faces were completely de-aged with a technique called 'digital skin-grafting', using photographs taken years before. The special effects made them look 20 years younger.

Vinnie's muscles, Patrick and Ian's face, and a full-scale section of the Golden Gate Bridge the size of a basketball court used for the end action scene of the movie, were some of the few computer generations involved in the sequel. It definitely wasn't a film that went overboard with special-effects technology, and

Hugh applauded Ratner for his insistence on using as much real action as possible: 'It was important to me because as someone who also watches films I can always tell when a double is being used and it takes me out of it. Maybe that's because I'm looking at it through slightly more introverted eyes than most. But it's the same thing with endless special effects; you instinctively know whether you're being tricked or not, so the more you can do, the better.'

Because of all the live action, there were a tremendous number of scenes where the actors had to fly around the set on wires. This called for extensive planning and wirework, where many of the actors were more than happy to perform some of their own stunts. The whirlwind wire-stunt performed by Halle Berry during one fight scene reportedly caused her to become so nauseated that she vomited. Later, when re-shooting more of the same action scene, someone from the crew apparently stood below her holding an empty bucket just in case.

Hugh again attempted to perform a lot of his own stunts. For the ones he didn't perform, he brought in his brother-in-law, Rich, to act as his body-double: 'It would be easy for me to tell everyone that it is me going 80 miles per hour into a tree and then falling down through all the branches, but usually it's Rich, my brother-in-law. But we're family, so it's kind of the same thing.' Rich had been working as Hugh's stunt double for several years. And while stepping in for him on the set of *Van Helsing*, he'd been sent home with a broken leg when something went wrong: 'So I got a call from big sis saying, "Start doing more of your own stunts, pal!"'

X-Men: The Last Stand completed shooting in January 2006, after six months of filming in Vancouver, Canada. According to associate producer Dave Gordon, it was one of the biggest productions ever filmed in Canada.

Hugh believed that *X-Men 3* would spell the end of the X-Men saga, just as the studio had always planned. Definitely the biggest film in every way, it felt like a fitting end to the trilogy: 'But if I was writing the story of how a movie got made and this was a case history, you wouldn't want this as your ideal way to do it. But it seemed to me that there was a little bit of chaos to all of these movies and it somehow seemed to create a winning formula. So funnily enough, it kind of ended up being a situation where everyone gave the best that they had to give and I think ultimately the movie has been good for it. I think it worked but it should be that big because it's the end of the trilogy. There have been three great movies and Bryan Singer pretty much started comic-book movies again. So you can be guaranteed that if there is another one it won't just be a kind of cash-in, or glorious swan-song moment of "I've got to get back in the game", that's for sure.'

The film was released on 26 May 2006 in the United States and Canada. Despite mixed reviews from critics and fans, it did well at the box office. Its opening-day gross of $45.5 million is the fourth highest on record, while the opening weekend gross of $103 million is the fifth-highest ever. It also had the biggest Memorial Day box-office opening ever, only to be beaten by *Pirates of the Caribbean: At World's End* in 2007.

It was quite apparent to the growing number of *X-Men* movie fans, that as the *X-men* trilogy progressed, Wolverine had increasingly become the main focus of the film, both on screen and off. Hugh's face became the face of the *X-men* movies, his name topped the list of stars and his interview time was longer than that of the other actors: 'I've always felt more comfortable being in the middle of it from the beginning to the end; I like working every day and being there. In this movie, there's a whole subplot with Ian McKellen's character that I wasn't in, and there was about three weeks where I didn't shoot, and it felt really weird. I would visit on set occasionally and just sort of pop in, and I came back to work and felt like, "Alright, I gotta get my legs back here."'

As for Hugh's son, Oscar, he found *Van Helsing* to be a little too scary but he really loved the Wolverine character and would don claws and cute sideburns to copy his dad on Halloween. 'He liked the Wolverine toy the most, the one which was about a foot and a half tall and says things like, "I'll slice you in half". He takes it to bed. I'll be in the other room and it goes off in the middle of the night. So he's getting these subliminal messages, "This kid will take you down" and "I'll slice you in half". He kisses and hugs it. I can see years of therapy coming my way!'

Hugh and director Brett Ratner became such good friends that after the film had been completed, the director decided to have some fun with the star. In secret, he teamed up with *Punk'd* hooligan Ashton Kutcher to set Hugh up in one of the biggest and best *Punk'd* stunts ever attempted. *Punk'd* is an American hidden-camera show featuring producer and host Ashton Kutcher, who plays pranks on celebrities.

Hugh's *Punk'd* experience began when he went over to Brett Ratner's home and the director showed him around the $14 million mansion, taking time to tell him how much everything cost. Then, before the two friends went out for a meal together, Brett told Hugh that he wanted to cook for his girlfriend later on and persuaded the star to take a peek at his barbecue grill because he wasn't sure how to use it. Hugh attempted to light the barbecue, but told Brett that it wasn't working properly. The pair left for dinner – only to find Brett's home engulfed in flames when they returned.

Hugh said, 'When we get back there are four fire trucks, one hundred firemen; the entire house is on fire. They had explosions, they had smoke, they were throwing couches out the window. After five minutes this guy came down and said, "We've discovered the source, it's coming from the barbecue." He admitted that he was physically shaking as it got worse and worse, and when they were informed that another three houses were also on fire, he thought his life was over, believing he had possibly killed someone.

'When the guy told me I'd been *Punk'd*, I was so into it I was like, "How can he be joking at a time like this?" When I finally realised what was going on, I just lay down on the ground. They handed me the release form to sign and I'm like, "Whatever." I was this close to throwing up.'

Kutcher did admit that he felt wicked when Jackman fell hook, line and sinker for the prank. But it was another example of how far Hugh had come in the world of showbusiness, because in Hollywood, you aren't really a star unless you have been '*Punk'd*'.

'*He's the perfect man. He's talented, bright, sweet, charming and gracious. Everyone loves him, and he's sexy as hell.*'

Rebecca Romijn, actress and co-star in *X-Men*

CHAPTER TWELVE

NO REST FOR MR NICE GUY

Aside from *X-Men*, 2006 would go down as an extremely prolific year in terms of film releases for the Australian heart-throb. Hugh's face appeared on every billboard in town it seemed, his name on the credits of numerous movies. Other, more established actors must have been shaking their heads in wonderment at how the guy from nowhere had suddenly landed so many plum roles alongside movie and musical legends such as Woody Allen, Michael Caine and David Bowie, as well as the new breed of stars like Christian Bale, Scarlett Johansson and a host of others. Hugh turned up on the big screen as a magician, a killer and part-astronaut, plus he'd been given the ultimate accolade for any Hollywood superstar of not one, but two voiceovers in two different big animation feature films.

Most of the movies were released in the second half of

the year and to many, Hugh must have appeared to be the hardest-working man in showbusiness at the time. And although he had been working fairly steadily, he was the first to acknowledge that he really wasn't working all that hard as a number of the projects, like the animation stuff, had actually been recorded during the year he was on Broadway. 'I probably had a month off in between each of them. But people say, "You must work hard". I'm like, most people work like 48 weeks a year, I'm lucky if I do 40.'

Scoop was released soon after X3. It gave Hugh the opportunity to work with the one and only Woody Allen (probably every actor's ambition before they die and go to Tinsel Heaven). The Australian star was surprised when out of the blue he received a call from his agent saying that the casting director for Woody Allen wanted to see him about a movie that was being shot in England. Hugh thought the writer/director only based and shot his movies in and around New York, but *Scoop* was actually Allen's second consecutive film to be set and shot in the English capital, following *Match Point* a few years before.

Before meeting the famous director, Hugh was informed that he should not be offended if his meeting with Allen took less than two minutes. The meeting actually took about three, which Hugh presumed to be a good thing. He remembered Allen to be shy and a little nervous, as if he was saying 'Well, I've got this movie and I know you've probably got more important things to do. But if you want to read it, you probably don't, but if you

do and you like it, then, you know, I'd love you to do it.'
And that was pretty much it. Hugh got the role and spent
the following few weeks smiling and repeating Allen's
name whenever anyone asked him what his next project
was going to be.

Allen himself confessed to never having seen Hugh
before they met. 'I had never seen Hugh Jackman or his
movies, or even knew what he looked like before I met
him. He was just one of those people who I'd never come
in contact with, for one reason or another. I only heard
wonderful stories about him and how great he was as an
actor. We called him and asked him if he'd be interested
in doing something, and he said "Sure." He came by to
say hello, and he walked in and not only is he fun to look
at, he is great-looking and he's also lovely and suave. I
offered him the role right away. I was very lucky that he
was free to take it, and wanted to take it.'

The picture was a typical Allen movie – smart, funny,
with moments of dark humour throughout. Following
the memorial service for irrepressible investigative
reporter Joe Strombel (Ian McShane), Strombel's spirit
finds himself on the barge of death with several other
deceased individuals, including a young woman who
believes she has been poisoned by her employer, Peter
Lyman (Jackman). She tells Strombel that she thinks
Lyman, a handsome British aristocrat with political
ambitions, might be the Tarot Card Killer, a notorious
serial killer of prostitutes, and that he killed her when she
stumbled onto his secret.

When Sondra (Scarlett Johansson), an American

journalism student, visits friends in London, she goes to see a stage performance by American magician Sid Waterman, played by Allen himself. She is shocked to find herself able to see and hear Joe from beyond the grave, and he gives her the scoop of a lifetime and urges her to pursue it. Sondra immediately starts chasing the big story, but ends up falling in love with the suspected murderer, Peter Lyman.

Classed as a romantic comedy/murder mystery, the audience is never sure if Hugh's character is really the killer until the end of the movie. The actor strived to make his character appear charming, but a bit reserved: 'I saw him as someone who you'd find in the pages of *Hello!* or *OK!* magazines in England.' He wanted Peter to be the debonair, about-town type, with a very well-established family, who dated the *models du jour* and drove expensive cars.

Hugh found Woody to be incredibly personable, fun and terrific to work with and he particularly enjoyed the easy atmosphere on set that Allen's presence created. 'He was very calm, and then all of a sudden, at three in the afternoon, he would send us all home. It was almost like bankers' hours. He didn't do a lot of takes; there was not a lot of rehearsal. I had to kiss Scarlett in this movie; it's a tough job, but someone's got to do it. And Woody didn't do a lot of takes of the scenes. However, on a personal note, it was good for me because when I went home to Debs, I could say, "Darling, one take, that's all it was…"'

The only slight problem he had to adjust to was Allen's

famous ad-libbing during takes. Hugh, of course, had worked with other actors who ad-libbed in the past, but no one did it better or funnier than the famous New Yorker himself. Hugh would end up laughing out loud, which on occasion would upset Allen: 'He'd be like, "No, no, no, please, my character is boorish, he's not funny." I said, "But if you keep ad-libbing like that and I'm in the shot, I'm going to laugh. You've got to be a little more boring!"'

Meanwhile, Woody Allen wouldn't be Woody Allen if he wasn't quirky. On one occasion while filming within a stately house, he suddenly disappeared. No one had any idea where he was until the sound of a clarinet came wafting through the air. Often he would turn to playing the instrument while thinking or waiting for a scene to be prepared, leaving the cast and crew lingering.

Allen also had an unusual disdain for filming directly in sunlight. He believed it to be too harsh and thought that it made for a slight ugliness in the actors. It was the first time that Hugh could recall everyone being thrilled to have cloudy English skies: 'I don't know if he'd been setting out sacrifices to the gods, but it was like four weeks of straight cloudy weather with hardly any rain, extraordinary. Normally, people complain a lot there about the weather, but I was around a lot of very happy people. The whole thing was a real thrill, and a great opportunity. I'm forever grateful for it.'

Despite his idiosyncrasies, Allen worked extremely well with everyone, especially Scarlett Johansson. Apparently, he had even written the script for *Scoop* with her in mind after working with her on *Match Point.* And Hugh could see why because he too found the actress to be quite an extraordinary woman, who could do anything she put her mind to and who seemed to come alive when on film. 'On the set, we'd sing together. She can sing like an angel. She can dance, too. Pretty much everyone on the crew had a crush on her. She's unbelievably down-to-earth, incredibly talented, very poised. There was not a hard day's work on the entire movie when working with her.' The pair would go on to work together on the film *The Prestige* later.

Scoop did the same at the box office as most of Allen's other movies, breaking even financially, with critics either loving or hating it. For Hugh, the entire experience of filming in the UK with the quintessential American director was invaluable. Just to have a Woody Allen film on his CV was enough, as he noticed when a stream of very experienced British actors turned up on set, happy to do a day's filming and then leave. 'They would come in just because they wanted to work with Woody Allen. There was not a lot of film work that happened in London, and certainly not a lot of films of the calibre of a Woody Allen movie. So, everyone working on it felt privileged and honoured.' The unassuming Allen was just as bowled over by the calibre of actors he attracted. He would wander around the set muttering about how bad he felt because all he had for them was one line.

The respect between actor and director was reciprocated. When Allen was asked if Cary Grant had been the inspiration behind Hugh Jackman's character and performance, he simply replied, 'No, I think that's built into Hugh. He's such a dapper, sweet, likable guy who can dance and move gracefully, and is so handsome and can sing, that comparisons are inevitable. You could always. Just as there was a time Hugh Grant would be compared with Cary Grant because he also is very debonair and charming. Well, so is Hugh Jackman, and it is an inevitable comparison.'

Hugh's next motion picture was full of obsession, deceit and jealousy with dangerous and deadly consequences. It told the mysterious tale of two magicians whose intense rivalry leads them on a life-long battle for supremacy. *The Prestige,* a British film directed by Christopher Nolan, adapted from Christopher Priest's 1995 World Fantasy award-winning novel of the same name was released on 20 October 2006, a week earlier than Touchstone Pictures' original planned release date of 27 October.

From the moment they first meet as young magicians on the rise, Robert Angier and Alfred Borden are competitors. But their friendly competition evolves into a bitter rivalry, making them fierce enemies for life and consequently jeopardising the lives of everyone around them. Set against the backdrop of turn-of-the-century London, Hugh Jackman and Christian Bale star in the dramatic thriller as the magicians engaged in a bitter war of one-upmanship, with Michael Caine as Jackman's mentor and David Bowie playing scientist Nikola Tesla. Hugh later stated that having the chance to work with Bowie was one of his main motivations for doing the film.

The Prestige also provided the first meeting on screen of two superheroes: Jackman, aka Wolverine, and Bale, who had just come off the back of playing the dark and moody crusader, Batman. Although most action-hero fans around the world would rather have seen the two square up in a winner-takes-all showdown, *The Prestige* offered the opportunity for both actors to put aside their comic book-based characters and engage in a little magic.

Hugh had always been a fan of Christian Bale, believing him to be a very dedicated and fearless actor. Although Bale's image is sometimes portrayed by the media as very serious and private, Hugh saw a much lighter side to the caped crusader: 'I think it's fair to say he's fairly low-key, relaxed, but he's got a very cheeky sense of humour and is quite naughty.' And the two shared a common interest at the time, which obviously helped. Both had new babies and spent their time between shots showing each other photographs and exchanging stories.

Up to that point, Hugh had always been a fan of magic and over the years he had read a lot about Houdini's life. He found the world of magicians fascinating, particularly around the Houdini era, where they were the celebrities of the day, treated like rock stars. Indeed, they had an incredible contact with the audience and were seen as mediators between this world and the next.

Hugh was keen to learn more about the secret art of magic and all the tricks of the trade. To prepare for the role, he spent a lot of time with magicians Ricky Jay and Michael Weber, learning how to carry out magic tricks convincingly and with the grace of a seasoned magician. He modelled his character, in terms of style, on a character called Channing Pollock, an American magician of the 1950s who actually became a film star in France later on in his life.

As well as the prospect of meeting and working with rock god, David Bowie, Hugh was also privileged to work alongside one of the world's most acclaimed actors, Sir Michael Caine. 'I learned a lot. You learn a lot from working with someone like Michael. I remember at drama school I watched Michael Caine's one-hour video on filmmaking. I was talking to him all about that and then I kept asking him more questions. He just kept giving me little acting tips and techniques all the time. Wonderful.'

The pair developed a great relationship on set and off, going out together many times while filming. Hugh found him to be a great person to be around – knowledgeable and passionate about cooking, with a strange infatuation for making one of England's best-known specialities: the chip. 'I didn't know he had several restaurants dotted about London and Miami. He taught me how to make good chips. He explained in great Michael Caine detail how to cook them just right, what oils to use and what are the best cooking times to get the perfect chip. He talked about them for ages.'

The Prestige was quite successful at the box office. On its opening weekend, it earned over $14 million in the United States, debuting at number one. It proceeded to gross $53 million domestically and earned an overall worldwide total of over $109 million. Generally, it received favourable reviews from film critics, with a consensus that it was full of plot twists that challenged the viewer throughout. The film received nominations for the Academy Award for Best Art Direction and the Academy Award for Best Cinematography, as well as a nomination for the Hugo Award for Best Dramatic Presentation, Long Form in 2007.

With the rabbit firmly back in the magician's top hat, Hugh finally got the chance to become involved in a project that he'd been dying to get his actor's teeth into for ages. It had started back in 2002 when Brad Pitt and Cate Blanchett signed up to appear in *The Fountain*, which was budgeted at $75 million. The script received positive word of mouth from online film websites and everything was looking good to go. Then Pitt suddenly dropped out, and despite the fact that sets had already been constructed, the film was shut down. Warner Brothers, who were producing the movie, had become nervous and wanted a co-financier to help fund the risky project before production could begin again.

Visionary director Darren Aronofsky re-wrote the script so that it could be made on a smaller budget of $35 million and he recruited the less-expensive Hugh Jackman and Rachel Weisz before the film was eventually given the green light.

Part of the appeal for Hugh was the chance to play three incarnations of the same character in his quest for eternal youth and the love of his life, or lives. The movie involves three parallel stories about love, death, spirituality and the fragility of existence, as told through the odyssey taken on by one man in his 1,000-year struggle to save the woman he loves, played by Rachel Weisz. The epic journey begins in 16th-century Spain, where, as conquistador Tomas Creo, Hugh commences his search for the 'Tree of Life', the legendary entity believed to grant eternal life to those who drink its sap. As modern-day scientist Tommy Creo, he desperately struggles to find a cure for the cancer that is killing his beloved wife, Isabel. In the last section, he travels through deep space as a 26th-century astronaut trying to grasp the mysteries of life that have consumed him for more than a century.

Hugh, who first met Aronofsky earlier on his road to stardom while playing Peter Allen, admitted that there was no question about him taking the role when the opportunity presented itself: 'When I read the script I was so blown away by it, I was crying at the end. Though I didn't fully understand it on the first read through,' he conceded, with a wry smirk. 'But I got the feeling of what he was trying to say, and it really moved me. Now, I understand movies, and with a lot of scripts I get 'em within the first ten minutes, but they don't move me. This is the first time I've ever cried reading a script. I also found it very engaging, and I did find myself flicking backwards and forwards a little bit.'

Fans of Jackman saw a far more raw and emotional side to the actor than they had ever witnessed before. To get to those dark places was a greater challenge than pulling off the emotional side of the Wolverine character.

Hugh had never really been given the opportunity to play scenes that required that rawness before, and it was emotionally very draining for him as well as slightly uncomfortable to watch at the première.

He credited Aronofsky with creating an atmosphere on set that was very private and comfortable: 'The scenes were raw. But we worked a lot on them and I think I had a great relationship with Rachel and with the director, Darren Aronofsky, and he wanted me to be this guy dealing with the death of his wife. I mean, it's pretty full-on, you know. And the script was very weighty, so I thought finally I had a script which took me emotionally to my limit. And the script was equal to that, you know what I mean? There's no point in putting it all out there on a script that really doesn't demand it, and this one did.'

To reach the real emotional parts, he forced himself to think heartbreaking thoughts such as the idea of something tragic happening to his own wife or children: 'I mean, I think anyone who has loved or has a kid or wife or whatever, you feel you'll do anything, if you could. You know, there are stories all the time of people jumping in front of buses, lifting cars, so human possibilities are immense. But of course as an actor you put yourself in that situation; it's a funny mix of techniques, I suppose.'

And it worked. During one emotional scene he cried so much that Aronofsky was amazed, telling him he'd never seen snot bubbles on film before. Sadly, after much debate, that particular shot didn't make the final cut.

Unpredictably, the physical demands required of the role were equally as tough as the mental ones. One of the most amazing physical feats was when Hugh, shaved bald, hovers in outer space, surrounded by a transparent bubble. It saw him in full lotus position, spinning upside down, stretching out into a traditional Superman flying pose, before floating away. Many commented that it was just a standard Hollywood effect shot. But it wasn't. He performed the stunt without any effects or stunt crew. According to Aronofsky, what people saw in the film was take 19: 'We had Hugh in that tank for three days. He never complained once.'

In fact, it took him over a year of training to achieve the lotus position and another three months to be able to hold it long enough for the underwater takes. He blankly refused a body-double. 'Oh, by the way, this was probably the most physical role I've ever done. I know it probably looks easy, but I don't know if you've tried to get into the lotus position, And T'ai Chi, I did T'ai Chi for a year in order to pull off what is ultimately about ten seconds of film. And the last three days of shooting I was in the lotus position, 20ft underwater, locked into this bar. I was underwater for eight hours a day. And the lotus position took me 14 months to get. I did an hour and a half a day of yoga to be able to get there without injuring myself.'

It was exhausting work. One lunchtime, Hugh went back to his trailer and he was so tired that he couldn't even eat; he just fell asleep lying on the floor. Many nights, he went straight to bed, only to rise the next morning at the ungodly hour of 4am to do yoga for an hour and a half before work. He was living the life of a monk in a Hollywood superstar's body.

'I dropped quite a lot of weight for the whole thing... yeah, I was pretty lean. Darren really wanted for me to be lean, as lean as I could be. I was working so hard I wasn't that hungry and didn't eat.'

Unfortunately, *The Fountain* didn't exactly set the box-office alight and disappeared after only one week. The advertising campaign was seemingly non-existent. When it came out in the UK, despite the generally better reviews, it was only shown in one London cinema. Yet Hugh was positively upbeat and incredibly proud of what he had achieved in the role. He knew that because of the subject matter and the way it was shot, it would be one of those love-it or hate-it movies.

He was disappointed, however, when news broke that the film was actually booed in Venice. At the press screening, about 80 per cent of the audience gave a standing ovation and only about 20 per cent booed, causing a fight to break out between certain members of the press. Two of them had to be pulled apart. Hugh thought that that in itself was a great story.

Next on the horizon, he took his chance to dip not only his toe, but to dive headfirst, fully-clothed and without the aid of a life jacket into the special and wonderful world of animation. First up came the British film *Flushed Away*, where the super-busy Jackman provided the voice of pampered house mouse, Roddy St James.

Flushed Away is a computer-animated British film

partnered between Aardman Animations of Wallace & Gromit fame and DreamWorks Animation. It was directed by David Bowers and Sam Fell, and because of the large number of water scenes, it was Aardman's first completely computer-animated feature as opposed to their usual stop-motion action done with clay figures.

Naturally, Hugh was excited to be working with the Aardman crew, who he described as the best in the business. What's more, not only did it have an impressive cast with Kate Winslet as Rita Malone, Sir Ian McKellen as the Toad, and a host of other British stars, the writing team assembled were top drawer, with Dick Clement, Ian La Frenais and Christopher Lloyd leading the pack. It was a match made in animation heaven, with many predicting a first-rate film with numerous awards to follow.

The story focuses on Roddy St James, a decidedly upper-crust pet rat, who makes his home in a smart Kensington flat. When a common sewer rat named Sid comes spewing out of the sink and decides to stay, Roddy schemes a way to get rid of Sid by luring him into the 'jacuzzi' – actually the toilet bowl. Sid may be an ignorant slob, but being a sewer rat, he does know his plumbing. He plays along and when given the opportunity pushes Roddy into the toilet instead and flushes him away into the sewers. Roddy gains the assistance of Rita Malone, an enterprising scavenger rat, who works the drains in her faithful boat, the *Jammy Dodger*. Roddy's aim is to get home, while dodging the evil Toad.

Fascinatingly, the original concept for the movie

involved pirates, but when it was pitched to DreamWorks in 2000, Aardman was told there was no market for pirate films. A few years later, *Pirates of the Caribbean: The Curse of the Black Pearl* was released to unprecedented success.

Flushed Away became Hugh's first attempt at swimming in the animation pool and he loved every minute of it, although he did miss the interaction with other actors as he often found himself alone in a sound booth. Although he shared lots of voice time on screen opposite the Kate Winslet character, Rita, they hardly met during the filming process: 'I do know Kate and we do actually get on very well together. The thing is, to be honest, Kate is one of the best actors around, so she can make anything work and I think we did. What happened was once she started to record more and I was recording, I would listen to her a lot. Sometimes they would even play her to me so I could hear her.'

But the studio didn't leave him entirely alone with a microphone. He worked with a fantastic woman called Susan, who would read opposite him in New York or in the UK. She was a rare talent and at every session she would read every part, going from Toad to Rita, to Sid to Whitey, with so much ease that it really helped him get to grips with the situation. Jackman also enjoyed being able to ad-lib and play around with the character a bit, although he admitted he wasn't half as good as the master himself, Woody Allen.

To make the actors feel at home, the writers included as much as they could get away with from past roles. In one scene, Roddy is looking for an outfit to wear and he goes into the wardrobe and picks up a Wolverine costume. Then, in another clip, Rita (voiced by Kate Winslet) watches her boat sink in the same way as Rose does in *Titanic*.

The voiceover work was exciting for Hugh, and for the first time ever he really appreciated the fact that he didn't have to sit through hair and make-up everyday. As with most animation projects, videotapes of the actors performing with their voices in the booths are shot so the gestures can be incorporated into the character drawings. Hugh was amazed when he saw the final result: 'I did see some similarities. It's a little frightening to see yourself looking like a rodent, but it's an adorable one, right? A pampered pet, shall we say. But no, there are some things definitely and they were filming it all the time. It was great going back in to see how these scenes were evolving, to see how they were using that. Anyway, it was interesting.'

Flushed Away collected $64 million in the United States on its release, which was below the average of other CGI films from DreamWorks, but a healthy $111 million from international markets to give a worldwide total of $176 million. It was the second of two Aardman-produced films released by DreamWorks, but things didn't work out and Aardman's experience with DreamWorks during the making of the movie led to a split between the two studios.

Last, but not least for Hugh in this phenomenal year was the release of the long-awaited Warner Bros animated film *Happy Feet*, which was set deep inside the icy land of Antarctica. This was an American-Australian computer-animated comedy-drama with music, directed and co-written by George Miller. It was produced at Sydney-based visual effects and animation studio, Animal Logic.

The storyline was simple, if not a little wacky. Two emperor penguins have a baby named Mumble, who develops an amazing skill for tap dancing, even though this is not acceptable for penguins. Even worse, he can't sing, unlike the rest of the emperor penguins. As a teenager, Mumble is torn apart from his mom, dad and best friend Gloria, and ventures off into the icy landscape only to be rescued from a leopard seal by a group of Adélie penguins. They take him to their home and discover that all their fish is being taken by an unknown 'alien' source, so they ask Lovelace, the unwise and cocky leader of the Adélies, to help them. Unfortunately, he proves no help at all, which leads to an incredible adventure as they try to discover the threat to their food source and their survival. Using courage and bravery, Mumble teaches everyone that uniqueness isn't a burden, but a gift to be treasured.

Hugh plays Memphis, Mumble's father and wannabe king of rock and roll: 'I'm a penguin who thinks he's Elvis.' He found it bizarre and said he had no intention of doing more Elvis-style work. 'I don't want to raise your hopes too high because when I first went in there, the character's name was Elvis and the second session I went in, all of a sudden this character was called Memphis. I said,

"George, is this a reflection on my ability?" He goes, "Oh, I was only ever after the essence of Elvis, really." I'm like, "Thanks, mate!"'

The film opened at number one in the United States on its first weekend of release (17–19 November) grossing $41.6 million and beating *Casino Royale* to the top spot. It remained number one for the Thanksgiving weekend, making $51.6 million over the five-day period. In total, the movie was the top grosser for three weeks, a 2006 box-office feat matched only by *Pirates of the Caribbean: Dead Man's Chest*. As of 8 June 2008, *Happy Feet* had grossed $198 million in the US and $186.3 million overseas, making about $384.3 million worldwide against the production budget of $100 million. It won the Academy Award for Best Animated Feature and was nominated for the Annie Award for Best Animated Feature, an award presented by the International Animated Film Association.

With two animated films in the bag, Jackman was now hooked on voice work and couldn't wait for his next opportunity in the strange, but fascinating world: 'I loved it. I wouldn't say it was easy. It was actually difficult, the acting part, but it was lovely to go to work. You walk into the studio, they turn on a button and you record everything. There's no hair, no make-up, no nothing, and for four hours you can do the entire script. You ad-lib, you play around, you do things and you get a lot done. It's sort of easy in that way but I really enjoyed it and I love these movies. Look, I've got a six-year-old and a one-year-old, so probably almost at least twice a week

I've got an animated movie of some description playing in my house. It's good to be actually involved in one of them. I think I've seen *Shrek* a hundred times.'

Within 12 short months, he had achieved more than most actors do in a decade. It was also rumoured that he actually turned down the role as James Bond before it was offered to Daniel Craig. He later said he wasn't offered the role directly – the Bond people don't do things like that – but it was floated in his direction. However, he floated it back and asked to see the script first. Again, the Bond people just don't hand out scripts and so after some contemplation, he decided against the role: 'Part of me thought, I'd love to play him. It was a childhood dream, but the other part of me wasn't passionate enough about it.'

'When he's on set with the baby, Hugh is just like he is with adults. He's interesting. He cares. He's full-bodied with people.'

John Travolta

CHAPTER THIRTEEN

THE FILM FROM OZ

For the third time in his career, Hugh found himself taking over the role of a leading man in a big production when *Moulin Rouge* director Baz Luhrmann cast him to replace Russell Crowe in his much-publicised film, *Australia*. It co-starred Nicole Kidman in an epic tale that galloped through his native country's dusty wartime history.

Crowe, Luhrmann's first choice originally, accepted the part and even went so far as to build a set of stables on his own sprawling ranch to house the massive herd of horses, before production delays and talk of possible budget cuts alienated the A-list star. All of which proved good news for Jackman, who, as a native of Sydney was desperate to be involved in the ambitious project. 'Of course, for me to be part of an Australian movie on this scale, that's the most important thing, to tell a story that looks at its history.' And in typical Jackman-style he remained very philosophical about again handling a script that had someone else's fingerprints on it: 'No problem at all. That's like saying I'll never do Hamlet because Gielgud did it 500 times. When people watch the movie, it's your role. Maybe I'm arrogant, but I can't audition unless I feel I'm the right person for the part. I don't compare myself to anyone else: Russell would have been different in *Australia*, Brad would have been different in *The Fountain*. I don't mind coming off the bench to pinch-hit.'

Luhrmann had talked to him three years previously about the then untitled film. He explained the story as if they were two friends sitting comfortably around a campfire, but never sent Hugh the script. Later, Hugh met Nicole Kidman at a Super Bowl party in the US, where she told him that she had overheard that he was going to be in Luhrmann's new movie. Hugh hesitated and replied that he hadn't even read the script yet and didn't know anything about it. 'Nor me,' Nicole answered, 'but it's Baz... just sign on.'

And that was what Hugh intended to do, given the opportunity. So later, when he received a call from the director, he quickly blurted out, 'Man, I'd love to be part of it.' He genuinely couldn't wait and on talking to the rest of the cast, discovered that they also felt the same when invited to star in the epic. The crew and everybody just wanted to be a part of it, knowing that it was a once-in-a-lifetime opportunity.

In the role, Hugh plays a tough, independent cattle drover, who reluctantly helps an English noblewoman in her quest to save both her philandering husband's Australian cattle station and the mixed-race Aboriginal child she finds there. The drover, the Australian version of a cowboy, is a man of few words who expresses everything through the flicker of an eye or a purse of the lips, like a Clint Eastwood character from the great spaghetti-western days.

The tale centres on Kidman's character, Lady Sarah Ashley, an aristocratic English woman who travels to the Outback on the eve of World War Two in search of her missing husband. Learning of his demise, she sets out to claim her family inheritance: a huge cattle station spreading out over a territory roughly the size of Belgium. Ashley is then forced to team up with Jackman, known only as 'the Drover'. Together, they embark on an arduous journey, driving a herd of 2,000 cattle across 500 miles of harsh terrain towards Darwin until they get caught up in the bombing of the Northern Territory capital by the Japanese.

'Movies on this scale, these big, epic romantic adventures simply don't happen very often,' said Hugh. 'It eclipses anything that has ever been done down there. Baz has been very open about it, making comparisons to *Out of Africa* and *Gone with the Wind*. And if you put those epic films in a melting pot, I think you'll understand the relationship between the two lead characters pretty well. It's been a laugh working with Nicole. She and I have known each other for almost 15 years; she's best friends with my wife.'

The cast and crew read like a Who's Who of Australian talent. It included Jack Thompson, Bryan Brown and

David Wenham. There was even a place for Rolf Harris and his wobble board on the end credits. But the real star, however, was the spectacular scenery of the Northern Territory and the outback of Western Australia with its wild and mysterious landscapes. Tourism Australia spent $40 million on a campaign, with commercials, directed by Luhrmann, linked with the release of the motion picture in the United States, Canada, Japan, Europe and South Korea. It was all part of the plan to help halt the recession and combat fluctuating international fuel prices. Tourism Australia worked with Luhrmann and Twentieth Century Fox on a publicity campaign called, 'See the Movie, See the Country', based on movie maps and location guides to transform the film into a real-life travel adventure.

The tourism industry hoped that Luhrmann's film would deliver visitors from all over the world in the same kind of numbers that came to the country following the 1986 release of *Crocodile Dundee*, or to New Zealand after the release of the *Lord of the Rings* films. Federal Tourism Minister Martin Ferguson said, 'This movie will potentially be seen by tens of millions of people and it will bring life to little-known aspects of Australia's extraordinary natural environment, history and indigenous culture.'

The opening scene set the background for the most expensive and most eagerly anticipated Australian film ever produced. When Lady Sarah Ashley (Kidman), the uptight English aristocrat, arrives in Darwin in the Northern Territory in search of her husband, Maitland Ashley, his drover (Hugh), swaggering in moleskin trousers and a battered Akubra hat, is sent to meet her. They stop at a bar, where Drover gets involved in a pub brawl. In the chaos that ensues some of Lady Ashley's luggage (designed by Prada for the film) is ransacked; her underwear, corsets, brassieres and stockings all thrown up in the air like confetti. 'Welcome to Australia,' the bloodied Drover replies, leaving the audience with a taste of what is to come.

The film was shot in destinations all around Australia, such as Sydney, Camden and the Queensland sugar town of Bowen. Bowen was considered an ideal location to recreate Darwin because of the two huge vacant lots near Bowen's Wharf and also because the local government provided Luhrmann with $500,000 to film there. About 600 Bowen residents were cast as extras and another 100 worked as volunteer guides for tourists visiting the town during filming over the year.

In addition to increasing tourism in the country, everyone involved with the movie hoped that it would become the one to represent their native country, doing the same for the people Down Under as *Braveheart* did for the Scots. Luhrmann meticulously researched the entire history of Australia for the film, even prior to the European settlement. He put together detailed notes that he made available to the actors on request; he also read every book about the country that he could find and settled on two dark and unappreciated points in history on which to base his work. The first was during the Japanese attack on Darwin, which was, surprisingly, twice as big as the one on Pearl Harbor. Japan actually attacked Darwin 64 times. Strategically, it was an important target due to the amount of oil that fed the American war ships. Casualties were reported to have reached 3,000 yet Aboriginal people were never officially put on that list, so the toll was actually a lot higher.

This led to the real heart of the movie, and the second and probably most significant point in Australian history in the film: the social injustice to the Aboriginals and their culture. Indeed, the film's strongest storyline lay with the character Nullah, a mixed-race Aboriginal boy played brilliantly by thirteen-year-old newcomer Brandon Walters. Nullah was trying to escape the cruel fate of forced separation from his Aboriginal family. Unbelievably, up until as late as 1973, Aboriginal children were snatched by the authorities and brought up in church missions to 'breed the black out', thus becoming known as the 'Stolen Generation'.

For Hugh, like many others who grew up in the country, the Stolen Generation was something he had never learned about in school, but he found out about it later when he spent some time working in the Outback in his late teens: 'To go out there and meet those people and work with them was wonderful. It gave me a great appreciation for how tough life is and about the indomitable spirit that the Aboriginal people have always possessed.'

Interestingly enough, the Australian government, which had never really apologised for the indignation, did so the year the film came out.

Australia was the first time that Hugh had teamed up with Nicole Kidman in a film. She also just happened to be best friends with his wife, Deborra-Lee. In fact, when Nicole first moved to Hollywood, she lived with Deb just before she made *Days of Thunder* with Tom Cruise. It was Deb who answered the phone when Tom called to ask Nicole out on their first date. 'So it was a great situation because, although we knew each other, there was still quite a lot of mystery there,' Hugh said, mentioning also that although it's easier to work with people you know, this can also present a problem: 'It's one thing you've got to watch when you're working for a long period of time; familiarity breeds contempt in terms of the camera. If you really like each other you can become too comfortable and for this movie our relationship had to have tension and passion to throw us together. If you're too laid-back, somehow all the air goes out of the room. With Nicole you're never quite sure what's coming, which is fantastic. She's like that in life too and she's an amazing actor.'

The film's success depended largely on the chemistry between the pair. Hugh recalled: 'I don't think there was a day we shot where there wasn't a moment of magic and it's the thing we all live for, the hairs on the back of your neck standing up, so the result was something beautiful.

'While it's never particularly comfortable making out with someone in front of 70 people, it was not the toughest day at the office! When I saw the movie for the first time, my wife was next to me, and just after the very first kiss, Deb went, "That was great!" So if your wife gives you the thumbs-up, you know you're on the right track!'

He remembered one particular kiss that he and Nicole shared. It was really hot and his lips were dry. When they parted a bridge of saliva spanned between them and kept going and going until it broke, causing everyone to burst out laughing.

It wasn't just their friendship that made the love scenes awkward. Hugh explained that it was because the scenes were so highly choreographed by Luhrmann. The couple got confused trying to align what they were doing with what the camera wanted: 'He [Luhrmann] wants it to be beautiful and sensual and that takes choreography with the camera. He didn't necessarily give me tips in bed, but he did tell me where to put my arms and how to arch my back, for example.'

During one love scene, Nicole saved Hugh from a poisonous scorpion – for real. She was about to join him in a sleeping bag when she noticed the scorpion crawling up his leg. She calmly instructed him not to move, scooped it into her hat, and walked over to the woods and released it. Everyone applauded and when she was asked why she hadn't just stamped on it. She said, 'I would never kill an animal. Every creature here has its purpose. This one just didn't belong in Hugh's bag!'

She confessed that she was a big fan of Hugh's work and that working with him was a ball: 'He was such a movie star and so fantastic to work with. There was a lot of mystery to Hugh, which was good. He was tough and romantic at the same time. Australian men are a different breed. They're rugged and they sweat.'

Although she had worked with the talented director in

the past on the musical *Moulin Rouge*, it was the first time for Jackman and it took a while for him to get used to his habits. Hugh said, 'With Baz, as soon as you arrive on set, even in costume fitting, you're in character because there could be a camera on you at any point. Apparently in *Moulin Rouge* there were quite a number of shots from the costume fittings that made the final film. For him there is no separation. He would talk to me as the Drover, which helped create a bit of mystery. Baz is also a perfectionist and it's not uncommon for him to do 30, 40 or 50 takes, but because of the way he does it, I don't find it annoying.'

Luhrmann is not just a perfectionist who wants everything to be just right; he is very thoughtful and leaves nothing to chance. Every day he would sit down with Hugh to discuss how filming had gone and talk about the scene the following day. Every day there would be a cup of tea in front of Hugh. It took him about three months to notice that the tea he was being served was actually his favourite. Then it hit him that sometime during pre-production months earlier, Luhrmann had asked him what tea he liked. Hugh had mentioned Lapsang Souchong, and sure enough Lapsang Souchong was there without fail, proving the director's dedication to detail both on and off the set.

'When I was doing Baz's film *Australia* I discovered rowing. Baz said to me when we started, "You look good and strong, but you're playing a cowboy and these guys are lean. I want you to lose some weight. Quickly." I had a trainer at the time who used to be a rower for New

South Wales. He said he would tell me how to keep all the muscle and drop all the fat. All you do is seven minutes, twice a week. You have to do 2,000 metres in seven minutes, which is actually the trial for the New South Wales team. So I do it - and it almost made me throw up, but it was a short, sharp shock. That's probably the best thing for burning fat.'

Luhrmann used Hugh's sex appeal quite a bit in the production. He wanted the actor to set the female audience's heart racing with a tongue-in-cheek washing scene out in the bush. Despite Hugh's initial concerns, Baz's direction made this a shot to remember: 'With the washing scene, I did question it at the time. I said to him, "Mate, I'm not sure people will laugh in the right way at this and might just think I'm a complete wanker." I had more fake tan and oil on my body than I thought possible, but he said if I went for it one hundred per cent then people would understand. I was very relieved on the night of the première when people seemed to laugh in the right way.'

Talking about the washing scene Nicole said, 'Oh, my God, not only did the women's jaws drop, so did the men's on the set when Hugh took his top off!'

On the other hand, there was more to the Drover than sex appeal, he also had to be an expert horse rider and Hugh's experience in *Kate & Leopold* wasn't quite enough. Jackman spent several months in Texas learning how to ride among some of the toughest cowboys he could find although, this still didn't prepare him for galloping alongside 1,500 stampeding cattle across the blistering Kimberleys in remote north-western Australia, where some of the five-month shooting took place: 'Of course they asked about horse riding and I said, "Yeah I can ride", because I had done a little bit on a movie called *Kate & Leopold*.' But then he read the script and realised what was expected of him. 'This is how they describe my character's horsemanship, "The Drover, astride his horse, like a knight in shining armour corralling 100 wild horses at the back of the homestead, by himself." That freaked me out to begin with, and on the day, of course, it was 200 wild horses, not 100! Then the next page said, "The Drover rides along on the saddle, pursuing a bull across the plains. He leaps down, grabs his tail and, with one fluid movement, he heaves his weight down upon it to throw the massive beast onto its side. The Drover takes out a bush knife, grabs the bull by the balls and slices them."'

At that point, Hugh realised he had a lot of work to do. He rode every day for at least a year leading up to filming and then every day while filming took place. He also worked closely with horse trainer Craig Emerton. On the first morning, while Hugh was learning to ride on set, Emerton brought him a motorcycle helmet and a full motorcycle jacket. Hugh was in an enclosed yard with soft sand and, because he'd been riding for a long time, he said, 'Guys, this is a little humiliating.' Emerton replied, 'Just wear it. You never know. It's an insurance thing.'

The first time the horse reared up, it snapped its head back so fast and hard that it caught Hugh right on the helmet and knocked him off. On video it looked as if Hugh had being yanked off by a cable. He landed on his back, seeing stars. When he came to, he was glad he had taken Emerton's advice and put on the ridiculous-looking motorbike helmet. Although Hugh's head didn't suffer too much, his wallet did because in the horse-riding world, there is a rule that if anyone falls off, they have to buy a bottle of whisky for everyone on the team, unless that person can say, 'Just taking a piss' before they hit the ground. Hugh was at least five cases of whisky down before he finally got it right.

Unfortunately for the star learning to ride a bucking bronco was the easy part: 'I remember one scene where Baz said, "Okay, Hugh, you're the leader, you bring in the cattle and bring them down to the camera, and when you get close, take the mob to the left." The director called action and all the cattle went the other way. It was hysterical trying to control those cows,' he recalled.

Yet nothing was quite so nerve-wracking as riding with a pack of real wild horses, called 'brumbies'. And even though Hugh's trainer warned him that he'd done a lot of work with the horse that he was riding, he couldn't guarantee anything once it joined the pack. The horse guys had rounded up 200 brumbies – crazy horses that had never had a saddle on them – and Hugh was absolutely flying during the scene in which the horses stampeded: 'There was so much dirt flying around that I couldn't see in front of me, but when the dust cleared out of the corner of my eye I saw some horses break away. About a hundred were coming right at me. You know the theory that horses don't step on people in a stampede? It's not true. My horse reared up, scared shitless like me. I thought, we're going over and we're getting trampled. I closed my eyes, hunkered down and pulled him with all my might to face the oncoming horses. Because of that, they went around us. Then I jumped off the horse because I could feel it wanted to go with the crowd, and it did. A few years of my life flashed before my eyes. Afterwards, my sound guy said, "If you ever need to act scared, I'll give you the tape."'

Equally demanding, but less life threatening, was the business of arranging Hugh's beard every day; it takes a lot of careful tailoring to be rough-hewn. Indeed, Luhrmann is fanatical about hair: 'I said to him, "Baz, what's with all the hair thing? I've never had so much attention!" Which must have sounded a bit weird coming from a man who'd played a hairy Wolverine for the last few years. Baz said, "In a close-up, your hair is a third of what's on screen. You look at the Mona Lisa, no one ever thinks about the hair, but that frames the face. About a quarter of that picture is hair."'

With this in mind, Jackman's beard underwent critical screen testing, which led to intense discussions about the length. One suggestion that they settle for stubble was deemed a little ridiculous for a guy who lives in the outback. In the end, ever the perfectionist, Luhrmann sent for Maurizio Silvi, who was nominated for an Academy Award for the make-up on *Moulin Rouge*. Jackman recounted how Silvi was the only person on earth who could put a beard on someone, hair by hair, and no one could tell. 'And what soon became clear was that Baz preferred my fake beard to my real beard.'

Filming *Australia* was physically very tough for everyone, especially out on location. It was sometimes like being on Mars, with temperatures soaring to the low forties. The heavy costumes worn by the cast and the hours of riding and sleeping in tents didn't help. It was not the usual pampered lifestyle that the stars were accustomed to.

While Nicole stayed in town during the two months of filming, Hugh and Luhrmann set up their trailers on the edge of the remote set and never left. Down the bank from Jackman's trailer was a creek teeming with crocodiles: 'I'd been out there when I was nine or ten and just loved it. I slept in my trailer and loved being with a campfire every night and a cliff overlooking a river full of crocodiles. And I'm not saying I'm a method actor, but there's something about the landscape, the magic of that landscape out there, and just living there and working with the guys was the real deal.'

Despite the less-than-perfect conditions, Kidman was very professional during the entire production, working herself to the bone every single day to get everything out of the scene. According to Hugh: 'Nicole's incredibly glamorous. I've known her for a long time. Even at casual barbecues she always looks like a million bucks and has a great sense of glamour. But Nicole is also an incredibly tough girl who wants to do every stunt. Her first day out she was wearing a three-piece woollen suit. It was 125 degrees, and we were standing in the sun in the middle of the day for a long time. I rode up, looked over and said, "Are you okay?" and she went, "Yep, fine." I said, "If you weren't okay, would you tell me?" and she said, "Nope." She doesn't play that "Oh, poor me, I'm just a girl."'

When shooting moved to Sydney, Hugh's son made his film debut in the background of a scene between Nicole's character, Lady Sarah Ashley, and her Aboriginal surrogate son, Nullah. Hugh wasn't working that day and so he was able to stand at the back to watch Oscar perform as an extra. 'He was looking very serious because I told him the story and he knew it was set in wartime. His school was just around the corner and he knew when he finished here he was back to school, so I think he wanted it to last longer.'

Hugh had planned to keep Oscar out of the film business but made an exception under the circumstances: 'During filming I had this high idea I would not pull rank, so I sat at the back with the parents of the other extras for a while,' he confessed sheepishly on his new role as a stage parent. 'But then I found out they didn't even get to watch the monitor, or see anything, so I gave up on egalitarian Hugh and came back up front.'

It was rumoured that Baz Luhrmann's obsessive attention to detail not only caused the project to go over budget, but created several scheduling problems too. The film took nine hard months to finally complete, which included some costly re-shoots. Indeed, the overly long production saw the birth of 15 babies to cast and crew members, one being Nicole Kidman's daughter.

To be fair it wasn't all Luhrmann's fault, and to add further to the production's difficulties, Australia itself was not very cooperative either. On one occasion, the largest and most expensive of the sets for the film was completely flooded when heavy showers hit a part of the country that rarely gets any rain at all. On other occasions, filming had to be delayed for days on end because of bad weather or poor lighting. Every delay was especially costly since Luhrmann employed hundreds of crewmembers and had a herd of 1,500 cattle that needed to be fed and cared for. This completely drained the budget, which led to production improvisation. Luhrmann was forced to go begging for more cash and certain compromises had to be made; he even had to move the filming of the final scenes of the movie from Darwin, where it was supposed to take place, to Bowen.

A worrying statistic of the Australian film industry was that before the release of the film, only 2 to 4 per cent of the films viewed by Australians were actually made in Australia, which is incredibly low compared to a country like France, where it is around 60 per cent. In the past, the Aussie film industry hadn't had the budget, the scope or the size of the big Hollywood production studios. *Australia* did, though, and there were expectations that it would be a huge success in Australia and the rest of the world when it was released in late November 2008. Thankfully for everyone involved, it did exceptionally well at the box office despite a disappointing gross in the US. The film grossed $211 million in its partial worldwide releases and profits stood at just over $133 million. Back home, the hype was such that when *Australia* premièred in Sydney, one film critic described it as 'the biggest thing this town has seen since the Olympics.' Sadly, it didn't catch the attention of the Academy Award Committee and was only nominated for one Oscar, and that was for Catherine Martin for Best Achievement in Costume Design.

For Hugh, though, it was a satisfying achievement to work in the country of his birth, only 10 minutes from where he grew up, and to go to locations that he had always dreamed of visiting. In fact, he enjoyed filming so much in Australia that he filmed another blockbuster there a year later. As for the long production time, Hugh said he would have stayed on for another two years because Baz was so good to work with and there was such a special atmosphere about the whole thing. It was everything he ever wanted as an actor.

'This is pretty much one of those roles that had me pinching myself all the way through the shoot. To be one of the leads in a film called Australia *with Nicole to kiss and Baz to direct me is a dream. I got to shoot a big-budget, shamelessly old-fashioned romantic epic set against one of the most turbulent times in my native country's history, while at the same time, celebrating that country's natural beauty, its people, its cultures… I'll die a happy man knowing I've got this film on my CV.'*

Hugh Jackman

CHAPTER FOURTEEN

DANCING WITH WOLVERINE

No one can claim that Hugh Jackman is the type of person to sit back and rest on his laurels, and so it wasn't long before he was looking to do something even more different to what he already had. In 2005, he embarked on a directing-and-producing career when he formed Seed Productions in partnership with his wife and long-time friend/producer, John Palermo. The inspiration for the name came from the notion that every little idea comes from a seed. To seal the partnership, Palermo designed matching rings for each of them that bore an inscription meaning 'unity'.

Regarding the trio's collaboration, Jackman stated on the launch of the business venture, 'I'm very lucky in the partners I work with in my life, Deb and John Palermo. It really works. We all have different strengths. I love it. It's very exciting. With the production company I have no agenda, as long as it breaks even. It's easier being an actor but it's important to be pro-active in life.'

The company worked in association with Twentieth Century Fox and established headquarters at the Twentieth Century Fox lot in the Century City area of Los Angeles. An Australian office was opened in 2006 at Fox Studios Australia in Sydney. Their dream was to produce quality feature films in their homeland of Australia as well as in the US, using local talent in all aspects of the filmmaking process. Besides producing, Seed also looked to represent filmmakers, actors and writers locally and overseas through a specialist artists' management division.

Hugh was well aware that being a producer was more than just a fancy title. He knew it would mean taking responsibility for each and every project, from conception to completion and beyond. And like everything else he does, he was determined to make it succeed: 'When you get to a certain point where you have that ability or power to be able to be in a meeting and go, "Oh, I think we should cast this person", I think you should step up and do it. I don't put my head in where I don't know what's going on. Marketing, I don't know about marketing. I really don't but I might want to make a comment about a trailer, or why this, or why that. But it's all so sophisticated on another level and I'm not going to be a pain in their ass about it, just try and learn and work with others.'

The company cut its production teeth by getting involved in several projects. It produced the short-lived television series *Viva Laughlin*, a film called *Deception* (2008) starring Ewan McGregor, plus three cricket documentaries involving Jackman's best friend, Gus Worland.

Their first production, an American TV musical-drama in 2007 called *Viva Laughlin*, was adapted from the popular BBC series *Blackpool* and written by Bob Lowry and Peter Bowker (creator of the original British series). *Viva Laughlin* was an ambitious musical murder mystery where the characters occasionally burst into song. Filmed on location in part at the Morongo Casino Resort & Spa in Cabazon, California, it features businessman Ripley Holden (Lloyd Owen), whose ambition is to run a casino in Laughlin, Nevada. Ripley invests all his money into opening a casino, but when the business is nowhere near completion, his financing suddenly falls through. Needing an investor, Ripley approaches his rival, wealthy casino owner Nicky Fontana (Jackman, who appears to the strains of 'Sympathy For The Devil'), but when Ripley turns down Fontana's request for sole ownership of the casino and someone turns up dead, Ripley becomes the number-one suspect in the murder.

Unfortunately, *Viva Laughlin* wasn't well received, and Hugh's golden-boy image took a battering, with US critics lambasting the new television series. The opening line of *The New York Times* review said, '*Viva Laughlin* on CBS may well be the worst new show of the season, but is it the worst show in the history of television?'

CBS cancelled the show on 22 October 2007 after airing only two episodes. The Nine Network in Jackman's home country followed suit the very next day, after just one episode.

The scathing reviews and the speed with which it was pulled from US line-ups within weeks of the première came as a major blow to the three directors of the company. 'We are obviously disappointed, but you have to take risks in this business,' Deborra-Lee commented. 'Doing a drama that was a musical was always going to be a huge risk, but if you don't take risks, you will never know. If I'm going to fail, I want to fail spectacularly, and it seems like we did.'

Next up was something closer to home and even closer to Jackman's heart. It involved a series of reality-style cricket documentaries, which aired on the pay-TV channel Fox8 in Australia. The series featured cricket-mad fan Gus Worland, who had been best mates with Jackman since they attended the same kindergarten. Together, they had moved to Knox Grammar School, paired up for an overseas adventure in a gap year before starting university, and acted as best man and godfather to each other's children.

Worland didn't hesitate when Hugh suggested to him that he should throw in his job and help make the TV series that would be produced by Seed. The show was shot from a fan's point of view and followed the fortunes of the Australian cricket team while they played against the other major cricketing nations in the world: England, India and the West Indies.

Worland described the work for Seed as if he was living in a dream: 'Jacko and I were in the under-11 cricket team together at Knox prep school, and went to all the big Test matches at the MCG in our youth. All through our lives, cricket has been the one thing that has been central to it. We talk about it all the time; we talk in commentators' voices. Jacko's wife just looks at us and walks out of the room because she thinks we are being silly, but it is something that we have grown up with from being mates.'

The first episode filmed in 2006, *An Aussie Goes Barmy*, features Gus infiltrating the Barmy Army, an organised group of supporters of the England cricket team. It was narrated by Hugh, who also helped to devise and produce the series with Granada Productions and Foxtel. The premise of the series was that Worland, who had lived in England for 20 years and had an English wife, follows the Barmy Army as they travel from the UK to Australia for the 2006/7 Ashes series. During filming, Jackman made a bet with his friend that if England won the test series, Worland must join the Barmy Army permanently and become an England supporter. Luckily for him, Australia won the series easily, 5–0.

A year later, in 2007, Gus followed the cricket team on a tour of India for *An Aussie goes Bolly*, followed later by *An Aussie goes Calypso*, where Worland follows the team to the West Indies and mingles with the crowds, interviews famous ex-cricket stars and samples the local delicacies. All three shows were a huge success in Oz and a welcome boost for Seed.

Meanwhile, during that time the production company became ready to move onto bigger things. When they received a script which intrigued them, for a movie called *Deception*, and learned that director Marcel Langenegger had put up his hand to become involved with it, they decided to go for broke and create their first feature film.

At first, the thought of actually having the courage to attempt a venture on this scale blew Hugh away. He was apprehensive but excited at the same time: 'Here was a film which was a genre film, but slightly left of field in terms of the genre. It just had enough difference to interest me, I suppose creatively, and not just be a down-the-line formulaic film. It also was reasonable in its scope. It wasn't too massive and we knew it would be realistic to make. And we found a way to fund it outside the studio system. So on the first day of filming, we were already in the black from foreign sales, which was, for us, an amazing position to be in as first-time producers. We didn't have studios breathing down our necks day in, day out.'

It was shot in New York and proved a great way for the production company to learn about the tricks of the trade. To reduce costs, they shot in digital and largely at night. For Seed, part of the deal was that Hugh would play one of the lead parts. Surprisingly, he opted for the role of the villain, who was a real charmer with a dark and malicious side to him.

Deception stars Scottish actor Ewan McGregor and Jackman in a cat-and-mouse style murder mystery. Jonathan McQuarry (McGregor) is a nerdy accountant auditor in Manhattan, tasked with auditing and checking the books of various companies. While working late one night, a smooth and well-dressed man named Wyatt Bose (Jackman) stops to chat with McQuarry, offering him a joint. Soon they become good friends and when their mobile phones are 'accidentally' swapped, Jonathan answers a series of Wyatt's calls from various women asking if he is free. Jonathan discovers that Wyatt and the women are part of a sex club for busy, powerful people. He becomes involved and falls for one of the club members, whom he knows only as 'S'. When S goes missing, Jonathan faces demands involving violence and lots of cash.

But the film received negative reviews from critics: in its opening weekend, the film grossed $2.3 million in 2,000 theatres in the United States and Canada, averaging only $1,155 per theatre and ranking number 10 at the box office. When all was said and done, it grossed just under $10 million, which wasn't that bad a return considering there was the added bonus that Hugh and his partners were able to use the film as a stepping stone to much greater things.

The next – and much greater – project for Seed came in the shape of the spin-off from the hugely successful X-Men series, called *X-Men Origins: Wolverine*. The end of *X-Men 3* had left fans and audiences hanging, and no one, including Hugh, knew exactly what was going to happen next as far as a fourth film was concerned. Meanwhile, Seed Productions received a fantastic script from David Benioff, one of the great writers in Hollywood, for a spin-off movie. Hugh thought his ideas were brilliant and steeped in a deep love of the character and comic-book history – exactly what he himself was looking for. He felt the script answered any questions left about his character's origins, and more importantly it gave Seed Productions a damn good reason to make the fourth movie.

The script pitched Hugh not only as the undisputed star, receiving approximately $20 million for his troubles, but also the co-producer of the $135-million motion picture. 'As a producer, I feel much more attached to how this movie will be received,' he announced. 'This was how I saw the Wolverine character and I haven't been quiet or shy about saying I wanted to make this movie, so it became more personal. If it fails, I can't lay the blame on anybody else.'

With the previous three *X-Men* films grossing over $1 billion, Jackman and company knew they would be under huge pressure to deliver another hit. 'I'm my father's son,' said Hugh, turning into the astute businessman. 'He was an accountant, and I love dealing with budgets and the machinations of the film-making process.'

Even so, his motivation had nothing to do with getting more cash for his behind-the-camera role. For him it was all about having a bigger say in the casting, deciding who should direct and ensuring the script was loyal to the spirit of the comic books. Personally, he wanted to take his Logan character to the next level while helping to make the best and most exciting adventure movie he could, with even more enhanced special effects than before: 'That was what was important to me. But I don't find producing the most fun. I find it quite difficult. It's quite a lot of conflicts. You probably get to know things about people on a crew that you probably prefer not to know. And as an actor, you probably don't need to know.'

Although nervous about its success, being the producer did have certain perks, such as a say in the location. While some scenes were shot in New Zealand and Canada, the bulk of the footage was filmed in Hugh's hometown of Sydney: 'Our aim is to support Australian filmmakers, to stimulate the creative community and provide international opportunities for Australian artists,' Hugh said when the location of the filming was announced.

Obviously it had major benefits for the rest of the Jackman household as well, because it meant they didn't have to uproot and live a nomadic existence while filming. For once, Hugh could more or less walk to the office each day.

The storyline for the *X-Men Origins: Wolverine* focuses on events that took place before the first three films and tells the back-story of Wolverine's violent past. It explores the mutant's lifelong rivalry with his brother Sabretooth (Liev Schreiber) and his quest for revenge after the murder of his schoolteacher girlfriend, Kayla Silverfox (Lynn Collins).

'To make films like *X-Men* work commercially, and still have some class, is one of the hardest things there is to do,' Hugh commented. 'I wanted to be seen to be able to cut across a lot of the genres, and still be "fair dinkum" as we say in Australia, which means genuine and true and, well, unique.'

To get that 'fair dinkum', he entrusted the role of director to Gavin Hood, a South African filmmaker, whose low-budget *Tsotsi* won the Oscar in 2005 for Best Foreign Language Film. However, even with all of Seed's diligent work and planning, things still didn't go as planned and four months into shooting, *Wolverine* was dogged by problems. Hood's initial vision of a Wolverine who suffers the superhero equivalent of post-traumatic stress disorder led to clashes with the studio and Hood was forced to admit that he had struggled with the logistics of working with so many special effects and a big budget.

At one point, nervous Fox executives in Los Angeles flew co-producer and experienced director Richard Donner (*Superman, Lethal Weapon*) to the Australian set to work with Hood. 'There were discussions between myself and the studio about style and I think we were all very happy with the way the film ended up,' said Hood tactfully. 'I was the new kid on the block and I welcomed Dick Donner's expertise. He was my mentor figure.'

The production also ran into trouble in Queenstown, New Zealand, where an environmental controversy arose over a scene involving the blowing up of a farmhouse and the storing of explosives at a local skating rink, which was eventually sorted out.

When the cameras finally did start rolling, Hugh couldn't keep the smile off his face. For him, it was a great feeling to be walking on set as a producer: 'There were two thoughts that came into my mind. The first thought was like, "Wow, look at all these jobs I've created, all these people, it's so fantastic." Then a minute later I'm like, "Why are they all standing around? Let's go, come on, people." Whereas as an actor, you're like, "Oh, no problem, we'll finish it tomorrow." Now I see it differently, I know now what's at stake. I know what the budget is. I know how many days we can go over and how many we can't. It's actually a thing that I think all actors and directors should be aware of.'

It was the fourth time that he had played Wolverine. He hadn't realised until after the film was released that he was the first actor to play the same comic-book hero in four consecutive movies since Christopher Reeve in *Superman*.

Hugh really wanted to lead from the front and trained extremely hard to be in tip-top condition for the role without going over the top. His vision was to make this Wolverine even darker and edgier than he had been in the other films, but he didn't want to go overboard in the muscle department: 'I wanted audiences to say, "This guy could easily rip someone's head off," but I didn't care about being massive, like Schwarzenegger massive. I wanted to be lean, and not seen as a freak of nature.' He pictured Logan to be lean but not pretty, more like De Niro in the remake of *Cape Fear*. His eyes lit up as he explained: 'You remember when you saw De Niro in that convertible as Max Cady, smoking cigars and then without his shirt, doing chin-ups, with those tattoos. You were like, "Oh shit, I'm scared as hell of this guy." That's what I wanted.'

His friend and personal trainer, Michael Ryan, set about turning him into a lean, mean fighting machine with some really insane workouts: 'We're very competitive and he trash-talked me the entire way. He would say, "I'm gonna smash you, that's pathetic." We played that game.' Hugh also found it got him in the mood if he listened to music. 'My favourites were AC/DC, Godsmack and Metallica played very loud. When I'm training I'm fairly obnoxious and I make a fair bit of noise. I beat my record on the bench, which is about 300lb, but I only trained for an hour. It's the intensity that counts. It is interesting because I think I am Wolverine when I'm training because then I can lift more weight and that's what it takes to feel the rage.'

You are what you eat, so the saying goes, and it soon became apparent to him that physique is 30 per cent training and 70 per cent diet. It meant that he had to wake up at 4am and eat egg whites followed by chicken or salmon, with steamed vegetables and brown rice every three hours. He cut out most breads, sugar, beer and pizza, which he hated because he loves bread. Also, there were no more carbs after lunch. Unbelievably, he got leaner while still packing on 15lb of pure muscle for the role. Which was just as well because at times during filming, Jackman needed every inch of that extra muscle to combat the high levels of testosterone flying about – especially during the fight scenes between Wolverine and his brother, Sabertooth, played by an equally vicious-looking Liev Schreiber. It was a case of both actors pushing themselves to the limit. The real savage intensity between the pair shocked the cast with the sheer force of the punches they exchanged. 'We would look to see if the other one was fading and then both of us always say, "No, I'm fine, let's go again. Come on, you can hit me harder than that!"' recalled Hugh.

In one big confrontation in a bar, Hugh stood at one end while Liev was at the other. On the count of three they just ran at each other. BANG! Liev got knocked to the floor, but then like a cat on all-fours he tackled Hugh, bringing him to his knees. Hugh remembered thinking at the time, 'Shit, I've broken a couple of ribs! But I'm an Aussie and getting injured is a point of pride. Liev's a physical guy who could have played pro football. We worked out together and became competitive on everything down to diet. We just punched the shit out of each other.'

Their competitiveness carried on throughout the movie. Liev, originally no match for the muscular Hugh, had requested the chance to gain real muscle after being humiliated by the need to wear a muscle suit for his role in an effort to make his physique look comparable to Hugh Jackman's 225lb. The suit was similar to that worn by Vinnie Jones in X-Men: The Last Stand. After three months of training while on the set of Defiance (2008) in Lithuania, a diet packed full of protein (which Schreiber called the genocide of chickens) and eventually more training with Jackman on the set of the film, Schreiber gained 35lb and had to buy some new suits due to his back gaining several inches in width: 'I can't fit into my favourite suit now! But I felt like I owed it to the genre to be big.'

In another fight scene, this time with twenty-eight-year-old Taylor Kitsch, who plays Gambit, aggression was again the order of the day but this time it ended up with bloodshed. 'We were having this fight,' Hugh recalled, 'and Kitsch had this staff, and he went to hit me and I stopped him with my claws, and he reeled back very quickly and someone called, "Cut!" I looked down at my claws and there were only two claws left, and I looked over at Taylor and it was sticking out of his thumb. He just looked at it before saying, "Whoa, dude, something I said?" then he pulled it out, wiped the blood away on his jeans and goes, "Let's go."'

X-Men Origins: Wolverine was not all about getting lean and 'punching the shit' out of one another, however. Hugh also attempted to make Wolverine look more natural than in any of the films so far, mainly because he didn't want to sit in make-up for quite so long. Before the shoot, he grew out his beard and sideburns, which proved a success. Unfortunately, even though all the hair was his this time around, it still took about three bottles of hairspray a day to get the style right.

There was also another first for Hugh in this fourth instalment of *X-Men* – a nude scene. He bared it all several times over while filming a scene where he jumps off a waterfall. Sadly for the hordes of female fans who later streamed to the cinema to catch a glimpse of his Jack-man-hood, all Hugh's best bits found themselves on the cutting-room floor as the movie's PG-13 rating meant it couldn't show nudity. Hugh stated, 'It's easy to jump off a waterfall naked, but for a PG-13 movie? It took a lot of choreography!' After filming finished, the director gave him a bag that contained the clips of his private parts, which had been cut from the scene. Hugh held the film to the light and said, 'Okay, now I know why that's in a bag!' He later admitted to locking the footage away in his safe.

X4 finished filming on time and within budget, which was a major plus as far as the production company was concerned. Then, while organising the première and all the sexy stuff that goes along with it, disaster struck as an unfinished print of the movie was leaked online. Within hours, tens of thousands had downloaded it. The only saving grace was that the pirated print lacked most of the special effects and more than 10 minutes of additional footage according to Hood, who described the leak as 'excruciatingly painful'.

It was devastating for everyone involved. Hugh was obviously heartbroken and more than a little angry that it had been leaked a month before the official release: 'It is a serious crime and there is no doubt it is very disappointing. The FBI is onto it and they're taking it very, very seriously,' he said. 'Rest assured that the persons will be found. I was heartbroken by it, but obviously people are seeing an unfinished film. It's like driving a Ferrari without a paint job.'

He was heartened by the fact that the majority of the online community of fans condemned the leak and assured Hugh that they would still go and see it at the movies on its release. Also, he was lifted by the fact that, even with film piracy being rife within the industry,

Hollywood was having a great year, registering its biggest homeland take in history with $13.59 billion, topping its 2007 total of $13.58 billion, which had also been a new high.

And so he put the disappointment behind him and travelled the world promoting the film. His first stop was Sydney Harbour's Cockatoo Island, where much of the movie was shot. There, he unveiled 20 minutes of completed footage to about 600 fans. Hugh thrilled fans by arriving by helicopter before catching a flying fox (a cable car) from a cliff top to the ground. During his speech, Sydney-born Jackman used the opportunity to address reports that he'd mistakenly called the Sydney Opera House the Opera Centre while communicating with fans on the social networking website Twitter that same week – tantamount to treason in his beloved country: 'I communicated it over the phone and when that got translated by someone in my office it came out all wrong. I do know the Opera House is called the Opera House. I think I had my high-school leaving assembly at the Opera House when I was eighteen so I should know that one.'

During the première, he again showed how kind and considerate he is towards his fans. While most Hollywood stars try to avoid obsessive fans, Hugh did the opposite. The actor spent almost £3,000 on breakfast and coffee for a group of Wolverine enthusiasts in Arizona, who had camped out to see him at the première of his latest blockbuster. After hearing that hundreds of fans had waited hours just to catch a glimpse of him at the event, he decided to reward them for their patience. The generous Australian heart-throb headed to the Paradise Bakery in Tempe to buy 67 breakfast trays, including platters of bagels, muffins and croissants and over 80 gallons of coffee. One fan who received the star treatment said, 'Everyone was so overwhelmed by it. It was just a really generous thing to do.'

His appreciation for the fans also shone through when, following the postponement of the country's première of *X-Men Origins: Wolverine* because of an outbreak of H1N1 influenza (swine flu) in Mexico, Hugh returned to the country. Praising the perseverance of the nation's people through the health crisis, the star stated, 'Mexico is standing: this makes me happy, Mexico is indestructible, just like my character.' He was treated as more of a superstar than he already was by thousands of Mexicans, including the President Felipe Calderón.

The worldwide opening for the film grossed over $158.1 million. Considering the leak, the mixed reviews from critics and the outbreak of swine flu in Mexico, this was a financial success, with overall estimated sales at the box office totalling $363.4 million worldwide. It was time to celebrate: Seed Productions really had achieved the first stage of its plan.

After all the excitement of the release had died down, Hugh didn't know if there would be a sequel. He admitted that he was afraid of flogging a dead horse: 'I have no interest in that. No matter how much I love the character. So there are many prerequisites. Ultimately, there are a few storylines that are running around my head which I think would be really cool, but unless the script is right, then I just don't see the point in doing it. I'm probably at the point in my career where I don't need it. And the last thing I want to do is just to push it on people if it doesn't warrant a full feature movie.'

Despite this, there were considerable rumours that a trip to the Land of the Rising Sun could be next in line for the mutton-chopped mutant hero!

'Hugh Jackman is incredibly impressive in the movie. You know, he's this six foot three Aussie bloke, who is well-conditioned. He looks like a weapon or one of those Marvel toys. He actually looks like one of those things you pull out of the box. He just owns the movie. He's in almost every scene and is just incredible in it.'

Dominic Monaghan, Barnell Bohusk
in *X-Men Origins: Wolverine*

CHAPTER FIFTEEN

MR X-APPEAL

'The praise is nice, of course, but you can't let stuff like that to go to your head,' Hugh admitted after he topped the list for *People* magazine's Sexiest Man Alive award in 2008. Not knowing what to make of it, he wasn't sure what it would mean to his already-flourishing career: 'Who knows? It may help, but I don't waste time thinking about it. It's a blip. It's a little bit of attention. Maybe some people who didn't know who I was now know who I am.'

At 6ft 3in, all smiles and biceps, he easily beat off his nearest rivals including some of the hottest guys in the industry, younger and older alike. He won the annual award ahead of Daniel Craig, the British spy James Bond, who had wowed female fans in *Casino Royale* with his muscular body and striking blue eyes. Jon Hamm, the star of hit US TV show *Mad Men*, came in third, while *High*

School Musical heart-throb Zac Efron and *Lipstick Jungle* hunk Robert Buckley rounded off the top five. Footballer David Beckham, Oscar-winner Javier Bardem, *Twilight* star Robert Pattinson, former *Dawson's Creek* actor Joshua Jackson and Olympic swimmer Michael Phelps all featured in the list. In their summing up of the contest, *People* magazine rather saucily described Hugh as a triple threat: a star who can sing, dance *and* wield a weapon.

Not fazed, the actor joked tongue-in-cheek that a lot of campaigning and dirty tricks had gone on to ensure he got his hands on the crown: 'I can admit it now but there was a lot of campaigning that goes into that. I was never strong in the swimsuit competition, but I think the baton-twirling put me at the top. We're the first ones to run a negative campaign and we spent years bringing Clooney, Pitt, Damon and McConaughey down to size. I was prepared to do absolutely anything and I'm not proud of it.'

Amusingly, his victory robbed 'Gorgeous George' Clooney of a three-year sweep. The same George Clooney who Hugh once confessed on a TV interview that if he did turn gay, it would be for him and no one else! Hugh revealed that the former Sexiest Man Alive champion couldn't resist a rib-tickle to let his feelings be known: 'George Clooney rang me at two in the morning. I was half asleep and I said to him, "Ah, George sweetie, good to hear from you." He goes, "Shut up, Jackman! I know what you did! You started this big campaign that's been going on and you took the title away from me. Who do you think you are? That first place is mine, don't you get it?"' He sniggered and hung up.

Of course, outwardly Hugh joked about joining the prestigious club of previous winners, which included the likes of George, Brat Pitt and Matt Damon, especially when the news broke and the text messages came flooding in from his mates. One of the more printable ones simply said, 'Hell, mate, my tennis racket is sexier than you!' But inwardly, the star who was two weeks shy of reaching forty, said, 'Let's face it, it's better than getting a kick in the teeth!'

However, there was little chance of him letting the title go to his head – not only his mates, but also his family could always be relied upon to put him firmly back in his place. Even Oscar gave his father a weird look and asked him, 'What? It's you?' on learning of the new title.

Deborra-Lee also revealed what she thought of her husband's new-found heart-throb status: 'The first thing I said was that I could have told them that years ago. But then I followed it up with, "Obviously Brad [Pitt] wasn't available this year was he?"' She added, 'But I like what's inside best, he's a romantic who sings ballads at home and makes pancakes for the kids.' Yet always happy to end on a wicked note, she also mentioned that the sexiest thing about her husband was that he came to her fully trained!

Hugh took all the ribbing in his stride, appreciating the fact that Deb and the others help keep him grounded, with his wife reading out the worst reviews, which really does keep his feet on the ground: 'She is my anchor, together with my children, who don't care whether I am a movie star or an accountant. We lead a pretty normal life, like everyone else.'

Others close to the actor found the whole thing a little

too weird to discuss. 'My old man travelled over with me and we landed in America, and all of sudden we stopped at the airport and saw the Sexiest Man Alive magazine, and everyone was talking about it,' recalled Hugh. 'My father found it really uncomfortable. He said to me, "I can't really talk to you about being sexy. It's a little weird." Mind you, I'm still waiting for the birds and the bees pitch from him. That hasn't happened either.'

Being the Sexiest Man Alive did have its advantages and disadvantages for the star. He suddenly discovered he was now not only living in the world of film and theatre but also walking tall in the world of style and fashion. His presence – with and without his shirt on – in trendy magazines grew, and he commented that it was quite tough and lots of hard work trying to look sexy. On saying that the fashion media found him to be a rare breed. Someone who could make anything from a Valentino suit to a worn T-shirt look great. Costume designer Catherine Martin, who created the clothes for *Australia*, said that Jackman's style works because of his self-confidence: 'Not everyone who has self-confidence has a good essence of style, but in Hugh's case the two go hand in hand. He has a proud posture and a winning smile, and he keeps to classic clothes that make him look handsome and super-trendy.'

Hugh admitted he wasn't, and hoped he never would be, the kind of guy to dye his hair and put on a glittery 1970s jacket and a pair of flares: 'Some people look really cool in those kinds of clothes. I would look crazy. I know my limitations. I like blue, like a blue T-shirt with jeans and boots. You can't go wrong. Black always works too, for me at least. I can wear a black shirt, black trousers, a black leather jacket and maybe a purple scarf as the only splash of colour.'

Although more comfortable and relaxed in jeans and T-shirts, he has been known on occasions to wear Ferragamo's leather shoes and Valentino suits from Ralph Lauren's super-exclusive 'Purple' collections (dubbed 'the world's most expensive suits') when attending opening nights and other official events. At the London première of *Australia*, Jackman stepped out of the limousine on Leicester Square to thousands of adoring fans and camera flashes going off like fireworks. Wearing a black suit, white shirt and black tie, he signed autographs, joked with journalists, hugged people affectionately, and was friends with absolutely everyone. Any media coach who could ever manage to capture the Jackman charm and put it in a bottle would surely make a fortune.

The great thing about Hugh is he isn't affected or artificial; no one taught him how to play the guy next door – that's just the way he is, it comes naturally. For example, when *X-Men* was about to be released, the studio told him to hire a publicist because it would make things easier during the promotional tour. He did what they said and got a publicist. She told him not to wave his hands about in interviews. She may have been right, but he didn't want to live that way; if succeeding as an actor depended on whether he waved his hands just right during an interview, he didn't want it.

'I'm like most Australian men. In Hollywood you're spoiled with personal assistants, personal trainers and luxurious trailers, and so on. Then you go to Australia, where you are lucky to be given a chair to sit on between takes. It's nice because as an actor you're just one of the team, there is no hierarchy.' With his laid-back attitude, he shines brightly and believes there is something untamed about the Australian soul: 'We have an inherent pride and we don't like to be controlled by people in positions of authority. Australians usually have a positive outlook on life; they're social and have a relaxed attitude. We work to live, we don't live to work. You won't meet a single Australian messing around on his BlackBerry on his day off.'

Although winning awards such as the Sexiest Man Alive puts Hugh in the spotlight even more, he doesn't think it's hard to maintain his privacy, unlike many other major Hollywood actors. In fact, he believes it's easier since he's become famous. Whether this comes with experience or it's something to do with turning forty, he definitely feels more centred. In the beginning, he felt the whole Hollywood showbiz thing was a bit like walking a big dog and having that dog take off, pulling him by the leash, but now he says, 'I have a firm grip on the leash now.' Even when handling the paparazzi, the biggest problem he has is in trying to explain to his kids while they are growing up why the photographers are only interested in taking his picture: 'They don't understand why they don't get photographed too. They think the photographers don't like them. My son said, "Yeah dad, but I just want my photo taken."'

He moved on from the prestigious honour of Sexiest

Man Alive to even more acclaim as host of the 81st Academy Awards in 2009, when the organisers promised to shake up the show's old format with a new look and feel. The announcement of the Australian actor to be the lynchpin of the event marked a departure from the Academy's standard big-name comedians. Jon Stewart, who hosted in 2006 and 2008, and Ellen DeGeneres (2007) were the latest in a line of funny MCs since 1990. Billy Crystal did it eight times, Whoopi Goldberg took on four, Steve Martin appeared twice and David Letterman and Chris Rock each had a shot.

Producers Laurence Mark and Bill Condon were excited to get their man because they knew Hugh was a consummate entertainer and an internationally renowned film star, who certainly fitted the theme of what they were looking for. He also had style, elegance and a sense of occasion. Mark and Condon announced: 'Hugh was the ideal choice to host a celebration of the year's movies, and to have fun doing it.'

While many actors would have shrunk away from the entertainment world's toughest and most scrutinised gig in town, the Australian actor couldn't wait for the evening to come. Hugh wasn't even fazed by the prospect of coming face to face with a room packed full of the film industry's most elite, including many of his peers, or the one-billion-plus TV audience. Instead, he felt honoured and extremely grateful to the Academy for giving him the opportunity and he was excited to work with the producers on what he hoped would be a memorable celebration. He knew when the time came for him to emerge from behind the curtains and take centre stage inside Hollywood's Kodak Theater for the 81st Annual Academy Awards, he would be living a dream: 'Thirty years ago, when I was in Sydney, my first memory was my dad letting us all stay up late and me watching Johnny Carson [the US TV talk show king] host the Oscars. Then years later, being in awe of Billy Crystal hosting and doing his trademark singing and dancing opening numbers. He hosted it eight times – I feel like I remember every single one of them and I never imagined that I'd one day have the chance to be up on that stage myself.'

Two months previously, while he was in London promoting his epic *Australia*, he received the call asking if he wanted to host the Oscars, which was to be aired on US network ABC on 22 February. The phone in his hotel room rang at 1.30am, when Hugh and his wife Deborra-Lee were asleep: 'My reaction was, as they say in Australia, like a stunned mullet. I was shocked and very excited. I said to my wife, who was sleeping beside me, "Baby, you're in bed with the host of the 81st Academy Awards!" She started jumping up and down, and I started jumping on the bed. Neither of us got to sleep for three or four hours after that. I felt like I had arrived, but way, way before my time.'

Even his son got in on the act when he found out and commented, 'You know what the headline should be, Dad? "Oscar's dad hosts the Oscars."' A scriptwriter in the making?

One of the first things Hugh did when he returned to the US was to go out and get fitted for a new tuxedo. He owned up to trying the suit on day after day and to not really taking it off for two months.

Notwithstanding all the hype associated with his appointment, there were some critics who believed selecting Jackman to present the show was a huge mistake. Some had their knives out ready to slice him to shreds even before he had stepped out into the spotlight. *Los Angeles Times* TV critic Mary McNamara wrote: 'Will the Oscar gift baskets include smelling salts? Yes, Jackman was just named *People*'s Sexiest Man Alive, and yes, he is Wolverine of *X-Men*, but do we want Wolverine hosting the Oscars? Probably not.'

All the same, the Academy knew what they were doing when they tapped into the Jackman appeal. TV ratings had been on the slide in recent years. In 1998, when the most popular film of all time, *Titanic*, swept the ceremony, 57.25 million Americans tuned into the US broadcast. In 2008, when the critically acclaimed but little-watched *No Country for Old Men* won Best Picture with Jon Stewart as host, the US TV audience was a mere 31.76 million. The year before, when *The Departed* won Best Picture, 39.92 million watched.

The Academy was aware that the Australian had been solely responsible for recharging the flagging Tony Awards in his first year as host in 2003, and had then been rehired in 2004 and 2005, and had actually won an Emmy for his 2004 hosting job. It was Hugh's quick wit and ability to make off-the-cuff remarks at unrehearsed moments that won over the producers of the Oscars. One year, he famously wandered down into the Tony Awards crowd, grabbed Sarah Jessica Parker, pulled her on stage and then began thrusting his pelvis, *à la* Peter Allen, at the *Sex and the City* actress. Everyone loved it. Nicole Kidman was in the audience watching, probably wishing she could disappear in case her co-star plucked her out: 'Nic is notoriously shy. I'll never forget, at those Tonys, Nicole was sitting in the front row, and she looked up at me and mouthed, "Don't you dare!" But I do love things going off-script. I hope there will be some spontaneity. If people know what to expect, then your party's dead,' commented Hugh.

He aimed to have a good time, turning the night into a big celebration. A sense of community was the key: it pleased him that the producers planned to take the show in a different direction and they had asked him to take the first step. They all knew the outcome of the show wasn't changing. There were 24 awards to give out, yet everyone agreed that the show should be less about the business of award-giving and more about putting the 'show' back into showbiz.

He also appreciated the Oscars was a completely different beast to the Tony Awards. It was much bigger and could be a lot nastier! There was so much hype, so much anticipation – one wrong move and it could spell the end of someone's career. He chatted with ex-host Steve Martin on the phone and he gave him some great tips: 'The first five or six minutes you're going to have possibly the best audience you've ever had in your life, because all of them know they're going be on camera at any moment, none of them have lost yet and they're all sort of generally ready for a good time.' He advised him from that point on to just move it on quickly.

Jackman also sought advice from other past hosts, including Whoopi Goldberg and celebrities renowned for working a room for laughs, such as British comedian Ricky Gervais, who co-wrote and starred in the hugely successful comedy shows, *The Office* and *Extras*. And it was apparent from listening to Hugh's lines in the opening sequences that the Gervais influence was written all over them.

Hugh knew he wasn't a stand-up comedian and didn't intend to be. The pressure was taken off slightly because no one expected him to come out and do seven minutes of bang, bang, bang jokes. Instead, the producers encouraged him to do what he did best, and to be himself.

Like everything he does, Hugh worked hard at getting it just right. He spent hours and hours in rehearsals, first in New York before jetting out to Hollywood for a final week of run-throughs; he appeared focused on the role, rarely eating or stopping for rest. It was the first time an Australian had hosted the movie industry's big night. In addition to working with a group of writers, he doubled up on his regular once-a-week singing lessons.

It was obvious to everyone involved that even the most professional showman can struggle with nerves: 'There have been moments in my life where I've been nervous going on stage, that's for sure, and I know I'll have a butterfly or two, 'cause yeah, you wanna have a couple.' But he knew he had to enjoy it, too. 'The way I see it is if I'm not going to have a good time, then how can anyone else have a good time? You know, you're the host

– it's not really about you. Ultimately, it's your job to set the tone and I always used to say to myself, I'm glad I do what I do. Because imagine being a hundred metre runner in the Olympics, everything has to be perfect on that day. But I suppose in showbiz, this is about as close as I'll come, because there'll never be so many people watching something that I do, at one time, ever.'

The content of the ceremony was kept a well-guarded secret. On arriving to do the show, Hugh was impressed with how intimate the Kodak Theater was. It was a different kind of layout to what he had been used to when performing in the musical shows. This was more like the nightclub of his dreams, where he could be close to the audience.

On the night itself, much was riding on his broad, gym-sculpted shoulders, but there was really no need to worry since everything went perfectly. 'I was scared. I was like "Wow man this is a billion people" and then I just thought, "Ok whatever you do just remember you are a kid from Wahroonga in Sydney, you're hosting the Oscars, just have fun".' He wanted to open with a bang, and he certainly did. He breathed much-needed life into the ailing Oscars ceremony as he sang, danced and joked his way through the best opening routine since Billy Crystal's priceless parody of *Jerry Maguire* and *The English Patient* in 1997.

In his opening skit, and in a reference to the global economic crisis, Jackman announced his opening number had been cut from the show. Undaunted, the song-and-dance man of *Boy From Oz* fame then launched into a hilarious musical semi-extravaganza, adorned by cheap sets made of cardboard, pizza boxes and gaffer tape. 'Everything is being downsized because of the recession,' Hugh remarked. 'Next year, I'll be starring in a movie called *New Zealand*.'

He pushed the usual irreverence to extremes by pulling Best Actress nominee Anne Hathaway out of her seat for a Frost/Nixon segment, and singing 'I haven't seen *The Reader*', striking a chord with most people watching. With dashes of Australian informality, he often left the stage to banter light-heartedly with nominees in the front row, including Kate Winslet, Angelina Jolie and Meryl Streep.

In a top-hat musical tribute to Old Hollywood, singer Beyoncé joined Jackman and cast members of *Mamma Mia!* and *High School Musical*. The number was directed by Baz Luhrmann, whose *Australia* got more than its fair share of mentions despite being nominated only for Best Costume.

As for the winners that night, as expected, the late Heath Ledger took a posthumous Best Supporting Actor award for his ground-breaking performance as The Joker in *The Dark Knight*. A standing ovation greeted the announcement as the award was accepted by his father Kim Ledger, mother Sally Bell and sister Kate Ledger. Everyone seemed to get into the celebration and party mood, even a humble Sean Penn, who uncharacteristically delivered the funniest line of the night when accepting Best Actor for *Milk* by admitting, 'I do know how hard I make it to appreciate me often.' He also brought perspective to the giddy mood by mentioning the homophobia still staining American life. Yet the dominance of *Slumdog Millionaire* fed perfectly into the optimistic vibe of the first post-Bush Oscars, which seemed designed to promote a less arrogant America.

Some US TV critics may disagree, but Hugh Jackman's performance as Oscar host received a big thumbs-up from the American public, and from the celebrities themselves. New York newspaper *Newsday* asked its readers to rate the Australian host's performance and 65.5 per cent deemed it 'excellent', 21.5 per cent 'good', 8.1 per cent 'satisfactory' and just 5 per cent gave him a 'fail'. *Entertainment Weekly* asked its readers if Hugh should return as host – just over 70 per cent said he should and only 29 per cent said not.

The affable Aussie's singing, dancing and stand-up comedy performance had spearheaded a reverse in the troubling slide in US TV ratings for the film industry's glitzy night of celebration. Viewing figures pointed to a 6 per cent rise in American viewers for the Jackman-led US TV Oscar telecast over the dismal performance a year before. And in Australia, the distinct Aussie flavour helped boost television ratings by 300,000 on the Monday night from a record low the previous year.

A few months later, the star was back for some more excitement at the same theatre, but this time to be inducted into the Hollywood Walk of Fame. It was a whirlwind time in the Jackman family.

'Women, men, children and dogs completely went to pieces when Hugh took his shirt off.'

Maureen Lipman, actress

CHAPTER SIXTEEN

WALKING ON BROADWAY!

'Quite often I get a feeling of being a bit over-whelmed, but I'm just in this bit of a purple patch at the moment, I suppose, where the opportunities I'm being offered are really exciting to me,' said the highly versatile, talented and hard-working Mr. Jackman. His ever expanding portfolio now included a long list of diverse and challenging roles on screen and on stage which ensured he got the Hollywood 'A' list treatment wherever he went.

From the outset however, 2009 and 2010 seemed a much quieter period as far as big budget film releases were concerned for the Australian even though behind the scenes there were a lot of things happening to keep the star busy.

Around that time there were several proposed movies which in the end were either put on ice as far as Hugh's involvement was concerned or were canned. *Drive,* based on the James Sallis novel of the same name, seemed to be on his radar for ages. There was much anticipation for the movie where Hugh was to play a stunt driver by day, a getaway driver by night. Yet after numerous delays, Hugh declined the part and it was eventually filled by Ryan Gosling.

In another project, Hugh was pencilled in to play the major lead role in Kevin Bisch's comedy *Avon Man.* The film would have seen the star swap his sharp claws for the world of beauty products. Along with his Seed Productions co-partner John Palermo, he was to also produce the movie about a laid-off car salesman who is reluctantly recruited as a salesman for the cosmetic company, Avon. Again after various reasons and production stretching into 2011, Hugh dropped it off his project list to get himself into shape for some bigger and more familiar roles to follow.

Despite all, there were still a number of movies he did do which would be released in 2011 or 2012. So with the business of clocking up films ticking along nicely, Hugh channelled his energy and effort not for the first time (and probably not for the last) back to his first love, the theatre. In September 2009, he starred in a gritty dramatic piece to kick off his return to the boards of New York – a play called *A Steady Rain.*

In *A Steady Rain,* written by Keith Huff, Hugh returned to Broadway to act alongside Mr Bond himself, Daniel Craig. The press notes stated, "It was a new American play that told the story of two Chicago cops who are lifelong friends and their differing accounts of a few harrowing days that changed their lives forever."

The story centred on two cops, one of which inadvertently returned a Vietnamese boy to a cannibalistic serial killer who claimed to be the boy's uncle; a story line similar to an incident that happened in real life to serial killer Jeffrey Dahmer.

'It's very raw,' said Jackman, 'there are not many plays like it on Broadway. I suppose the roles are different from others we've done, but that's what you want. To be remembered for different things is something that motivates both of us.' Jackman added, 'I loved the idea of returning to the basic of the spoken word, two actors and the audience.' Even in the more restrained world of the theatre, news of the production caused a tremendous buzz, and not just because the two major megastars were going to be sharing the same stage at the same time.

Jackman played Denny, an aging and racist cop with a wicked temper not helped by a strained and stressful marriage. 'Denny is very unpredictable, very explosive,' Jackman commented, 'and it ain't all Mr Nice Guy, that's for sure.'

Craig stepped into the role of his partner, Joey, a recovering alcoholic with some dark secrets of his own. Both actors turned down significant film roles for the chance to work together in the two man play. 'I'm just really excited to be working with Daniel Craig, and to just be working on Broadway again, but this time in a play,' Hugh commented.

On and off stage the actors got on extremely well and

were more than happy to share the limelight and the spoils equally. There were no egos, no tantrums, or infighting, just hard work and a friendly professional atmosphere. Allegedly, to create this atmosphere and help the actors bonding process, John Crowley, the director, installed a ping pong table backstage in the theatre so the superstars could play and relax during rehearsals breaks.

No one would deny that a high percentage of the audience gathered outside Gerald Schoenfield theatre each night for several hours before curtain call were not your usual theatre goers. Most were film fans there just to catch a rare glimpse of their favourite actors in the flesh. On more than one occasion, their appearance from behind the curtain prompted loud cheers and wolf whistles from the audience. It took several minutes until the commotion died down enough for the actors to start their dialogue.

In the first week of performances, most TV channels and newspapers picked up on the story that happened during the middle of a tense dramatic scene, when someone in the audience forgot to knock their mobile phone off and it rang. As cool as ice, Jackman, staying in character, pointed to the phone offender and said, 'You wanna get that? You wanna get that, grab it I don't care.' The person didn't move. He continued, 'Grab your phone it doesn't matter.' To everyone's relief the ringing stopped. Unbelievably a few seconds later it started to ring again. This time, evidently annoyed, Jackman, still using his fake Chicago accent, added, 'Come on, just turn it off unless you got a better story, you want to get up and tell your story?' Craig chimed in with, 'Can you get that, whoever it is can you just get it? We can wait just get the phone.' The end of the ringing was met with gentle applause from the other members of the audience.

During the two hour performance without an interval break, the audiences were served a compelling, and fast-paced ride through the tough streets of Chicago by Jackman and Craig. At the end of each night they received standing ovations for their raw, emotionally charged performance.

'I love New York,' Jackman commented. 'I have a home here; my kids go to school here. And Broadway audiences are different from any others that I've experienced. They're on your side to begin with. You can lose them quickly, but they've come to have a good time, and they give you the benefit of the doubt. That's part of the fun.'

The pair made a unique place for themselves in the history of Broadway Cares / Equity Fights Aids fundraising when between them they raised over $1,500,000 in the 21st annual Gypsy of the Year competition, from six weeks of curtain appeals at their hit Broadway drama.

The first week of preview performances took *A Steady Rain* into the top three at Broadway's box office, grossing $1,167,954. Only *Wicked* and *Billy Elliot* scored higher. It didn't stop and the twelve week stint proved extremely successful and highly profitable. It broke box office records for a non-musical play in Broadway. The critics also gave the play and its Aussie and Brit lead actors, which included very convincing Chicago accents, their seal of approval.

Due to its success, rumours have been circulating that Steven Spielberg is very interested in adapting the play into a big screen movie with the two actors set to play the lead roles. Talks are still continuing.

Hugh strongly believed another stage production would soon follow in 2010. A play based on the life and loves of the famous magician and escapologist, Harry Houdini. Hugh admitted he had always been deeply fascinated by the life of Houdini since he was very young but again it was put on hold. This didn't deter Jackman however who carried on treading the boards once more when he launched into a one man show called *Back on Broadway*.

Back on Broadway was the long time dream of the Australian to create and star in a Vegas-style, rat-pack kind of show with six female dancers / singers, an 18 piece orchestra and on a few occasions a quartet of indigenous Australian vocalists and didgeridoo players. 'I had it in my mind for sixteen years. I wanted to do something personal to try and show a bit of who I am and the things I love. I tried to share different styles of music, different parts of myself and I thought I wanted to share some of the gravitas and some of the emotion of really what being Australian is.'

There was just one problem. He had to convince his wife and family it was the right thing to do. 'I was like a guy who goes to his wife and asks her if she minds if he goes out to play golf. I went to Deb's and

said, "Hey Deb's do you mind if I did this show."'
Luckily she agreed.

The action packed stage show proved a perfect platform for the all action-movie star to remind the audience what else he had in his locker. 'I can't think of a time when I felt more relaxed than on stage, not even Sunday mornings. But even when dancing and singing unless I try to invent some kind of disguise for myself I feel naked.'

During the show he sang and danced, twirled, swung and pirouetted across the stage, no mean feat for such a big man. The show also delved into a bit of rap, a blast of tap and a slice of capella. And of course in true 'Boy from Oz' fashion Hugh happily interacted with the audience with his off the cuff moments of conversations and humour.

The one-man show started life at the Curran Theatre in San Francisco from 3-15 May 2011. Then he packed it up and moved it to the East coast to Broadway's Broadhurst Theatre where it energetically played out night after night to full to capacity audiences from November 2011 to January 2012.

Unbelievably even with such success, some people still find it hard to comprehend how Hugh wants to, and almost effortlessly does, flutter back and forth between stage and screen. There are some critics that feel he should just settle down in one medium or the other. He himself, on the other hand, shrugs his shoulders, knowing full well that he finds walking on either side of the genre street completely comfortable: 'That's just my taste anyway. When people say to me, "What type of music do you like, what do you listen to?" I always think it's such an odd question. I love all different types of music. But that's how I am with food, with people. I was reminiscing with an old mate and he said, "Oh my god, if I look back at all my girlfriends they're all the same!" I said if I look back on all mine, they couldn't be more different. I've never sort of repeated. So it's my natural state of being.'

Advance sales exceeded the $6 million dollars mark. After the tiring, but enjoyable, ten week show, sales eventually grossed well over $14 million giving him ten out of the eleven of the Broadhurst's highest earning weeks (the other being The Merchant of Venice in early 2011).

Then just to add another string to his bow a new type of project involving the star emerged. Far away from the producing, film work and treading the boards, Jackman took his new-found liking for comic books into new areas after getting hooked on the *X-Men* series and turned his hand to creating his own series, *Nowhere Man*.

Working with a US comic publisher, Virgin Comics, Hugh, along with Marc Guggenheim (writer of the Marvel comics *Wolverine* and *Amazing Spider-Man*) created a futuristic science-fiction odyssey series set in an era where men have traded their privacy for safety and security. Obviously, from where Jackman and his production company sat, there was hope *Nowhere Man* will one day become popular enough to warrant a movie, or four! Unfortunately Virgin Comics disbanded a year later and at present *Nowhere Man* is still no where to be seen.

In addition to his normal day job, Hugh's fame and popularity opened up new horizons and gave him the wonderful chance to help others. In the latter part of decade, he became goodwill ambassador of Seoul in South Korea. 'As a goodwill ambassador, Jackman will help raise the brand value of Seoul and publicise the city's policies to the world,' said a local official. 'He will play an important role in promoting Seoul's charm, especially to America and Europe.' Hugh himself was excited about the prospect when he visited the city to promote his latest *X-Men Origins: Wolverine* movie: 'As a goodwill ambassador to Seoul, which has unlimited possibility and charm, I will do my best to show people how beautiful Seoul is and why it is a city worth visiting.'

He also used his fame to try and get more people aware and involved in charity work throughout the world. As a philanthropist, Hugh is a long-time proponent of microcredit, the extension of small loans to impoverished prospective entrepreneurs in underdeveloped countries. He is a vocal supporter of Muhammad Yunus, microcredit pioneer and winner of the 2006 Nobel Peace Prize.

Hugh even took time out of his busy schedule to attend a UN Climate Summit with former British Prime Minister Tony Blair, where he urged world leaders to act on global warming before it becomes too late. The actor, an ambassador to World Vision, spoke about the effect climate change is having on the poor in Africa after returning from a trip to Ethiopia where he met coffee grower Dukalee and his family. He hoped to raise awareness on the issue, saying, 'I will use the best weapon I have, which is not Wolverine claws or mutant powers, but my voice to speak on behalf of Dukalee and a billion other people in developing countries, who contribute the least to climate change and yet are hit the hardest by it.' He described how it gelled for him on this trip: 'You can't separate the issues of climate change and poverty. They are inextricably linked. Having been to Ethiopia and seen these farmers, seen the battle they face from what is a problem that the developed countries have brought on many of these developing countries, there is a justice and there is a gap we need to fill.'

The Aussie actor admitted the trip to Africa was an eye-opening experience and it inspired him and his wife Deborra-Lee to live a greener life at home. He added, 'It's humbling, it's embarrassing sometimes, when you go to Dukalee's farm, who has nothing and who's doing no harm by shovelling manure, and there's me in my lovely apartment.'

To go along with his stance, he narrated a video for the Global Poverty Project, as well as a documentary, *The Burning Season*, about global warming. In addition, Jackman gave his support to The Art of Elysium, a non-profit organisation founded in 1997 which encourages working actors, artists and musicians to voluntarily dedicate their time and talent to helping children who are battling serious medical conditions, as well as supporting the Motion Picture & Television Fund. He and his wife are also patrons of the Bone Marrow Donor Institute in Australia.

Like lots of Hollywood stars, Hugh now finds himself a regular 'Twitterer' on the internet, frequently updating his army of fans on what's going on in his life. More importantly, he often uses this media to focus people's attention on charity work. On his Twitter page, Jackman once posted: 'I will donate $100K to one individual's favourite non-profit organisation. Of course, you must convince me why by using 140 characters or less.'

Within minutes of his call to arms, thousands upon thousands of responses were received. Suggestions included Jackman giving the money to charities involved in homelessness, fighting disease, child welfare and towards developing impoverished nations. After much thought, he decided to donate $50,000 to Charity: Water and $50,000 to Operation of Hope.-

Charity groups were not deterred by the possibility that Jackman, who has almost 36,000 people following him on Twitter, could be making the pledge as part of a public relations exercise. 'Quite possibly, it's a PR stunt, but at the end of the day a community organisation is going to get a significant amount of money that they wouldn't have otherwise got,' commented Philanthropy Australia CEO Gina Anderson. '$100,000 is a large amount of money; he doesn't have to give it. It's fantastic. On the other hand, $100,000 sounds like a lot of money to be making a decision about based on 140 characters.'

For Hugh, it was more important that people saw him getting involved and not just giving money away. He wanted them to ask themselves the question, 'Why? Why is he giving money there, why is that important?' His aim was to encourage people to show passion towards a charity, to persuade them to get support from friends, to teach them the importance of it. He, and many of the charity organisations, are quite excited about using this new kind of media, one which connects with a new demographic and encourages personal participation.

'I don't know how much smoke I should blow up his a—, but Hugh's tremendously talented. When you're on stage, you want to be looking at someone who's intelligent and who's got your back. It makes my job that much easier, lazy actor that I am.'

Daniel Craig, aka Mr Bond

CHAPTER SEVENTEEN

THE REAL DEAL

2011 started out rather quietly on the movie front for Jackman, but finished up very hectic by the latter part of the year. First off, he stepped rather calmly into the role of Arthur in an indie production called *Snow Flower and the Secret Fan,* based on an historical drama set in 19th-century China.

Next up came a very small part, but in more familiar territory. With the announcement of the fifth instalment of *X-Men* movies due for release in the summer, many fans were surprised and disappointed to learn that Hugh Jackman would not be playing any part in the production. *X-Men: First Class*, directed by Matthew Vaughn, aimed to be a prequel to the original film and followed the lives of the X-Men at a much younger age.

In spite of this, Jackman appeared in a fifteen-second cameo near the end of the movie. During his on-screen time he delivered a single line, which not only got the biggest laugh in the entire film, but also won him a 2011 Scream Award for Best Cameo. 'Basically, I was asked a long time ago if I would do a cameo. Way before shooting happened. They pitched me the idea and I remember saying, "Does anyone else swear in the movie?" They said, "No," and I said, "I'm in." It sounded perfect to me. The actual line they used in the end, "Go f**k yourself," was a bit of an ad-lib by me. The line was originally "f**k off". We did about eight takes, and I said, "Matthew, let me do just one more."' It was Hugh's line that didn't end up on the cutting room floor.

It wasn't until October of the same year that he punched his way back into a big blockbuster movie. *Real Steel* is an all-action film loosely based on the 1956 short story *Steel* by Richard Matheson. Set in the year 2020, robot boxing is all the rage and commands enormous worldwide audiences. The story follows the ups and downs of a struggling robot-boxing promoter Charlie (Hugh) trying to get ahead in the world.

'He's a little bit of a broken man,' admits the star. 'He's disappointed himself, and many people right throughout his life, and he's kind of used to that. He kind of expects to disappoint people. So he's one of those people who doesn't put himself in a situation to have people rely on him, you know, deliberately, because he lacks in self-confidence, or self-belief, I suppose. It was so much fun to see how far we could take Charlie. This is a DreamWorks picture being distributed by Disney, and our lead character sells his son in the first 20 minutes. I really liked that. When we showed it to the studio I thought they were gonna tell us to reshoot. I'd already asked Shawn Levy, the director: "Are we making him too much of an asshole?" The studio thought we'd pushed it, but that it worked.'

'What's interesting about casting Hugh,' said Levy, 'is he's a movie star who you believe in the physicality of the role. But he has such a built-in likeability that he can play a complete asshole. Hugh Jackman spends the first half of this movie behaving in ways that are unforgivable, and yet we never quite risk alienating the audience because Hugh brings such a sheer force of niceness! Hugh really enjoyed playing a d**k! When that character starts to find redemption in the latter half, it's tended to be a very emotional reaction from audiences.'

Although a film about robots basically bashing lumps out of each other, the underlying theme is centred around the relationship between Jackman's character (Charlie) and his 11-year-old son, Max (played by Dakota Goyo), who he hasn't seen in years after walking out on his mother. 'You know the way I've described it to people is *Rocky 1 to 6*, or whatever it is,' Jackman stated. 'Remember *Rocky 1*, which was like 70/30? If you saw it, there wasn't that many fights in it. And we're sort of in the same world here. It's really a character story. At first I didn't think it was for me. I don't really like special effects movies. But I started reading the script and I thought this is *Rocky*; more *Rocky* than *Transformers*, a great sports drama. It was the type of movie that gets everyone cheering and believing in it.'

And it proved to be a great family film for the Jackman household in more ways than one. The actor was quite pleased to point out during interviews that it was the first of his movies his kids had seen. 'It was such a joy doing a movie that my kids wanted to see. When I read the script for the first time I was reading it with him [Oscar]. So, that's bad parenting, basically! I was trying to do two things at once, but he loved it, and made me read it to him every night for the next 10 nights. But I was pretty much drawn in anyway, but it was a nice bonus that he liked it.' On the set, Jackman soon became a massive fan and was extremely impressed with his co-star, the 11-year-old Canadian actor, Dakota Avery Goyo. 'Well, I auditioned with him. I auditioned with a lot of kids. So, I got to know him. And then we had a couple of weeks of rehearsal where we got to know each other. We were on-set together every day and we were really working together a lot. He was a dream to work with. It's just effortless for him. Shawn [Levy] is a brilliant director of kids. He's done a lot of films with them, plus he has four kids, so he knows exactly what to do. So, for me, I just got to really enjoy being an actor with him. He was kind of more mature and present than a lot of the actors I've worked with. The only thing he got nervous about – and I don't blame him for it – was dancing in front of 5,000 people. I mean, he's just an 11-year-old kid, so right at that age where you'd be embarrassed by that kind of thing.'

The film was set in the year 2020, which surprised many people who thought it would be based further out in the future. The idea behind this was director Shawn Levy's: he knew the movie was going to be an underdog story, so he didn't want the distant futurism of extreme sci-fi to overshadow it. He wanted the world to have that really familiar feel to it, so the watching audience could completely relate to the characters – 'The cellphone we used five or ten years ago looks different from today, but a diner still looks like a diner.' That was exactly the image and the feel he set out to capture.

To get the film from concept stage to actual production took several years and many rewrites. Yet it certainly gathered momentum when the legendary Steven Spielberg came on board as executive producer. His impact was almost immediate. In Levy's first meeting with Spielberg, the *Jaws* director challenged him to do something different. He explained that when he made *Jurassic Park* many years before, computers were limited in what they could do. 'We built real dinosaurs that moved,' the superstar director added, 'I know it's an old-fashioned notion, but consider building real, fully animated, animatronic robots.'

And that's what was done. With over a $100 million budget, twenty-seven total live action robots were manufactured in various forms. To many, this definitely gave the film a big advantage over other similar high-tech movies around at that time. In the fight scenes they used, and directed, human boxers to produce the movements, then employed graphics to make it come to life as robots fought with each other. But in every scene in the movie where Jackman was interacting with one of the robots, if that robot wasn't walking or boxing, it was a real one, some controlled by around 20 puppeteers.

'I mean, it's so amazing,' the actor said during one interview. 'My first thought was that this looks so unbelievably good that they aren't going to believe it's for real. It's really exciting. A real sort of shock when we first saw those robots, my jaw was on the ground. People will think they're CGI [Computer-generated imagery] but it makes such a difference for us, as the actors, and just the overall look. And I think what Shawn [Levy] has done so brilliantly is create a world that's very real – very gritty, very timeless – and robots that are sort of very everyday. I know what's going to happen, and every kid is going to be really upset that it's not real, because it's so fun, and you totally could believe that this would be the biggest sport in the world.' It was the first time Jackman had worked with Spielberg. Even though the great director kept himself at arm's length and left most of the day-to-day production to Shawn Levy, from the outset Hugh was aware of the 'Spielberg Effect'. He described what it was like working with him. 'He took a kind of secondary position in the room. He was a quiet character. He didn't demand; he didn't take all of the air out of the room. He was very generous. Of course he was aware of who he was, but he didn't lord it, or use it in any way.'

Later he recalled almost getting busted by the police when the director called him soon after the film was made. 'I got a phone call from him as soon as he'd seen the movie and he was talking to me for half an hour while I was driving around Sydney. My wife was like, "You're going to get a ticket, you're going to get a ticket!" So, I replied: "Hang on, Steven…" and I turned to her and said: "I want a ticket! I want to be picked up and I want to be able to tell the officer that it's Steven Spielberg on the line. I want him to write that on the ticket so I could frame it!"'

Although always too modest to admit it, Hugh rarely lets himself get out of shape, even when he's not making movies. But for this role as an ex-boxer he discussed with Levy that maybe he should be out of shape and have a bit of a stomach. The director agreed. 'So I came in ten kilos heavier. I actually said to Shawn: "Man, I'm an ex-boxer, we should go realistic. I think I should come in big so that you can believe in him but maybe give him a bit of a paunch to show how he'd let things slip." And so I came in for a fitting a month before and he went: "Yeah, let's not go so realistic…" Obviously, I was too loose, so I had to get back in shape quite quickly. But Wolverine has been a part of my life for 10 years and it's much easier to stay in shape than to get into shape, and the Wolverine shape is ridiculous because it's so hard. So, even pulling back 20% felt quite easy.'

A massive bonus was getting to work very closely with one of his all-time heroes, the great Sugar Ray Leonard, a true boxing legend in every sense of the word. Having won titles in five different weight divisions throughout his career, Sugar Ray served as a consultant for the robots and as a trainer for Hugh.

'The biggest thing Hugh struggled with was to let go and surrender,' explained the former world champion, 'and drop his guard and be a fighter, and forget about Hugh and Broadway, and be the fighter and the trainer. That's really difficult. With fight films and boxing films, the only ones that come to mind where the actor and actress let go and become that fighter were *Raging Bull*, *Million Dollar Baby*, *Requiem for a Heavyweight*, and *The Fighter*. They were people who had dropped their guards, and that's very hard to do, for a superstar to let go of that thing. Once you do that, you know what it's like to be a fighter, for a moment.'

Hugh trained with Sugar Ray every day and like everything he approaches in life he was a fast learner and a model pupil. He also called on a little bit of his dad's experience. 'He was the Army champ when he was on National Service. From Army champ he went up one level, a Golden Gloves or something, but in his first fight he got knocked out and doesn't even remember where the punch came from. But he realised with that he was too slow and he opted out.'

Normally, the actor doesn't find himself in awe of many people but Sugar Ray Leonard, a boxer who Jackman had watched fighting while growing up back in Australia, was placed firmly in that category. 'Sugar Ray is like a freak of nature. I mean, he's ridiculously handsome. He looks younger than me. You can't believe he was ever hit. And he was very up-front with me. He talked to me a lot and really helped me out a lot, not only in looking like a boxer but thinking about the mentality of the cornerman, which is what I play. He was terrific. But the one thing he told me was that he used to know Angelo Dundee, a famous cornerman, and he would hire him two weeks before a fight. He said: "Angelo Dundee... he kept doing the De Niro thing... That look... without that, you feel like you're going to fall." It's not only what they say... the way they look at you from the corner is everything. And Angelo Dundee just gave you strength, just by the way he looked and [Sugar Ray] kept telling me that I must have that. Before every take he'd look at me like that. So, even though it's a robot, it's important that the audience feels for those robots and supports them just like humans.'

After the usual promotional tour, which included appearing on the WWF [World Wrestling Federation] wrestling show, both fans and critics alike gave the thrilling movie the big thumbs up. Jackman went on to win the People's Choice Award for Favorite Action Movie Star, while Dakota won the Young Artist Award in the Best Performance in a Feature Film – Leading Young Actor category. It proved to be a worldwide smash and a toy line of all the main robots quickly followed.

It wasn't long after that Hugh got to work with his *Real Steel* co-star Dakota again, when they both added voice-overs on the 3-D, computer animated, action movie *Rise of the Guardians*, based on the series of books by William Joyce, *The Guardians of Childhood*.

Next up was *Butter*, in which Jackman played Boyd Bolton in a bizarre story about a young orphan who discovers her uncanny talent for butter sculpture in an Iowa town where her adoptive family lives. The talent pits her against the ambitious wife (Jennifer Garner) of the reigning champion (Ty Burrell) in the annual butter sculpture competition.

Then came a role he was born for.

Of all the stage musicals that could possibly be given the Silver Screen treatment, *Les Misérables* was the one he would have moved heaven and earth to star in. So when rumours circulated that Universal Pictures, along with British film company Working Title Films, were considering doing just that, Hugh admitted he was the first in the queue.

'I was a late teenager when the musical came out, so I knew the score really well. Everybody did, it was playing everywhere, and my mate used to blare it in his car all the time. He was one of my only friends who had a car, so we heard it nonstop. I've seen it about five times. I've always been a massive fan. One of the first auditions I had for a musical was for *Beauty and the Beast*, and I sang "Stars," and the guy said, "Well, you can throw that away. You'll never be in that! So there you go." Actually Cameron Mackintosh, *Les Misérables*' producer, did ask me to play Inspector Javert several times in the past, so there!'

And he made more than a bit of a nuisance of himself when the rumours surrounding the making of the movie turned into reality. 'I was a huge fan of the stage version of *Les Misérables*, but I didn't think a film would ever get off the ground. When I heard it was happening, I rang director Tom Hooper and told him I needed a meeting with him... urgently! I met him, demanded an audition, and pushed him so hard for a part, harder than I had ever pushed for a part before. I think I was lucky he didn't call for security and have me slung out on my ear. In my enthusiasm to land a role, I didn't even realise that the poor guy hadn't signed to the film himself at this point! So I backtracked a little and we went from there. A three-hour singing audition later, one of the most gruelling, but exhilarating experiences of my life, and the role of Valjean was mine. I was the first person Tom auditioned, so it was more like a workshop. He was still getting his head around it. He picked up his chair, moved about five feet from me and said, "Imagine I have the camera. Let's just make it work here in this intimate space."'

Hooper also remembered the meeting well. He described Jackman as a 'tour de force' from his initial attempts to land the part through to his commitment to the project once it was being filmed. 'He smacked of utter devotion,' he added.

The film *Les Misérables* is the epic British drama based on the stage musical of the same name by Alain Boublil and Claude-Michel Schönberg, which in turn was taken from the 1862 French novel by Victor Hugo. It tells the story of Jean Valjean, an ex-convict who eventually becomes mayor of a town in France and owner of a factory in the same place. He is always on the alert to the risk of being captured again by police inspector Javert, who is ruthless in hunting down law-breakers. One of his factory workers, Fantine, blames him for being cast into a life of prostitution. When she dies, he feels responsible, and agrees to take care of her illegitimate daughter, Cosette, though he must first escape Javert. Later, when Cosette is grown, they are swept up in the political turmoil in France, which culminates in the June Rebellion.

Without question, the stage production became one of the most successful musicals throughout the world. The Broadway production of *Les Misérables* opened in 1987 and it alone ran for over 6,680 performances, making it the third longest-running show on Broadway. It has been nominated for thirteen Tony Awards, winning eight (Best Musical, Best Featured Actor (Michael Maguire), Best Featured Actress (Frances Ruffelle), Best Scenic Design, Best Costume Design, Best Lighting Design, Best Direction of a Musical, Best Score and Best Book).

As far back as 1992, producer Cameron Mackintosh excitedly announced to the world that the film would be co-produced by TriStar Pictures. However, the project was abandoned. Then in 2005, Mackintosh confirmed that interest in turning the musical into a film adaptation had resumed. He added that he wanted the movie to be directed by 'someone who had a vision for the show and that will put the show's original team, including himself, back to work.' He also wanted the film audiences to make it as 'fresh as the actual show itself.'

Fast forward to 2009, Mackintosh, producer of *Miss*

Saigon and *The Phantom of the Opera*, was not only happy to finally get the project off the ground, but also over the moon to get such a talented cast, 'Even though I have dreamt about making the film of *Les Misérables* for over 25 years, I could never have imagined that we would end up with the dream director Tom Hooper (*The King's Speech*, *The Damned United*) and the dream cast of Hugh Jackman and Russell Crowe as the two great protagonists, Jean Valjean and Javert. Not only were they born to play these roles vocally, but they thrillingly inhabit this great score.'

A cast of acting royalty supported Jackman and Russell Crowe. Anne Hathaway, Sacha Baron Cohen and Helena Bonham Carter were all handpicked to bring the musical to life on the silver screen. Apparently, a few others had been in the running for the role that Sacha Baron Cohen finally secured. Comedians like Rowan Atkinson, Billy Crystal, Ricky Gervais, Steve Martin and Robin Williams were all at one point considered for Monsieur Thénardier. But after Hooper saw Cohen star opposite Helena Bonham Carter in another musical, *Sweeney Todd: The Demon Barber of Fleet Street*, his name jumped to the top of the list.

Jackman couldn't wait to get his teeth into one of his favourite fictional characters of all time. 'He's obviously one of the great literary characters and I saw him as a real hero; quiet and humble,' the actor explained. 'Jean Valjean came from a place of the greatest hardship that I could ever imagine. I don't think any of us could. He manages to transform himself from the inside.

Obviously, on film, we wanted to show the inside changes as well but actually Victor Hugo uses the term "transfiguration". It's more than a transformation because he becomes more godlike; it's a spiritual change. It's something that happens from within. It's to me one of the most beautiful journeys ever written and I didn't take the responsibility of playing the role lightly. I think it was one of the greatest opportunities I've ever had and if I'm a tenth of the man Jean Valjean was, I'll be a very happy man.'

Being part of the project not only satisfied his passion for films but also gave him the adrenaline rush he frequently got from performing live on stage every night. The cast rehearsed together for around seven weeks before the three-month shoot began. 'Every day we recorded every take live, so, basically, the feeling of an opening night on Broadway was happening every day of my life.'

Russell Crowe starred as Javert, a police inspector who dedicated his life to imprisoning Valjean. Apparently, before being cast as Javert, Crowe was initially dissatisfied with the character. On his way to Europe for a friend's wedding, he came to London and met with director Tom Hooper. He told him of his concerns about playing Javert, but after the meeting went away more than happy and certainly determined to be involved in the project – 'I think it had something to do with Tom's passion for what he was about to undertake, and he clearly understood the problems and he clearly understood the challenge.'

Before Anne Hathaway was actually cast, there had been some resistance from the studio because she fell between the ideal ages of both the main female parts. They believed she was not mature enough for Fantine, but too old to convincingly play Cosette. Eventually, she landed the plum role as Fantine, a young orphaned *grisette* in Paris who becomes pregnant by a rich student, after reportedly blowing everyone away at her audition and leaving them in tears. Another plus was that Hugh Jackman had personally lobbied for Hathaway to secure the role of Fantine after the two performed together at the Academy Awards. It wasn't her first ever exposure to the role. In 1987, her mother, Kate McCauley Hathaway, played Fantine in the first US tour of the musical.

However, for the rich and famous Anne Hathaway, connecting to the agonies endured by Fantine presented a particular challenge, as she herself admitted: 'In my case, there's no way that I could relate to what my character was going through. I have a very successful life and don't have any children that I could give up, or keep, so what I did was try to get inside the reality of her story as it exists in our world. To do that, I read a lot of articles and watched a lot of documentaries and news clips about sexual slavery. For me, for this particular story, I came to the realization that I was thinking of Fantine as someone who lived in the past but she doesn't. She's living in New York City right now. She's probably less than a block away. This injustice exists in our world, so every day that I was her, I thought, "This isn't an invention. This isn't me acting. This is me honouring that this pain lives in this world". And, I hope that in all of our lifetimes, like today, we see it end.

'I remember there was a police raid on one of the brothels and a camera crew went along and there was a small, crawl space up in the ceiling. Oh my God, fourteen girls came out of it and they were all so tiny and crunched up and when they came out, they weren't shocked that there was a camera there. They weren't worried about getting arrested. They were gone. They were numb. They were unrecognizable as human beings and my heart broke for them. There was another piece where there was a woman who didn't want her identity revealed and she sat there and kept repeating, "I come from a good family. We lost everything and I have children so now I do this." And she doesn't want to do this but it's the only way the children are going to eat. Then she let out this sob that I've never heard before. She raised her hand to her forehead and it was the most despairing gesture I've ever seen.'

That was the moment when she realised the woman she had been watching wasn't playing a character. To her it was real life and she knew women like that deserved to have their voices heard. 'I needed to connect to that honesty and recreate that feeling. I'll never know who she was, but she was really the one who made me understand when Fantine says "shame," what it's like not just to go to a dark place, but to have fallen from a place where you didn't imagine anything bad was going to happen to you, and the betrayal and rage you feel at life. You've gone into a place that, by the way, I don't believe this woman would have gone to, that Fantine would not have gone to, if she didn't have children to support. I think she would have let herself die. So, Fantine is so heartbreaking and it all just layered within me.'

For her role, Hathaway allowed her hair to be shorn into a pixie cut on camera for a scene in which her character sells her hair, stating the lengths she goes to for her roles, 'Don't feel like sacrifices. Getting to transform is one of the best parts of acting. I offered Tom the option of cutting my hair. I always knew in the back of my mind it was something I was willing to do for a character if it was the right thing to do. So, when I got cast, and got the script, and knew they were keeping the hair cutting in, and I'd read the book, and it's such a devastating scene in the book, I thought that doing it for real might raise the stakes a bit for the character. I guess, in the back of my mind, I thought if it was a painful experience watching her hair be cut, then watching her teeth get pulled would be really painful and, of course, when she becomes a prostitute, I thought they [the audience] are going to be with her, feeling that alongside of her and, as an actor, it was great to authentically communicate a physical transformation.'

Hugh remembers the hair-cutting experience: 'I had my hair cut off with those gashes and Annie had been talking about cutting her hair. She came in for a consultation with Tom and she walked into the make-up room where I was sitting there with my head shaved and I saw the look on her face, the reality dawning on her as she was talking with Tom and her make-up artist. If you watch the movie, he is a man, but obviously, in the film was dressed in a dress because you needed an actual hair stylist to cut her hair, so if you notice man-hands in a dress, you'll see why. I remember Anne saying, "If you end up cutting my scalp and there is blood, fantastic, let's go for it!" I put up my hand and said, "For the record, I would like make-up. Fake scars, please!"'

As well as losing her locks, Hathaway had to shed 25 pounds for her portrayal of Fantine. The actress wasn't overweight to start off with so to lose so many pounds had a dramatic effect on her appearance. When asked in interviews, she refused to discuss how she lost the weight to play the dying woman, as she admitted her methods were life threatening, and she didn't want to glamorise or promote them to young women. However, she confirmed eating oatmeal paste was one of the reasons for her weight loss.

Despite reports of her finishing the sensational song 'I Dreamed A Dream' in one take, Hathaway confirmed in an interview that it took over eight hours to film. She added that she wanted to make the scene deeper and more emotional. In the end, the fourth take made it into the final cut.

Of course Jackman had to make sacrifices to get into character himself and he admits his portrayal of the convict-turned-hero was the most gruelling part he has ever played. The film provided the opportunity to fully dramatise the changes in Valjean's appearance in the long stretches of time between his encounters with Inspector Javert. The actor recalled, 'It's a very big part of the story, the relationship Valjean has with Javert, and they know each other right through the story. When they meet in the play it's probably five minutes in when they re-meet nine years later and Javert has no idea who this guy is. It's clear to everyone that the guy has taken a fake beard off and put on a greyer wig and it's exactly the same guy. Tom said we actually have an opportunity here for all the characters to show time, scale and all these things. I realised the sacrifices had been worth it, that the headaches, dizziness – and the grumpiness – had been a relatively small price to pay

'The scene is near the start of the film, when Valjean is about to be released from prison on parole after serving 19 years of hard labour, during which time he has often been close to starvation. So, of course, I had to look gaunt. The director Tom Hooper said I had to look so strikingly thin, in fact, so different from the way I normally look, that my friends would think I was ill. And I guess I achieved that, although there were times when I thought I had maybe pushed my body too far. I'd already shed 20 pounds, through exercise and a very lean diet, before I embarked on that 36-hour period in which I drank nothing and ate very little and I knew I was pushing myself and my body to the limit. But the non-consumption of liquids is a very clever bodybuilders' trick for giving one sunken cheeks and sunken eyes and boy, did it work. Maybe just a little too well...

'I told my wife, "This may be too much for me." She replied, "It will probably demand more of you than anything you've done, so it should feel frightening and uncomfortable. So use the fear. Work harder. Get in there!" I shaved my head, had to lose more than two stone in weight, and lived like a monk, nursing my vocal cords with a portable steam machine and avoiding dairy products. I went off coffee because it doesn't help the voice and if I didn't have eight hours' sleep a night, forget it. Some days I started singing at nine in the morning and was still singing at ten at night, so it wasn't easy.'

For inspiration, he looked closer to home than ever before. 'The more I looked into Valjean, the more I saw him in Dad. The really admirable thing I see in both of them is that real humility. I've never heard him say a bad word about anyone. When I was growing up, I thought he was quiet, uncommunicative; he didn't talk much. But in the end, I suppose he had no need to talk about himself and what he's done. He's done many great things, and didn't have the need to fish for compliments or any kind of acknowledgement about the incredible job he did. He never bemoaned, or whined, at any point, and what he did was Herculean, to bring up five kids with a full-time job. When I was about 14, it really struck me what my father had done and what he did every day in his life. And the other thing they had in common is that my father is a deeply religious man. He was converted in the Billy Graham crusade, and he didn't have deep exposure to religion until then. So church was a big part of our lives, though I don't think I ever really heard my father talk about God or religion necessarily. He was just one of those quietly religious people who believed actions spoke louder than words.'

Before filming began Jackman and the other leading cast members, Crowe, Hathaway, Amanda Seyfried and Eddie Redmayne, spent a solid two months rehearsing. 'You can't just turn up to a musical and hope to do it. This wasn't sitting around a table, chatting. This was a serious rehearsal so by the time we started filming we had a great ensemble feeling and we were all in it.'

While most major films like *Les Misérables* don't usually have especially lengthy rehearsals, a musical requires intense preparation, and as Jackman related, that meant extensive rehearsals. 'Tom Hooper told us all there were going to be rehearsals. I don't think any of us expected nine weeks of rehearsals and I've been on a film where the entire cast signs up for the entire time. I come from the theatre so, for me, rehearsal is vital and a way of life. There are many film directors and some actors who don't like to rehearse but with a musical, you have to. And with Tom, we would rehearse full out. It wasn't a half-hearted thing. Tom would be sitting here close by. He'd move his chair, often, to a very uncomfortably close place and do this [leaning in] the whole way. So everything we ended up doing was brilliant. By the time we got to the set, it was not uncomfortable having the camera that close. There had been times when I or Anne, or all of us had done a version of the song where there was snot coming out of our noses and Tom would say, "Alright, that's a little too much" so everything was tested properly. I mention that because I'm so grateful to Tom and everyone at Working Title and Universal that they spent the money and time on that to make it possible.'

He also loved Hooper's decision to have the actors singing as the cameras rolled, rather than lip-syncing as is usual in movie musicals, and especially attempting something on this scale. 'As a performer it was fantastic,' he revealed. 'The idea of singing live was daunting at first, but it gave me so much freedom. It was like being on stage. Instead of lip-syncing I could slow the tempo down, or speed it up, and do what I liked. I just had to worry about acting.'

Hooper explained his reasoning: 'I just felt, ultimately, it was a more natural way of doing it. You know, when actors do dialogue they have freedom in time; they have freedom in pacing; they can stop for a moment, they can speed up. I simply wanted to give the actors the normal freedoms that they would have. If they need a bit for an emotion or a feeling to form in the eyes before they sing, I can take that time. If they cry, they can cry through a song. When you're doing it to playback, to the millisecond, you have to copy what you do. You have no freedom in the moment – and acting is the illusion of being free in the moment.'

Recording the actors singing live as they performed may not be a first for this kind of film, but the scope, and especially the manner in which it was done, was. The actors all wore earpieces which fed the sound of a live piano being played off-stage to keep their singing in key. The main novelty here was that there was no count-in, or predetermined tempo, and the piano was following the pacing of the actor, not the other way around; a first for a filmed musical. Orchestral music was added post-production.

Typically, the soundtrack for a movie musical is recorded several months in advance and the actors mime to playback during filming. However, on this film, every single song was recorded live on set to capture the spontaneity of the performances. Everyone involved, from Jackman to Crowe, to producer Cameron Mackintosh, praised this approach as it allowed the performers to concentrate on their acting as opposed to lip-syncing properly.

Jackman explained, 'What a lot of people don't realise is that singing is very physically demanding, anyway. I've done a lot of action films and people assume musicals are easy to do by comparison, which they are not! And this particular part, in this particular musical, was both emotionally, and vocally, challenging, often at one and the same time, with the attendant discomfort vital in displaying the character's unhappiness. Cameron Mackintosh talked about the need to put yourself into a position of discomfort, not always to sing in the key that you find most comfortable, for example, so you have something to work against if you are searching for emotional angst, which I was, and he was spot on. I knew I had to go to extremes in my preparation and prove I could multi-task. When I went to the gym, I would sing loudly as I chalked up high-speed miles on the running machine, or as I bench-pressed. The people around me probably thought I was crazy, but I felt I had to do it. You're pushing, you're pulling, you are lifting, you are carrying and you are singing at the same time. The last thing I wanted to do when I came to the film was give the impression that any part of what my character was doing was not being competently undertaken. Looking stupid in the gym was a small price to pay for that conviction. If you're an actor, you sign up to make a fool of yourself on a regular basis anyway.'

He also revealed that the biggest bonus about the movie wasn't the cash ('To be honest, I have more money than I need') but working for the first time with old Aussie pal Russell Crowe, who played Javert. Hugh has always held a place in his heart for the gruff New Zealander ever since Crowe turned down the lead role in the action film *Wolverine* and recommended him for the part instead – 'He suggested me to the director, something for which I will always be grateful, and he has been a mentor to me for years. I've rung Russell on many occasions for advice and to work with him on *Les Misérables* was a dream come true. There's an old adage about great actors making other actors look good and Russell does just that! He would have soirées at his home on a Friday evening, throughout filming, for cast and crew, and the guitars would come out, we'd relax and have fun. He was very much the cheerleader of the production, the guy who kept our spirits up when we were cold, hungry and tired.'

Due to the physical demands of daily singing, none of the cast was allowed alcohol. Russell Crowe and Amanda Seyfried both admitted it was a challenge to not be able to drink, and Crowe bought Seyfried a bottle of whisky as a present once filming wrapped.

With Crowe calling the shots, the cast of *Les Misérables* soon became an uncommonly close team over the course of production. Anne Hathaway also had high praise for her co-actor: 'You cannot underestimate Russell's contribution and influence on this cast. He was the first one to say, "Hey, come to my house Friday night. My voice teacher is gonna play piano. We'll have a couple of drinks and sing!" That was such a key part of the process. Up to that point, we were in rehearsals with each other. We were very serious and spending all day crying but in between, I don't think we had gotten to the point where we thought of song as a way of communicating with each other. I think we thought, "This is a technical thing we have to accomplish" and through those nights, Russell let us approach it from a completely different perspective. This is the way we are going to communicate. This is the language we speak. These are our shared experiences. I know, for me, it made me so much more invested in the totality of the film and being in such a small part of the film that I am, I could have easily gone home and forgotten about it all but I cared so much that I needed to know how did "On My Own" go?' or "In My Life", how did that turn out?

I think it really cemented the bond between us. Now we kind of say we're "Camp Les Mis".'

The original film was to be four hours long, with a fifteen-minute battle scene, but it was shortened to two and a half hours in the end. It premiered in London on 5 December 2012, and was released on 25 December 2012 in the United States, on 26 December 2012 in Australia, and on 11 January 2013 in the United Kingdom. The movie received divided, but generally favourable reviews. It won the Golden Globe Award for Best Motion Picture – Musical or Comedy, the Golden Globe for Best Actor – Motion Picture Musical or Comedy for Jackman and the Golden Globe for Best Supporting Actress – Motion Picture for Hathaway. *Les Misérables* also won four BAFA Awards, including Best Actress in a Supporting Role (Hathaway). It received eight Academy Award nominations, including Best Picture (the first musical nominated since 2002's winner, *Chicago*) and Best Actor for Jackman, and won three awards for Best Sound Mixing, Best Makeup and Hairstyling and Best Supporting Actress (Hathaway), despite having just fifteen minutes of screen time and her character dying forty-three minutes into the film.

Les Misérables earned a worldwide total of $441,809,770. Robbie Collins in the *Daily Telegraph* gave the film five stars: '*Les Misérables* is a blockbuster, and the special effects are emotional: explosions of grief; fireballs of romance; million-buck conflagrations of heartbreak. Accordingly, you should see it in its opening week, on a gigantic screen, with a fanatical crowd.'

During his Golden Globes acceptance speech Jackman admitted to his *Les Mis* director Tom Hooper that he came close to quitting after a disastrous early rehearsal. 'I really thought I'd bitten off more than I could chew,' he said. 'My wife talked me off that cliff, like she talks me most days. "But baby, I'm going to say it now in front of the entire world: Thank you for always being right."' He also thanked the person who had stolen the wheels from his bike during his *Les Misérables* audition, promising to leave the frame in the same place for them!

'It wasn't hard work, but, you know, it was challenging. And we looked to Hugh every day and to his strength and to his indefatigable spirit. He never complained once. He did as many takes as need be, and he was absolutely our rock and our inspiration through everything and to me personally.'
Anne Hathaway

CHAPTER EIGHTEEN

THE BRIGHTEST STAR

'It was just a red dot on my nose, and I was like, "maybe I injured it in a fight sequence, or something", and lo and behold, it wasn't. It was a basal cell carcinoma,' said Jackman, concerning the cancer scare he had in 2013. 'I'm an Aussie; we have to get checked, but everyone should get checked. Particularly if you're my age. If you're 21, or older, you just go and get checked. It's simple.'

Basal cell carcinoma is the most common form of skin cancer and accounts for more than 90 per cent of US skin cancer patients. The basal cell carcinomas rarely spread, but if they are not removed, they can damage and disfigure surrounding tissue.

Hugh underwent surgery in November 2013 to remove the cancerous growth in the skin on his nose and soon afterwards he told the press that he felt good and the operation had been a complete success. He publicly thanked his wife, who he said had first noticed it and badgered him to get it checked out.

With the scare dealt with, it was back to business. The summer of 2013 saw the much-delayed release of the second *Wolverine* movie, and the sixth instalment in the *X-Men* series. But *The Wolverine* wasn't without its problems. After numerous delays it got to the point where it seemed the second instalment of Jackman's project would never go ahead. A number of painstaking rewrites, the director leaving, the massive Japanese earthquake and the Tsunami of March 2011, plus a certain movie about a French uprising extended the making of the film.

Darren Aronofsky (director of *The Wrestler*, *Black Swan* and *The Fountain*, which starred Jackman) had been hired to take control of the movie but bowed out unexpectedly, much to everyone's disappointment. He later said in a statement, 'As I talked more about the film with my collaborators at Fox, it became clear that the production of *The Wolverine* would keep me out of the country for almost a year. I was not comfortable being away from my family for that length of time. I am sad that I won't be able to see the project through, as it is a terrific script and I was very much looking forward to working with my friend, Hugh Jackman, again.'

In June 2011, James Mangold was brought on board as a replacement. Mangold had previously worked with Jackman on the film *Kate & Leopold* (2001), which also starred Meg Ryan; the movie for which Jackman was nominated for a Golden Globe as Best Actor in a Musical or Comedy. The experienced director had also co-written and directed the five-times Oscar nominated *Walk the Line*, a film about the life of the country music legend Johnny Cash and his relationship with June Carter.

Along with screenwriters Chris McQuarrie, Scott Frank and Mark Bomback, Mangold embarked on adapting the screenplay based upon Frank Miller and Chris Claremont's Japanese *Wolverine* saga: 'Following Darren seemed like a suicide mission. I felt like anyone who would even attempt to make it would get slaughtered. I say this as a great admirer of Darren – it would be like following Springsteen or something. Everyone was just going to imagine what could have been. But time went by. The project didn't get filled. I spoke to Darren Aronofsky a bit about it before I ended up taking it on,' recalled Mangold, 'but I will tell you that when Darren stepped off, I was in the middle of doing a lot of other things, and when it was brought up to me, I actually didn't even consider it. It was, oh, who wants to do that, and follow that? And I could hear all of the media swirl about it. Several months went by and I hadn't even really read the *Wolverine* script, and later when they came back to me and I kind of took it in, and a lot of that hand-wringing had kind of died down what I saw was some really promising material, and to me an interesting character played by a great friend of mine who's a terrific actor, Hugh Jackman.'

One of the factors that changed Mangold's mind was the idea of placing such a unique character as Wolverine in such a truly unique environment as Japan – 'I mean, the fact that half of the characters in this movie spoke Japanese, this was like a foreign-language, superhero movie that's as much a drama and a detective story and a film noir, with high-octane action, as it is anything like a conventional tent-pole film. I think part of the reason I did the picture was because it isn't, to me, a conventional superhero movie. It wasn't an original story, so I'm freed from that burden, and it also wasn't a save-the-world movie, which most of them are. It was actually a character piece; I actually think it had more in common with *The Outlaw Josey Wales* and *Chinatown*, what we did, than the conventional, "will Wolverine and his compatriots save the world from this thermonuclear device?" question.'

Mangold insisted on bringing a touch of realism back to the character and the storyline. Talking about the previous movie he said, 'I don't think this hurt the first *Wolverine* film at all, but when he leaps up and brings down a helicopter, to me, that's too much. It's getting into Superman territory. He doesn't have frog's legs. He shouldn't be able to jump that high. My own idea of him is that there's tremendous strength, but that it's somehow still bound by physics in some way that we certainly pushed to the max too, but not quite that far. It turns into a video game, watching characters flip through the air in any which way.'

His vision was to make an adventure movie that he himself wanted to sit down and watch. A story he could believe in. 'I looked at images of Hugh in the previous movies and I felt like he looked like he was wearing a wig, frankly. He was, so that's why it looked like it.

'You're always trying to walk that line between some kind of relationship to the existing comic book art and at the same time having to physically make it work on human flesh,' he continued, 'so there's my own barometer of what I'll reject, and I didn't want *Wolverine* to look like *A Flock of Seagulls*.'

Mangold admits that Fox, the film's distributor, challenged some of his choices. 'When there had been six movies that have had his hair like that, and they're like, "Why can't we do that?" You're like, "Because I think it looks like shit, and I'd like to try and do it differently."' Eventually, he settled on a theme that wasn't merely unique, but almost revolutionary for a film of *The Wolverine*'s scale. 'It occurred to me that he was running from the fact that anyone he cared for died, either from the curse, the dark side of immortality, which is that you are forced to ride this very slow train in which you're watching everyone you care about die, or the most aggressive version, which is that people who want to get at him kill the people he loved. So when I came on the movie I wrote on the back of the script very early, "Everyone I love will die,"' he recalled. 'And then I thought, "Well, how do I make a movie, a tent-pole movie about death?"'

Jackman himself was thrilled about the project and with the choice and vision of his new director. They both wanted to make 'the ultimate Wolverine movie,' which to their minds hadn't been made yet. He intended the film to have a rawness, to feel gutsy and handheld and very urgent – 'I think what I was trying to do was make the most intense film I could, and I knew with some things I was on the very edge of what would be rated "R". But I wanted to play on the edge, because I knew fans were interested in the most intense Wolverine film we could possibly make. So, in a way the sandbox I was playing in was at the very edge of what I knew I could get away with. So, the extended cut is in some ways just the stuff that was trimmed and scenes that fell by the wayside as we were trying to get under the "limbo bar" of the MPAA [Motion Picture Association of America].'

The actor had first read the landmark 1980 comic book by Chris Claremont and Frank Miller that inspired *The Wolverine* while shooting Bryan Singer's original *X-Men*. He was immediately struck by the moody, introspective qualities of the saga and the nuanced portrayal offered of its angry, violent anti-hero and his exploits in Japan. Concerning the Japanese theme, Jackman stressed, 'For me the whole thing was worth the wait. I waited in a way 12 years for this chapter in this saga, for this Samurai story, from the very first week I had on *X-Men 1*. I was reading this comic and [producer] Lauren Shuler Donner and I were saying, one day hopefully we get to do this story. So I think maybe in the past we've had times where we've had late changes in director or whatever, but we had been backed into a release date, so we had to push. It was nice to know that we started with something really solid. There were so many areas of that Japanese story. I loved the idea of this kind of anarchic character, the outsider, being in this world full of honour and tradition and customs; someone who's really anti all of that, and trying to negotiate his own way. The guy who is the outsider, emblematic in a way of anti-authority, anti-tradition, anti-honour, anti-code, is in Japan with all these Samurai and Ninjas. The idea of the Samurai too, and the tradition there, it was really great. In the comic book he got his ass kicked by a couple of Samurai, not even Mutants.'

He had lengthy talks with the writers about getting every aspect of the Japanese saga correct – 'This I hoped was going to be out of the box. It was going to be the best one, I hoped, very different. This was Wolverine, this was not Popeye. He was kind of dark. But, you know, this was a change of pace. Chris McQuarrie, who wrote *The Usual Suspects*, had written the script, so that'll give you a good clue. I knew he was going to make it fantastic. There was going to be some meat on the bones. Something to think about as you leave the theatre, for sure.'

However, even with the new director in place and the script sorted, plans had to be put on hold still further to the spring of 2012 so that Jackman could work on *Les Misérables*. When filming wrapped, he finally got to slip on the steel claws and white vest. 'I think we got the chance to nail the character this time, to do the hole-in-one. We hadn't managed that yet. On the last movie, we complicated it with too many other characters. And there were more women this time, which was good. The last one was so masculine! The new film went more into the character. I don't think we ever saw his rage expressed properly. We let go with this one of the whole "Who am I? Where did I come from? Oh no, I've lost my memory" thing. I feel like that's sent us all to sleep. "Yeah, whatever, pal. We're bored! Fine, you were a sushi chef, whatever it was, can we just get on with the story now?"'

It went without saying that from the very start he knew he was onto a winner in doing the *Wolverine* sequel. The character in the comic book series was still incredibly popular, probably the most popular of all the *X-Men* characters. Plus, he knew the fans had embraced him to a point where he just couldn't do anything wrong in their eyes – 'I never thought my run would last this long. To be a guy who can't age, obviously there is a shelf life for playing this role, so I love it. I've always found it fascinating and slightly, I'll admit, frustrating that I feel we've never really delivered what I would say is the core of the character. And I think in this story, you get to see the ultimate Wolverine. You get to see who he really is. You definitely see him at his most vulnerable, both physically and emotionally. As we were saying before, we had the preparation time so we were really in great shape, and I may be going off the question a little bit, I'm sorry. I feel really blessed in a way to have had the opportunity. I know a lot of the *Wolverine* fans. I've met many of them. They've told me exactly what they think of the movie, every scene, whatever. Lucky for me so far, there hasn't been major disappointment because I'm pretty sure I'd get spat on in the street. That's the level of passion involved. So I'm happy.'

More than anything he hoped the movie would be the springboard for a new direction for his character. He deliberately didn't want to simply title it *Wolverine 2* because he wanted it to be placed and to feel like a standalone picture, a completely different *X-Men* film. And he wanted to give himself the space to explore Logan's (Wolverine's) inner angst more deeply than ever before; it provided a welcome window into the soul of the character who had launched him to stratospheric stardom.

'Yeah, it definitely feels like a standalone movie in every way. I always hated the idea of saying "*Wolverine 2*" – I didn't know what it was going to be called. It was the studio, I think, who came up with the idea of the title, and I was like, "Fantastic." Because in a way, I knew that everybody, from studio down, was embracing this idea of this movie being different, and it needed to be. I mean it was one of the reasons why the comic books are so popular. I was so happy with it. I definitely thought it was the best I've been in the character. This is not jam packed with Mutants, this is not a massive, special effects movie, and nor should it be. It doesn't need to be. For a while it's felt like a rock ride. I think it's the best idea we've had, the strongest script we've had, and that now we really have an opportunity to make something really great.'

When the project finally did go ahead of course most

of the action took place in Japan, although a small part was filmed in Australia, where Jackman's character went on an adventure in and around Tokyo, battling deadly Samurai as well as his inner demons. As previously mentioned, the plot was based on the 1982 limited series *Wolverine* by Claremont and Miller and followed on from the events of the previous *X-Men* movie, *The Last Stand*.

As with his previous roles, Jackman's preparation involved pushing himself to the very limit. In this regard he contacted Dwayne Johnson, also known as 'The Rock', the American actor and semi-retired professional wrestler, for advice on bulking up for the movie.

'It was hard, let me tell you. Basically, one of the great things about having the preparation is I really probably started months ago, when I first thought we were about to gear up and go. I changed my training for this. Over the years, I've got smarter with it. Unfortunately, I realized I needed to train a little more to get what I wanted for this, which was a leaner, more animalistic look. And I'd wanted to be as big as I possibly could be, which was hard for me because I'm skinny. So I started eating six, seven meals a day from January and training about three hours a day. I rang Dwayne for help because I saw him between these two movies, the two *Fast & Furious* movies, and he put on 25 pounds, which in muscle is a lot. It really is hard to put on that amount of muscle. He did it in six months. He sent me his entire thing [programme], so I followed that. You got to adjust to yourself.'

Johnson suggested that he should (and could) gain a pound a week over six months by eating 6,000 calories a day of 'an awful lot of chicken, steak and brown rice'. The end result was that he felt with this film that he had finally achieved the physique he had always envisioned that Wolverine should have. He said that for some reason, on each of his five prior takes at the character, he felt that he never had enough time to get in shape; for this particular movie he finally had enough time, and got his body exactly the way he wanted it to look. Co-star Will Yun Lee also said that it was Jackman's best physique for the role of Wolverine.

For his shirtless scenes, Hugh wanted to look 'as ripped and cut as possible' so he adopted a dehydration diet (used in bodybuilding), as he had with *Les Mis*, where he did not consume any liquid for 36 hours before filming. He said it made him feel 'headachy' and faint, but he was pleased with the results as dehydrating tightens everything up and gave him the exaggerated muscle definition and vascularity that he wanted to show.

'It was tough, but I had more fun than ever,' Jackman said, during one interview. 'I don't know what it is, maybe being a little older helps playing a character who is two or three hundred years old.'

The Wolverine was released in July 2013 worldwide. It received generally positive reviews from critics and became a commercial success, making roughly triple the $120 million production costs so far. With a worldwide total of roughly $413.6 million, it is now the second highest grossing film of the franchise.

In November 2013, it was reported that 20th Century Fox had begun negotiations with both Jackman and his director James Mangold to return for a third solo film starring Wolverine.

At the end of the year, the edge-of-your-seat thriller *The Prisoner* saw Jackman play a father who takes the law into his own hands after his daughter is kidnapped over the Thanksgiving holidays. 'People will go and see a movie that is gripping and entertaining and keeps you on the edge of your seat. There is a whodunnit but it also demands something of you as a viewer. Films like this are not made that often in Hollywood, you have your big blockbusters and small indies and there's something in between. I'm really proud of it.'

So it proved to be another blockbuster year for the extremely likeable Australian. The great thing about Jackman is that even though he might be one of the biggest actors on the planet, he really seems to understand what is important in life, and what truly matters. Thankfully, he feels it's not all about being a busy movie or stage star, or even a producer. In fact, for him, it's quite the reverse. He still maintains the most important part of his life is being so much in love with his wife Deborra-Lee Furness and the joy of being a father-of-two. It's quite easy to see that, in an industry riddled with insecurities, he manages to balance his frequently chaotic life and still remains genuinely grounded. It is also refreshing, in a world obsessed with worshipping celebrities who are often badly behaved and who frequently pop in and out of rehab, to see a star as affable and clean-cut as Jackman emerge from the shadows to shine brightly.

'There are a few things that I have to do every day without which I will lose the plot,' admitted the actor. 'Firstly, I meditate every day, and that brings me back to the essential me, where no matter what role I'm playing, I forget it all for a little bit twice a day. Then, of course, my wife and family are a very big part of anchoring me to what is essentially the most important thing to me, which is their wellbeing and our happiness. I've realised that if you're doing something you love, that's amazing to watch, but you can do twice as much because you just love it, you have passion, it's not exhausting, you don't complain about it or you don't get sick.'

Deborra-Lee also feels that their relationship is as strong now as it's ever been: 'We're still like kids going, "Wow! Look at this! Look at that!" It's been a joyride. We've got to work with amazing people, we've got to travel and meet extraordinary people. When we first met, we said, "Let's travel the world." It's great we can make this work, career and travel, and a creative life together. We're like this nomadic tribe, but, believe it or not, we have incredible routine and normality. The kids always have the same routine. I feel blessed that I have such a great relationship.'

Obviously, there is a lot of pressure on them as a family who move around a lot, but the pair understand that travelling is the nature of the beast. While Hugh continues to juggle lots of balls in the air at the same time, they maintain a firm grip on what matters, while often relying on their sense of humour to help them through.

Although they try their best to live outside the 'normal' celebrity lifestyle, Hugh and Deborra-Lee have a slew of A-list buddies, a nanny and nice cars, and their everyday conversation is often littered with references to influential friends from Nicole Kidman to Sting or Rupert Murdoch. Hugh has a passion for collecting fine wines, but an equal passion for sharing them out among his friends at dinner parties, while Deb loves to be the life and soul of any occasion. And, truth be told, they are not averse to attending the odd glitzy Hollywood event every now and again, as it is all part of the networking process. However, even among all the celebrity trappings, right down to paparazzi lurking for shots of the family in unguarded moments, they both have a matter-of-fact lack of pretension.

Hugh says: 'I lived on a hundred bucks a week as a drama student until I was 26. It was fine, but I remember walking past a good restaurant and thinking I'd love to be able to walk in there without having to worry about the bill. I still go into a five-star hotel and jump up and down on the bed. And when I go into a plane and turn left into first class, I go, "Woo hoo!" None of this happened until *X-Men*, so absolutely none of it is lost on me.'

He believes the older and more famous he gets, the easier it is to separate the over-hyped role of an actor from what it really means and where it fits in the real world. He sometimes finds it amusing but worrying when an actor's every word is translated as gospel, with millions of people not able to tell the difference between the real and fake world of Hollywood: 'It's a dangerous position to think, as an actor, that your opinion matters. You're out there dressing up, pretending to be someone for others' entertainment. You're an entertainer. Actors were fools in the old days. Like the jesters in Shakespeare, you could affect people. Now your whole life is there for people to talk about, and you get paid well for it... So much about being an actor is just being alive and listening and entertaining and providing a service. Ultimately, great actors are conduits for great scripts and great stories. They're not the centre of the world.'

With this last thought firmly planted in his mind, both he and Deb work hard on not allowing their kids to turn into Hollywood brats on the back of their success: 'The hard thing with my kids is I'm terrified of them getting on a plane and saying in reference to people not flying first class, "Daddy, what's behind the curtain?" They've been brought up with more privileges than I ever had.' But knowing the well-grounded couple from Australia, no matter how famous they become, or how much money they have in the bank, their kids will never be allowed to forget how different life could have been.

On his future plans, oddly enough Hugh says that he has little idea of what he wants to do next. However, at this stage and position in his life, he is more than happy to see where the road takes him and he jokes that he is open to suggestions so long as he gets time to play the odd game of killer tennis with one of his best mates every now and then.

There is talk of more proposed films in the pipeline to be released over the next two years. *Selma* is a movie about Martin Luther King, Jr and the US civil rights movement. Jackman has been pencilled in to star alongside Robert De Niro and rock star Lenny Kravitz. *Unbound Captives* will see him star alongside his former co-star Rachel Weisz, as well as *Twilight* and *Harry Potter* heart-throb Robert Pattinson. There are also plans afoot to transform the Aussie star into a police detective who reluctantly helps protect a spoilt teen heiress (reportedly to be played by Miley Cyrus), who is receiving kidnap threats, in *Personal Security*. Then there is further talk of a potential blockbuster in the works: a big film version of the hit stage musical *Carousel*, with Hugh set to star as carousel barker Billy Bigelow, the part he played in the stage version, as well as a role in another musical film, *The Greatest Showman on Earth*, as P.T. Barnum himself. For the modest man from Sydney it's all systems go!

There are rumours from some quarters that he will keep on playing Wolverine until he's old and grey, while others are convinced that he will leave all that behind him to concentrate on serious roles, going forward and getting more involved in directing and producing. Whatever the outcome, it is certain that he will do everything in his power to succeed. One of the more amusing reports doing the rounds is that the man from Oz may be a candidate to play the lead in a film about the life of Hugh Hefner, the American magazine publisher and founder of Playboy Enterprises. Jackman smirks when asked what he would bring to the role.

'I think Hef is an embodiment of the male American dream. He pushed that in the 1950s and said, "Come on, this is what you really want. Let's be honest, I'm living what you really want." If I read the script right, he was a dreamer and not particularly the ladies' man as a teenager. Hef became an alter ego, who he wanted to be.'

He went on to say that all of us have those dreams, but few attempt to achieve them, and that he admired Hefner's ambition and his courage in not caring what anybody else thought: 'He was a real fighter who prevailed. He also has the ability to kind of laugh at himself, which from the Australian point of view is probably the most important thing.'

A visit to the Playboy mansion to put on the famous purple robe may, or may not come off, but one thing is certain: Hugh Jackman is surely a unique talent, particularly in comparison to many of the one-trick-pony crop of today's Hollywood stars. Often he is referred to as a throwback to the actors of a golden generation and compared to two of Hollywood's legends, the laid-back and loveable Cary Grant and the rough-and-tumble action hero, Clint Eastwood. He knows it's definitely no bad thing because as he himself has said there are worse actors to be compared with.

Jackman tells a funny story about meeting one of his heroes a few years ago: 'I did *Swordfish* for Warner Bros, and Clint's a Warner guy. We went to ShoWest, the Comic-Con for exhibitors, in Vegas. I was not a star at that point. We were lining up backstage, and in front of me was Sylvester Stallone. I was like, holy shit, Rocky's in front of me! I look behind, and there was Clint Eastwood. My heart really dropped. I thought, "What do I say? This is the man, Dirty Harry! And he's really tall!" So I turned and said, "Hi Clint, my name's Hugh," and we shook hands. And then I said, "Listen, mate, I'm not sure if you've seen *X-Men*, but people have said I look a bit like you." Of course, what could he say to that, anyway – some schmuck in front of him saying, "I look like you"? So he said, "You're holding up the line, kid." I turned around. Stallone had already gone onstage, and I was just holding up the line. I was humiliated but later I thought, "Did he deliver a great line or what?"'

Even if Eastwood didn't recognise him, it's still been a wonderful journey for Hugh Jackman. There's a certain irony that Jackman, the abandoned boy, chose acting, a profession whose currency is both adoration and rejection. And he admits that it shows a need of some kind: 'I saw the play *Riflemind* about fame and the need for love, and there's a great quote by Bono, which goes something like, "Any person who has to get up on stage to have unanimous, instantaneous love yelled at them from 70,000 people obviously has some massive hole within them". On some level all of us have the need for acceptance and respect, and dare I say it, attention. My mother often joked around that as the youngest, I used to stand up on a chair and make a lot of noise and throw my arms around, and she used to say, "Hugh, you don't have to show off to get attention." Now, in the light of my career, she says, "Well, what do I know?"'

He truly is a mega-superstar who is just an ordinary nice guy, the boy from next door, and it's quite easy to see why everyone loves him. In fact, he's actually quite an open person, who wears his heart on his sleeve a lot more than many other actors. Although a little more circumspect in talking about matters than he used to be, especially things that affect other people, he doesn't feel he has a lot of secrets and he's not that preoccupied with trying to keep them locked away.

He's a star who sits comfortably in his own skin, while always looking to stretch himself. In showbiz land there is more than a feeling that the world hasn't yet seen the best of Hugh Jackman, and everything that he's done so far has simply been the foundation for much bigger things to come. And who would bet against it? With the determination and drive he's shown in the past, plus love and support of his family, he can do anything he wants. So watch out, Prime Minister of Australia, Hugh may be lining up for your job next!

He is one of the bright stars, if not *the* brightest star, in the Hollywood sky, commanding fees in the region of $25 million per movie. There is no doubt he has colossal charisma and matinée-idol good looks and is extremely bankable. A multi-edged individual who can sing, dance, act, produce, host and much more – the list is endless. He's proved to be a breath of fresh air in an industry that can easily become clouded by inflated pay cheques and gigantic egos. Nevertheless, he's learned to take it all in his stride with a huge smile on his face. Probably the most important thing that the success of Hugh Michael Jackman, the boy from Wahroonga, has brought to the world is proof indeed that sometimes the good guys do make it to the top – and he has gone a long, long way to prove it.

'Acting is something I love. It's a great craft that I have a lot of respect for. But I don't think it's any greater challenge than teaching eight-year-olds, or any other career. In my life, I try not to make it more important than it is and I just hope that rubs off on the people around me.'

Hugh Jackman

FILMOGRAPHY

Film/TV Credits:
The Wolverine (2013) Logan/Wolverine
Prisoners (2013) Keller Dover
Movie 43 (2013) Davis
Les Misérables (2012) Jean Valjean
Rise of the Guardians (2012) Bunnymund
Butter (2012) Boyd Bolton
Real Steel (2011) Charlie Kenton
X-Men Origins: Wolverine 2 (2011) Logan/Wolverine
Unbound Captives (2010)
Guardians of Ga'Hoole (2010)
X-Men Origins: Wolverine (2009) Logan/Wolverine
Australia (2008) Drover
Deception (2008) Wyatt Bose
Uncle Jonny (2008) Uncle Russell
Viva Laughlin (2007) (TV) Nicky Fontana

Happy Feet (2006) Memphis

Flushed Away (2006) Roddy

The Prestige (2006) Robert Angier

The Fountain (2006) Tomas/Tommy/Tom

Scoop (2006) Peter Lyman

X-Men: The Last Stand (2006) Logan/Wolverine

Van Helsing (2004) Van Helsing

Making the Grade (2004) (TV) Mr. Slattery

Standing Room Only (2004) Roger

X-Men 2: X-Men United (2003) Logan/Wolverine

Kate & Leopold (2001) Leopold

Swordfish (2001) Stanley Jobson

Someone Like You... (2001) Eddie Alden

X-Men (2000) Logan/Wolverine

Oklahoma! (1999) (TV) Curly McLain

Erskineville Kings (1999) Wace

Paperback Hero (1999) Jack Willis

Halifax f.p: Afraid of the Dark (1998) (TV)
  Eric Ringer

Snowy River: The McGregor Saga Duncan Jones
  (TV – five episodes, 1996)

Blue Heelers Brady Jackson (one episode, 1995)

Correlli Kevin Jones (TV – ten episodes, 1995)

Law of the Land Charles 'Chicka' McCray (TV –
  one episode, 1994)

Producer:

The Wolverine (2013)

X-Men Origins: Wolverine (2009)

Deception (2008)

An Aussie Goes Bolly (2008) TV series

Viva Laughlin (2007) (executive producer)

What a Whale Wants (2007) TV episode (executive producer)

The Directors' Series (2007) TV series (executive producer)

An Aussie Goes Barmy (2006) TV series (executive producer)

Awards:

2013 Golden Globe Award for Best Actor – Motion Picture Musical or Comedy – *Les Misérables*

2013 Donostia Award in San Sebastián International Film Festival

2012 Tony Award Special Award for Extraordinary Contribution to the Theatre Community.

2012 People's Choice Award for Favorite Action Movie Actor – *Real Steel*

2011 Scream Award for Best Cameo – *X-Men: First Class*

2010 People's Choice Award for Favorite Action Star – *X-Men Origins: Wolverine*

2009 Jackman had his hand and footprint ceremony on the Hollywood Walk of Fame

2009 Best Performance By A Human Male at the 2009
Spike Video Game Awards as Wolverine in *X-Men Origins: Wolverine*

2008 Teen Choice Award for Choice Actor in an Action Adventure *X- Men Origins: Wolverine*

2008 Australian GQ Man of the Year

2008 People magazine's Sexiest Man Alive Award

2008 Australian Film Institute Award Readers' Choice

2008 Australian Dance Award for Outstanding Performance in a Stage Musical – *The Boy from Oz*

2008 WAAPA – Chancellor's Alumni Award for Excellence, UTS Towering Achievement Award

2006 Mo Award for Australian Performer of the Year

2006 ShoWest Award for Male Star of the Year

2005 Emmy Award for Outstanding Individual Performance in a Variety or Music Program – 58th Annual Tony Awards Ceremonies

2004 Australian Showbusiness Ambassador of the Year

2004 New York International Independent Film & Video Festival – Short Film Award for Best Actor – *Making the Grade*

2004 Tony Award for Best Leading Actor in a Musical – *The Boy from Oz*

2004 Theater Fans' Choice Award for Best Leading Actor in a Musical – *The Boy from Oz*

2004 Outer Critics Circle Award for Best Actor in a Musical – *The Boy from Oz*

2004 TDF-Astaire Award for Best Male Dancer in Theatre – *The Boy from Oz*

2004 Drama League Award for Distinguished Performance of the Year – *The Boy from Oz*

2004 Broadway Audience Award – *The Boy from Oz*

2004 Theatre World Award – *The Boy from Oz*

2004 Drama Desk Award for Outstanding Actor in a Musical – *The Boy from Oz*

1999 Australian Movie Convention, Australian Star
of the Year

1998 Mo Award for Best Actor in a Musical –
Sunset Boulevard

1997 Variety Club Award for Best Actor in a Musical
– *Sunset Boulevard*

Other Nominations:

2013 Academy Award for Best Actor – *Les Misérables*

2013 BAFTA Award for Best Actor in a Leading Role
– *Les Misérables*

2013 Critics' Choice Award for Best Actor –
Les Misérables

2013 Critics' Choice Award for Best Song –
Les Misérables

2013 Screen Actors Guild Award for Outstanding
Performance by a Male Actor in a Leading Role –
Les Misérables

2013 Screen Actors Guild Award for Outstanding
Performance by a Cast in a Motion Picture –
Les Misérables

2012 People's Choice Awards for Favorite Movie
Actor

2010 MTV Movie Awards for Best Fight – *X-Men
Origins: Wolverine*

2010 People's Choice Awards for Favorite Movie Actor

2010 People's Choice Awards for Favorite On-Screen
Team – *X-Men Origins: Wolverine*

2010 SFX Awards for Best Actor – *X-Men Origins:
Wolverine*

2009 Emmy Award for Outstanding Special Class Programs – 81st Academy Awards

2009 Teen Choice Awards for Choice Movie Drama Actor – *Australia*

2009 Teen Choice Awards for Choice Movie Hissy Fit – *X-Men Origins: Wolverine*

2009 Teen Choice Awards for Choice Movie Rumble – *X-Men Origins: Wolverine*

2007 Australian Film Institute for Best Actor – *The Prestige*

2007 Academy of Science Fiction, Fantasy & Horror Films for Best Actor – *The Fountain*

2006 Teen Choice Awards for Choice Liplock – *X-Men: The Last Stand*

2006 Teen Choice Awards for Choice Actor – *X-Men: The Last Stand*

2006 Green Room Award for Best Male Artist in a Leading Role – *The Boy from Oz*

2006 Emmy Award for Outstanding Individual Performance in a Variety or Music Program – 59th Annual Tony Awards Ceremonies

2001 CFCA Award for Most Promising Actor

1998 Olivier Award for Best Actor in a Musical – *Oklahoma!*

1997 Mo Award for Best Actor in a Musical – *Beauty and the Beast*